SECOND EDITION
Challenger

Teacher's Manual

ADULT READING SERIES

FOR STUDENT BOOKS 1-4

New Readers Press

Challenger Teacher's Manual 1–4, 2nd Edition
ISBN 978-1-56420-576-6

Copyright © 2010, 1994, 1991, 1986 New Readers Press
A Publishing Division of ProLiteracy
1320 Jamesville Avenue, Syracuse, New York 13210
www.newreaderspress.com

Printed in the United States of America
9 8 7 6 5 4 3 2 1

All proceeds from the sale of New Readers Press materials
support literacy programs in the United States and worldwide.

Developmental Editor: Terrie Lipke
Contributing Editor: Terry Ledyard
Contributing Writer: Practical Strategies, Inc.
Creative Director: Andrea Woodbury
Production Specialist: Maryellen Casey
Cover Design: Carolyn Wallace

Book 2

INTRODUCTION

LESSON NOTES

Book 3

INTRODUCTION

LESSON NOTES

Book 4

INTRODUCTION

LESSON NOTES

Answer Key for Writing Books

INTRODUCTION TO THE *CHALLENGER SERIES*

The *Challenger Adult Reading Series* is a program designed to develop reading, writing, and reasoning skills in adult and adolescent students. The first four books in the *Challenger* series emphasize *learning to read*, developing basic decoding, vocabulary, comprehension, and writing skills. Beginning with Book 5, the emphasis shifts to *reading to learn*, developing higher-level comprehension and reasoning skills while expanding the student's knowledge base.

Components of the Series

The *Challenger* series contains:
- 8 student books
- 2 teacher's manuals
- 8 writing workbooks
- online *Challenger Placement Tool*
- online puzzles correlated to the student book lessons

The Student Books

Each book in this controlled vocabulary series contains 20 lessons, plus reviews. Each lesson includes:
- word study
- a reading selection
- a wide variety of exercises and activities

In Books 1, 3, 5, and 7, each lesson begins with a word chart that introduces new words according to specific phonics principles. In all books, new words that appear in the lesson are listed before each reading selection.

The reading selections in the odd-numbered books are mostly fiction. Books 1 and 3 contain original stories about a group of adults in a variety of situations. Most reading selections in Books 5 and 7 are minimally adapted well-known works of fiction. The even-numbered books contain engaging informational readings. The selections in Books 2 and 4 are on topics similar to those in magazines and encyclopedias. Most selections in Books 6 and 8 are adapted from highly respected works of nonfiction that enable students to broaden the scope of their knowledge.

The varied exercises and activities help students to develop their reading, writing, speaking, and listening skills and to increase their basic knowledge. Comprehension exercises based on the reading selections focus on the development of literal, inferential, and applied comprehension skills. In addition, comprehension exercises in Books 5 through 8 develop literary understanding, interpretation, and critical reading skills.

Other exercises are designed to increase vocabulary and develop reading and reasoning skills. They include vocabulary reviews; word associations; classifying, sequencing, and categorizing exercises; using context clues; forming analogies; using dictionaries and reference materials; and several types of puzzles.

There are reviews after every four or five lessons, except in Books 1 and 3. Each book has a final review. Also included in Books 1 through 5 are indexes of the words introduced so far in that book. The word indexes for Books 6 through 8 are included in the teacher's manuals. These word indexes can be used in developing reinforcement activities and vocabulary reviews.

The Teacher's Manuals

There is a single teacher's manual for Books 1–4 and a single teacher's manual for Books 5–8. These comprehensive manuals explain the concepts underlying the *Challenger* series and offer practical suggestions about procedures and techniques for working with students. Separate chapters deal with preparing to teach, teaching the lessons, writing, doing reinforcement activities, and using the lesson notes. These chapters should be read before you begin to use this program. Individual lesson notes containing suggestions for pre-reading, post-reading, and writing activities, and comments on specific exercises should be read before teaching the lessons. In the teacher's manuals, there are also introductions to each book and scope and sequence charts for each book.

Finally both teacher's manuals contain charts of the common phonics principles and elements in English words.

Student Writing

Students are encouraged to write from the very first lesson. Early in the series, exercises focus on writing at the sentence level and are designed to simultaneously improve spelling, sentence structure, and students' skill in expressing themselves clearly. Most lessons in Books 5 through 8 have exercises that require students to write brief paragraphs. Suggestions for providing additional writing activities are given in the individual lesson notes.

Significant Educational Features

FLEXIBILITY AND ADAPTABILITY

The *Challenger* series has been used successfully with students in many different types of instructional settings:

- adult volunteer literacy programs
- ABE, pre-GED, and GED programs
- secondary remedial reading programs
- secondary special education programs
- community college reading programs
- educational programs in correctional institutions
- workforce tutorial programs for employees

Challenger can be used in one-to-one tutoring situations, as well as in a variety of group settings. The lessons can be adapted to fit a variety of formats, allowing you to introduce additional activities and topics related to individual student interests and needs.

An Integrated Approach

Challenger integrates reading, writing, speaking, and listening skills. Reading comprehension is developed through oral discussion of inferential- and applied-level questions. These discussions help students to develop speaking and listening skills. Students build writing skills through follow-up writing activities. Critical thinking and reasoning skills are developed as students discuss the readings, the exercises, and their writing activities.

Sequenced Skill Building

Each lesson builds on the skills developed and the content introduced in previous lessons. Students are continually challenged as the lessons increase in length and difficulty. As reading selections become longer, the content, vocabulary, and sentence structure become more sophisticated and demanding. The exercises and writing activities build on and expand students' knowledge and abilities. Students experience a sense of progress as they learn to apply their skills to new situations.

Highly Motivating Material

Students who have used the *Challenger* series have commented that this reading program has many characteristics that help to hold their interest and maintain their motivation. The characteristics they most frequently cite include:

- exceptionally motivating reading selections
- mature and diverse material
- information that increases background knowledge
- emphasis on using reasoning powers
- challenge of increasingly difficult materials
- feelings of success and confidence generated by the program

Placement

The *Challenger Placement Tool,* used in conjunction with information you have about a student's background knowledge, speaking and writing abilities, and motivation, can help you to decide where to place the student in the *Challenger* series. Scores on standardized reading inventories can also be used. For the first four books, scores in the following reading level ranges are appropriate:

Book 1:	2.0
Book 2:	2.0–3.0
Book 3:	3.0–4.5
Book 4:	4.0–5.0

Keep in mind that numerical reading levels by themselves are not adequate descriptors of adult reading abilities. For students already using the series, scoring 85 percent or better on the final review in each book indicates that they are ready to go on to the next book.

COMMON PHONICS ELEMENTS AND PRINCIPLES IN ENGLISH WORDS

The English phonics system includes the sound-symbol relationships for the various vowels, consonants, consonant blends, and digraphs in English, plus the letter sequences and syllable patterns that indicate how words are most commonly pronounced. This chart lists single letters and common letter combinations together with key words that indicate how the letter or letters usually sound. When letters represent more than one sound, example words are given for each common sound. In addition, common short and long vowel syllable patterns are listed, along with basic spelling rules for adding endings to words.

Consonants
CONSONANT LETTERS THAT REPRESENT ONE SOUND

b	bed	l	lake	t	ten
d	dime	m	man	v	vase
f	feet	n	name	w	woman
h	hat	p	pen	y	you
j	job	qu	queen	z	zoo
k	kite	r	rope		

CONSONANT LETTERS WITH MORE THAN ONE SOUND

s	sun, rose	**Note:**	s can sound like /s/ or /z/.
x	six, example, xylophone		x can sound like /ks/, /gz/, or /z/.
c	can, cop, cup	**Rule:**	c followed by *a*, *o*, or *u* sounds like /k/.
	cent, city, icy		c followed by *e*, *i*, or *y* sounds like /s/.
g	gas, got, gum		g followed by *a*, *o*, or *u* sounds like /g/.
	ginger, germ, gym		g followed by *e*, *i*, or *y* can sound like /j/.
	get, give, fogy		g followed by *e*, *i*, or *y* can also sound like /g/.
gu	guard, guess, guilt, guy		*gu* followed by a vowel sounds like /g/. The *u* is usually silent.

CONSONANT BLENDS

Consonant blends are two or three consonants (or a consonant and digraph) that commonly occur together. Each sound can be heard.

Initial Blends					
bl	blue	pl	plate	sp	spoon
br	bride	pr	price	spl	split
chr	Christmas	sc	scar	spr	spring
cl	clock	sch	school	squ	square
cr	cry	scr	scream	st	step
dr	drop	shr	shrunk	str	street
fl	flame	sk	skate	sw	swim
fr	friend	sl	sleep	thr	throw
gl	glass	sm	smart	tr	track
gr	groom	sn	snow	tw	twin

Final Blends					
ct	act	nd	hand	rm	farm
ft	left	nge	range	rn	corn
ld	gold	nse	sense	rp	burp
lf	self	nt	front	rse	course
lk	milk	pt	kept	rt	smart
lm	film	rb	curb	sk	ask
lp	help	rce	force	sp	clasp
lt	melt	rd	card	st	last
mp	lamp	rf	scarf	xt	next
nce	chance	rk	bark		
nch	lunch	rl	girl		

CONSONANT DIGRAPHS

Consonant digraphs are two consonants that represent one sound.

ch	chair, machine, Christmas	ph	phone
		sh	she
ng	ring	th	thing, the
nk	bank	wh	whale, who

SILENT CONSONANT COMBINATIONS

These are common consonant combinations that contain one or more silent letters. Hyphens indicate initial or final combinations.

-ck	clock	-mb	climb
gh	high, rough, ghost	-mn	autumn
-ght	sight, thought	rh-	rhyme
gn	sign, gnat	sc-	scent
kn-	know	-tch	catch
-lk	talk	wr-	wrong
-lm	calm		

Vowels
VOWEL LETTERS AND THE SOUNDS THEY REPRESENT

Each vowel letter represents several vowel sounds. The most common sounds are represented in the words listed below. All vowels can represent the *schwa* sound in unstressed syllables. The schwa is represented in many dictionaries by the symbol /ə/.

	Short Sound	Long Sound	Other Sounds	Schwa Sound
a	man	name	all, father, water	about
e	bed	me	cafe	open
i	six	time	ski	April
o	job	go	son, do, dog	second
u	but	rule, fuse	put	awful
y	gym	fly	any	

VOWEL COMBINATIONS AND THE SOUNDS THEY REPRESENT

Listed below are common vowel digraphs or vowel-consonant combinations. Many of these combinations produce long vowel sounds. If a combination represents more than one sound, a key word is given for each sound.

Long Vowel Sounds		Other Vowel Sounds	
ai	rain	ai	against
ay	day	au	auto
ea	meat, great	aw	saw
ee	feet	augh	taught, laugh
ei	either, vein	ea	head
eigh	eight	oi	boil
eu	feud	oy	boy
ew	blew, few	oo	book, blood
ey	key, they	ou	you, country, out, soul, could
ie	field, pie		
igh	high	ough	though, thought, through, enough, bough, cough
ind	find		
oa	soap		
oe	toe	ow	own, town
oo	food	ui	build
ue	due		
ui	fruit		

r-CONTROLLED AND *l*-CONTROLLED VOWELS

When vowels are followed by *r* or *l*, the pronunciation of the vowel is usually affected.

air	fair	err	berry	ild	mild
ar	car, dollar, warm	ir	girl	ol	old, roll, solve, doll
		irr	mirror		
		oar	roar	ull	full, dull
arr	carry	oor	door	ur	fur, fury
are	care	or	horse, word, color		
ear	ear, earth, bear				
eer	deer	our	hour, four, journal		
er	very, her				
ere	here, were, there	urr	purr		
		al	pal, bald		
		all	ball		

OTHER VOWEL-CONSONANT COMBINATIONS AND THE SOUNDS THEY REPRESENT

-dge	badge	-ci-	magician, social
-ed	hated, rubbed, fixed	-si-	session, television, Asian
-gue	league	-ti-	caution, question, initial
-que	antique		
-stle	whistle	su	sugar, measure
		-tu-	picture

Common Syllable Patterns in English

Some patterns of letters in syllables signal short vowel sounds. Others usually produce long vowel sounds. Recognizing the common short and long vowel syllable patterns can aid in decoding and spelling unknown words. It is usually the letter or letters that follow a vowel that determine pronunciation.

Key: **V** = any vowel
C = any consonant
(C) = may or may not be a consonant

SYLLABLES THAT USUALLY PRODUCE SHORT VOWEL SOUNDS

Closed syllables (syllables that end with one or more consonants)

VC	at, Ed, is, on, up
CVC	(also called 1-1-1 syllables) had, let, did, lot, but
CVCC	hand, less, with, lock, bump **Exceptions:** find, child, high, sign, old, poll, bolt, most

SYLLABLES THAT USUALLY PRODUCE LONG VOWEL SOUNDS

VCe	(silent e syllables) name, eve, time, hope, rule
VV(C)	(double vowel syllables) paid, need, meat, die, boat, due, food
(C)V	(open syllables) ta/ble, fe/male, bi/cycle, go, o/pen **Exceptions:** Many unaccented open syllables: a/muse, to/day

A SYLLABLE THAT USUALLY PRODUCES THE SCHWA

Cle	(a consonant followed by *le*): table /ta bəl/, gentle /gĕn tǝl/

Rules for Adding Endings

THE DOUBLING RULES

1. If a word has one syllable, one vowel, and one final consonant, double the final consonant before adding an ending that starts with a vowel. Do not double a final *w* or *x*. (This is also called the 1-1-1 Rule.)

Examples:		
hop + ed = hopped	*but*	fix + ed = fixed
run + ing = running		row + ing = rowing

2. If a word has more than one syllable, double the final consonant if the last syllable has one vowel and one final consonant, is accented, and starts with a vowel.

Examples:		
forgot + en = forgotten	*but*	offer + ing = offering
begin + ing = beginning		

THE SILENT *e* RULE

If a word ends in silent *e*, drop the final *e* before adding an ending that starts with a vowel.

Examples:
joke + ing = joking
secure + ity = security

THE *y* TO *i* CONVERSION

If a word ends in a consonant plus *y* (**Cy**), change the *y* to *i* before adding an ending, unless the ending starts with *i*. Note that this rule does not apply when a vowel precedes the *y*.

Examples:		
lucky + er = luckier	*but*	cry + ing = crying
happy + ness = happiness		

SCOPE AND SEQUENCE: Student Book 1

Phonics	Lesson	1	2	3	4	5	6	7	8	9	10	11	12	13	14	15	16	17	18	19	20	R1	R2
1. Recognize long vowel sounds:	(CV and CVC¢)	●	●	●	●	●	▲	▲	●	▲	▲	▲	▲	▲	▲	▲	▲	▲	▲	▲	▲	▲	▲
	(CVVC)						■																
2. Recognize short vowel sounds:	(VC and CVC)	●	●	●	●	●	▲	▲	●	▲	▲	▲	▲	▲	▲	▲	▲	▲	▲	▲	▲	▲	▲
	(CVCC)						●											▲					
3. Recognize sounds for *y*:		▲	▲	▲	▲				●	●	▲	▲						▲		▲		▲	▲
4. Recognize sounds for vowel groups:	*ee*								●	●													
	ay, ey, oy, uy									●													
	ai, ie, oa, oi, ou, ue												●	■				▲					▲
	ea (as in *eat* and *bead*)												●	■	▲			▲		▲			
	oo (as in *food* and *foot*)												●	■									
														●									
5. Recognize *r*-controlled vowel sounds:	*ar, are, or, er, eer, ir, ur*											●											
	air, oar, oor													●									
	ear (as in *ear* and *bear*)													●									
	our (as in *sour* and *four*)													●									
6. Recognize vowel sounds followed by *l*:	*al, el, ild, ol, ul, ull*														●								
7. Recognize sounds for single consonants		●	●	●	●	●	▲	▲	●	▲	▲	▲	▲	▲	▲	▲	▲	▲	▲	▲	●	▲	▲
8. Recognize sounds for initial consonant blends:	*st, sk*							▲	▲		▲					▲		▲					
	bl, cl, fl, gl, pl, sl							●															
	br, cr, dr, fr, gr, pr, tr, str										●					●							
	sm, sn, sp, sw, thr, tw																●	▲					
	chr, sc, scr, shr, spl, spr, squ																		●	▲			
9. Recognize sounds for final consonant blends:	*nd, nt, ck, mp*						●																
	ng, nk								●							●							
	st, sk																	▲					
10. Recognize silent consonants:	*kn, wr, mb, ght, tch*										●									▲			
11. Recognize sounds for digraphs:	*ch, sh*																		●				
	th, wh																				●		
	dge																				●		
12. Recognize sounds for *c* and *g*																					●		
13. Mark long and short vowel sounds				●					●					■									

Word Analysis	Lesson	1	2	3	4	5	6	7	8	9	10	11	12	13	14	15	16	17	18	19	20	R1	R2
1. Recognize verb endings:	*-ed, -ing*	▲	▲	▲	▲	▲	▲	▲	▲	▲	▲	▲	▲	▲	▲	▲	▲	▲	▲	▲	▲	▲	▲
	-s		▲	▲	▲	▲	▲	▲	▲	▲	▲	▲	▲	▲	▲	▲	▲	▲	▲	▲	▲	▲	▲
2. Recognize noun endings:	*-s*		▲	▲	▲	▲	▲	▲	▲	▲	▲								▲	▲	▲	▲	▲
	-'s																					▲	▲

KEY: ● = Primary emphasis ■ = Secondary emphasis ▲ = Integrated with other skills

Word Analysis, cont.	Lesson	1	2	3	4	5	6	7	8	9	10	11	12	13	14	15	16	17	18	19	20	R1	R2
3. Recognize contractions for: not		▲				▲	▲	▲	▲	▲	▲	▲	▲	▲	▲	▲	▲	▲	▲	▲	▲	▲	▲
is				▲		▲		▲	▲	▲		▲	▲	▲	▲	▲	▲		▲		▲	▲	▲
am					▲							▲			▲						▲		
will											▲		▲			▲							
had													▲	▲					▲				
are												▲						▲	▲	▲	▲	▲	▲
have																		▲	▲				
would																							
4. Recognize abbreviations: Mr.		▲			▲	▲	▲	▲	▲	▲	▲	▲		▲		▲	▲	▲			▲		
Mrs., Ms.						▲		▲	▲	▲	▲	▲	▲	▲		▲	▲		▲				
Dr.															▲	▲		▲					
5. Recognize other word endings: –y, –ly									●														▲
–er											●		▲							●			
–ful, –less																							
6. Recognize common word beginnings: un–, re–															■								
7. Distinguish words that look similar/rhyme		■	■	■	■		■	■	■		■		■	■		■	■	■	■	■	■	■	
8. Form compound words						●																	

Vocabulary	Lesson	1	2	3	4	5	6	7	8	9	10	11	12	13	14	15	16	17	18	19	20	R1	R2
1. Learn unfamiliar vocabulary		▲	▲	▲	▲	▲	▲	▲	▲	▲	▲	▲	▲	▲	▲	▲	▲	▲	▲	▲	▲	▲	▲
2. Identify synonyms									■	■						■						▲	▲
3. Identify antonyms											■			■	■							■	■
4. Identify word associations										■	■			■					■				▲
5. Learn/review common expressions																			■				▲

Comprehension	Lesson	1	2	3	4	5	6	7	8	9	10	11	12	13	14	15	16	17	18	19	20	R1	R2
1. Decode words accurately when reading aloud		●	●	●	●	●	●	●	●	●	●	●	●	●	●	●	●	●	●	●	●	●	●
2. Pronounce word endings when reading aloud		▲	▲	▲	▲	▲	▲	▲	▲	▲	▲	▲	▲	▲	▲	▲	▲	▲	▲	▲	▲	▲	▲
3. Group words appropriately when reading aloud		▲	▲	▲	▲	▲	▲	▲	▲	▲	▲	▲	▲	▲	▲	▲	▲	▲	▲	▲	▲	▲	▲
4. Interpret punctuation correctly when reading aloud		▲	▲	▲	▲	▲	▲	▲	▲	▲	▲	▲	▲	▲	▲	▲	▲	▲	▲	▲	▲	▲	▲
5. Identify words using phonics and context clues		▲	▲	▲	▲	▲	▲	▲	▲	▲	▲	▲	●	▲	▲	▲	▲	▲	▲	▲	▲	▲	▲
6. Read silently		●	●	●	●	●	▲	▲	▲	▲	▲	●	●	▲	▲	●	●	●	●	●	●	●	●
7. Follow oral directions		▲	▲	▲	▲	▲	▲	▲	▲	▲	▲	▲	▲	▲	▲	▲	▲	▲	▲	▲	▲	▲	▲
8. Improve listening comprehension		▲	▲	▲	▲	▲	▲	▲	▲	▲	▲	▲	▲	▲	▲	▲	▲	▲	▲	▲	▲	▲	▲
9. Discuss story		■	■	■	■	■	■	■	■	■	■	■	■	■	■	■	■	■	■	■	■	■	■
10. Relate story to illustrations		■	■	■	■	■	■	■	■														
11. Develop literal comprehension skills: - Recall details		■	■	■	■	■	■	■	■	■	■	■	■	■	■	■	■	■	■	■	■	■	■
- Locate information in the story		■	■			■			■						■					■	■	■	

KEY: ● = Primary emphasis   ■ = Secondary emphasis   ▲ = Integrated with other skills

Comprehension, cont.

Lesson	1	2	3	4	5	6	7	8	9	10	11	12	13	14	15	16	17	18	19	20	R1	R2
11. Develop inferential comprehension skills:																						
– Infer word meanings from context clues		◄	◄	◄	◄	■	■	■	■	■	■	●	●	●	◄	●	●	●	●	●	●	●
– Infer information from the story	◄	◄	◄	◄	◄	◄	◄	◄	◄	◄	◄	◄	◄	◄	◄	◄	◄	◄	◄	◄	◄	◄
– Use context clues to predict correct responses	■	■	■	■	■	■	■	■	■	■	■	■	■	■	■	■	●	■	■	■	■	■
– Classify words under appropriate categories	■																●			■	■	■
12. Develop applied comprehension skills:																						
– Relate reading to personal experience	◄	◄	◄	◄	◄	◄	◄	◄	◄	◄	◄	◄	◄	◄	◄	◄	◄	◄	◄	◄	◄	
– Draw conclusions	◄	◄	◄	◄	◄	◄	◄	◄	◄	◄	◄	◄	◄	◄	◄	◄	◄	◄	◄	◄		
13. Recognize number words													■					●			■	■
14. Learn/review basic factual information																	■		■	■	■	■

Writing

Lesson	1	2	3	4	5	6	7	8	9	10	11	12	13	14	15	16	17	18	19	20	R1	R2
1. Write legibly	■	■	■	■	■	■	■	■	■	■	■	■	■	■	■	■	■	■	■	■	■	■
2. Copy words accurately	■	■	■																			
3. Copy sentences accurately	■	■																				
4. Spell words with greater accuracy					■	■	■	■	■	■	■	■	■	■	■	■	■	■	■	■	■	■
5. Form new words by adding the endings:																						
–*ed*					■	■																
–*ing*						■	■															
–*y*									●													
–*er*										●	●											
–*est*																						
6. Change the *y* to *i* before adding:																						
–*er*															●							
–*est*															■							
7. Write number words												■				■				■		
8. Use *a* and *an* appropriately								■										●			■	
9. Compose sentences				◄	◄	◄	◄	■	■	◄	◄	◄	◄	◄	◄	◄	◄	◄	◄	◄	◄	◄

Note: Specific suggestions for additional writing assignments appear in the individual lesson notes for Book 1 and in Chapter 3 of this manual.

Study Skills

Lesson	1	2	3	4	5	6	7	8	9	10	11	12	13	14	15	16	17	18	19	20	R1	R2
1. Complete exercises:																						
fill-in-the-blank	◄	◄	◄	◄	◄	◄	◄	◄	◄	◄	◄	◄	◄	◄	◄	◄	◄	◄	◄	◄	◄	◄
matching		◄	◄	◄	◄	◄	◄	◄	◄	◄	◄	◄	◄	◄	◄	◄	◄	◄	◄	◄	◄	◄
yes/no questions				◄																		
writing sentences								◄				◄				◄						
true/false questions																						
multiple choice questions												●										
analogies	■	■	■	■	■	■	■	■	■	■	■	■	■	■	■	■	■	■	■	■	■	■
2. Apply reasoning skills:																						
context clues	◄	◄	◄	◄	◄	◄	◄	◄	◄	◄	◄	◄	◄	◄	◄	◄	◄	◄	◄	◄	■	■
process of elimination								◄									◄	■	◄	◄	■	◄
3. Use word indexes to check spelling					◄	◄	◄	◄	◄	◄	◄											◄

KEY: ● = Primary emphasis   ■ = Secondary emphasis   ▲ = Integrated with other skills

SCOPE AND SEQUENCE: Challenger Writing 1

Lesson	STRAND 1			STRAND 2	STRAND 3		STRAND 4	STRAND 5	STRAND 6		STRAND 7
	Fill in the Missing Word (1)	Add Another Word	Fill in the Missing Words (2)	Choose the Right Word	Answer the Questions (1-word change)	Answer the Questions (multiple changes)	Unscramble the Sentences	Put These Sentences in Order	What Do You Think? (sentence completion)	Complete the Sentences	Personal Questions
1	X				X		X	X	X		
2	X				X		X	X	X		
3	X				X		X	X	X		
4					X		X	X	X		
5	X	X			X		X		X		X
6						X		X	X		X
7	X	X				X	X		X		X
8	X	X				X		X	X		
9	X			X		X	X		X		
10	X			X		X	X				X
11	X			X		X		X	X	X	
12	X			X		X		X			
13			X			X	X		X	X	
14			X	X		X	X	X	X		
15			X			X	X	X	X	X	
16			X			X			X		
17				X		X	X	X	X	X	
18				X		X			X		
19				X		X	X	X	X	X	
20			X			X		X	X		
Review	X						X	X	X		X

SCOPE AND SEQUENCE: Student Book 2

Phonics

Lesson	1	2	3	4	5	R	6	7	8	9	10	R	11	12	13	14	15	R	16	17	18	19	20	R
1. Use phonic skills to decode unknown words	●	●	●	●	●	●	●	●	●	●	●	●	●	●	●	●	●	●	●	●	●	●	●	●
2. Recognize long and short vowel sounds	◀	◀	◀	◀	◀	●	◀	◀	◀	◀	◀	◀	◀	◀	◀	◀	◀	◀	◀	◀	◀	◀	◀	●
3. Identify long and short vowel sounds	■	◀	◀	■	■		■			■			■											
4. Identify silent *e*	■																							
5. Recognize/contrast *r*-controlled vowel sounds		◀	◀	◀	◀		◀	◀	◀	◀	◀	◀			■		◀		◀		◀	◀	◀	
6. Recognize vowel sounds preceding *l*					◀					■		◀					◀	◀						
7. Contrast *ow* (as in *cow* and *slow*)			■															◀						
8. Recognize *aw* words													■											
9. Contrast *oo* (as in *food* and *foot*)									■								■	◀					■	
10. Contrast other vowel sounds																								
11. Recognize sounds for single consonants, consonant blends, and digraphs	●	●	●	●	●	●	●	●	●	●	●	●	●	●	●	●	●	●	●	●	●	●	●	●
12. Contrast sounds for single consonants, consonant blends, and digraphs		■		■	■	■		■	■	■	■	■	■	■			■		■					
13. Recognize sounds for *c* and *g*	◀	◀	◀						◀	◀	◀	◀	◀	◀	◀			◀	◀				◀	
14. Recognize silent consonants and vowels	◀						◀		◀	◀	◀	◀					■	◀						
15. Identify silent consonants and vowels										■								■						

Word analysis

Lesson	1	2	3	4	5	R	6	7	8	9	10	R	11	12	13	14	15	R	16	17	18	19	20	R
1. Use syllabication to decode words	■	■	■	■	■	■	■	■	■	■	■	■	■	■	■	■	■	■	■	■	■	■	■	■
2. Recognize abbreviations and contractions	◀	◀	◀	◀	◀	◀	◀	◀	◀	◀	◀	◀	◀	◀	◀	◀	◀	◀	◀	◀	◀		◀	■
3. Distinguish words that look similar/rhyme	■	■	■	■	■	■	■	■		◀	◀		■	●		●	◀	◀	◀	●	◀		■	■
4. Recognize noun endings							◀					◀					◀		◀		◀			
5. Recognize verb endings											■								■					
6. Recognize other word endings														■		■		■	■	■			■	
7. Recognize common word beginnings																						■		
8. Divide compound words				●			■	■						●						●				●
9. Form compound words								●	●															

Vocabulary

Lesson	1	2	3	4	5	R	6	7	8	9	10	R	11	12	13	14	15	R	16	17	18	19	20	R
1. Learn unfamiliar vocabulary	●	●	●	●	●	●	●	●	●	●	●	●	●	●	●	●	●	●	●	●	●	●	●	●
2. Infer word meanings from context clues	■	■	■	●	●	■	●	●	■	■	■	■	■	■	■	■	■	■	■	■	■	■	■	■
3. Identify antonyms		●	●	●				●									●	◀		●				■
4. Identify synonyms								●		■		■			■						■			■
5. Complete word associations									●															
6. Complete analogies							■										●				●			
7. Learn/review idiomatic expressions/common sayings	◀	◀			◀												●	◀				◀		
8. Learn/review collective nouns																	■							

KEY: ● = Primary emphasis   ■ = Secondary emphasis   ◀ = Integrated with other skills

Comprehension

Lesson	1	2	3	4	5	R	6	7	8	9	10	R	11	12	13	14	15	R	16	17	18	19	20	R
1. Follow oral and written directions	■	■	■	■	■	■	■	■	■	■	■	■	■	■	■	■	■	■	■	■	■	■	■	■
2. Group words appropriately when reading orally	■	■	■	■	■	■	■	■	■	■	■	■	■	■	■	■	■	■	■	■	■	■	■	■
3. Interpret punctuation correctly when reading orally	■	■	■	■	■	■	■	■	■	■	■	■	■	■	■	■	■	■	■	■	■	■	■	■
4. Identify words using context clues and phonics skills	■	■	■	■	■	■	■	■	■	■	■	■	■	■	■	■	■	■	■	■	■	■	■	■
5. Recognize title as topic of reading selection	●	■	■	■	◄	◄	◄	◄	◄	◄	◄	◄	◄	◄	◄	◄	◄	◄	◄	◄	◄	◄	◄	◄
6. Improve listening comprehension	◄	◄	◄	◄	◄	◄	◄	◄	◄	◄	◄	◄	◄	◄	◄	◄	◄	◄	◄	◄	◄	◄	◄	◄
7. Discuss the reading passage	■	■	■	■	■	■	■	■	■	■	■	■	■	■	■	■	■	■	■	■	■	■	■	■
8. Relate reading to illustrations	■	■	■	■	◄	◄	◄	■	◄	◄	◄	◄	◄	◄	◄	◄	◄	◄	◄	◄	◄	◄	◄	◄
9. Develop literal comprehension skills:																								
– Recall details	●	●		●	●	■	●	●	●	●	●	●	●	●	●	●	●	●	●	●	●	●	●	●
– Locate information in the reading passage	●	●		●	●	■	●	●	●	●	●		●								●	●	●	
10. Develop inferential comprehension skills:																								
– Infer word meanings from context clues	■						●		●	●		■		●	●	●	●	■	●		●	●	●	
– Infer information from the selection							■			■	■							■		■		■		
– Draw conclusions based on selection											■		■				■						■	
– Use context clues to predict correct responses	■	■				■		■		■														■
– Classify words under topic headings		●		◄			◄		◄	◄				◄										◄
– Determine topic headings for words																								
11. Develop applied comprehension skills:																								
– Relate reading to personal experience	■		■	■	■		■		■		■		■	■	■	■			■				■	
– Draw conclusions based on personal experience							■				■	■		■					■					
12. Learn/review basic factual information	■	◄				◄	◄		◄	◄		◄	◄							◄	◄			◄
13. Reorder words into meaningful sentences												■	■						■					■
14. Sequence events accurately																	■	■	■					

Writing

Lesson	1	2	3	4	5	R	6	7	8	9	10	R	11	12	13	14	15	R	16	17	18	19	20	R
1. Write legibly	◄	◄	◄	◄	◄	◄	◄	◄	◄	◄	◄	◄	◄	◄	◄	◄	◄	◄	◄	◄	◄	◄	◄	◄
2. Copy words accurately	■	■	■	■	■	■	■	■	■	■	■	■	■	■	■	■	■	■	■	■	■	■	■	■
3. Capitalize words appropriately	◄	◄	◄	◄	◄	◄	◄	◄	◄	◄	◄	◄	◄	◄	◄	◄	◄	◄	◄	◄	◄	◄	◄	◄
4. Spell words with greater accuracy	■	■	■	■	■	■	■	■	■	■	■	■	■	■	■	■	■	■	■	■	■	■	■	■
5. Use homonyms correctly	■	■		■		■					■													
6. Spell number words accurately		◄	◄																					
7. Form new words by adding the endings: -y													■	■		■								
-er																								■
8. Change y to i before adding -er, -est, -ly																			■					
9. Unscramble words/sentences														■										
10. Write sentence answers to questions	■			■	■		■	■	■	■	■		■	■	■	■	■		■	■	■	■	■	

Note: Specific suggestions for additional writing assignments appear in the individual lesson notes for Book 2 and in Chapter 3 of this manual.

KEY: ● = Primary emphasis   ■ = Secondary emphasis   ▲ = Integrated with other skills

Study Skills

Lesson	1	2	3	4	5	R	6	7	8	9	10	R	11	12	13	14	15	R	16	17	18	19	20	R
1. Increase concentration	■	■	■	■	■	■	■	■	■	■	■	■	■	■	■	■	■	■	■	■	■	■	■	■
2. Complete reading comprehension questions requiring: single word answers	▲	▲	▲	▲	▲	▲	▲	▲	▲	▲	▲	▲	▲	▲	▲	▲	▲	▲	▲	▲	▲	▲	▲	▲
phrases	▲	▲	▲	▲	▲	▲	▲	▲	▲	▲	▲	▲	▲	▲	▲	▲	▲	▲	▲	▲	▲	▲	▲	▲
complete sentences	▲	▲	▲	▲	▲	▲	▲	▲	▲	▲	▲	▲	▲	▲	▲	▲	▲	▲	▲	▲	▲	▲	▲	▲
3. Complete exercises: fill-in-the-blank	▲	▲	▲	▲	▲	▲	▲		▲	▲	▲	▲	▲	▲	▲	▲	▲	▲	▲	▲	▲	▲	▲	▲
matching	▲	▲		▲	▲				▲	▲		▲		▲										
multiple choice						▲			▲			▲												
analogies									■										■			■		
4. Apply reasoning skills to exercises: context clues	■	■	■	■	■	■	■		■	■	■	■	▲		▲	▲	▲	▲	▲	▲		▲	▲	▲
process of elimination	■	■	■	■	■			■	■	■	■	■	▲		▲									
5. Use a world map or atlas			▲		▲					▲														
6. Use an encyclopedia or the Internet			▲																		▲			
7. Use word indexes to look up correct spelling	▲	▲	▲	▲	▲	▲	▲	▲	▲	▲	▲	▲	▲	▲	▲	▲	▲	▲	▲	▲	▲	▲	▲	▲

KEY: ● = Primary emphasis   ■ = Secondary emphasis   ▲ = Integrated with other skills

SCOPE AND SEQUENCE: Challenger Writing 2

Lesson	STRAND 2 Choose the Right Word	STRAND 4 Unscramble the Sentences	STRAND 5 Put These Sentences in Order	STRAND 6 What Do You Think? (sentence completion)	STRAND 6 What Do You Think? (questions w/starters)	STRAND 6 What Do You Think? (questions w/o starters)	STRAND 7 Personal Questions	STRAND 8 Combine the Sentences (2 sentences)	STRAND 9 Use These Words in Sentences	STRAND 10 Complete These Paragraphs
1	X	X		X			X	X		
2	X	X		X			X	X		
3	X	X		X			X	X		
4	X	X		X			X	X		
5	X	X		X			X	X		
6				X			X	X	X	
7		X					X	X	X	
8	X	X		X			X	X		
9	X	X		X			X	X	X	
10	X	X	X	X			X			
11	X				X			X	X	X
12								X	X	X
13					X			X		X
14	X	X	X		X					X
15		X			X			X	X	X
16	X		X			X				X
17		X				X		X	X	X
18	X	X				X		X	X	X
19	X	X	X			X		X	X	X
20						X			X	X
Review		X				X				

SCOPE AND SEQUENCE: Student Book 3

Phonics

Lesson	1	2	3	4	5	6	7	8	9	10	11	12	13	14	15	16	17	18	19	20	R
1. Use phonics skills to decode unknown words	●	●	●	●	●	●	●	●	●	●	●	●	●	●	●	●	●	●	●	●	●
2. Recognize long and short vowel sounds	▲	■	■	■	■	■	■	■	▲	▲	▲	▲	▲	▲	▲	▲	▲	▲	▲	▲	▲
3. Recognize sounds for vowel combinations:																					
ai, ee, ĕa, ĕa, ui								●													
oa, ou, oi, oo									●	●											
au											●										
r-controlled vowel combinations															●						
4. Recognize sounds for consonant blends:																					
st	●	●																			
bl, br, cl, cr, fl, fr			●																		
gl, gr, pl, pr, sl, str				●																	
dr, tr, thr, sc, sk, sw					●																
sm, sn, sp, scr						●															
5. Recognize sounds for digraphs:																					
ch, sh						●															
th, wh						▲															
6. Recognize sounds for *c* and *g*	▲																				
7. Recognize vowel sounds preceding *l*													●								
8. Recognize silent consonants							●			▲				■							
9. Recognize *r*-controlled vowel sounds											●			●							
10. Recognize *gh* and *ght* words												●									
11. Recognize *ow* sounds (as in *cow* and *slow*)																■	■				■
12. Contrast vowel and consonant sounds																					

Word Analysis

Lesson	1	2	3	4	5	6	7	8	9	10	11	12	13	14	15	16	17	18	19	20	R
1. Use syllabication to decode words	●	●	●	●	●	●	●	●	●	●	●	●	●	●	●	●	●	●	●	●	●
2. Recognize abbreviations and contractions	▲	▲	▲	▲	▲	▲	▲	▲	▲	▲	▲	▲	▲	▲	▲	▲	▲	▲	▲	▲	▲
3. Divide compound words	■	■	■	■	■	■	■														
4. Form compound words								■				■									
5. Divide words into syllables													■	■	■	■	■				■
6. Combine syllables to form words																					
7. Recognize common word endings:																					
-er				▲																	
-est		■																			
-y					■	■															
-ly			■																		
-ful and -less							■	■													
-en									■	■											

KEY: ● = Primary emphasis   ■ = Secondary emphasis   ▲ = Integrated with other skills

Word Analysis, cont.

Lesson	1	2	3	4	5	6	7	8	9	10	11	12	13	14	15	16	17	18	19	20	R
8. Recognize common word beginnings:																					
re–											■	■									
in–													■					●			
mis–																		●			
de–																●	●				
ex–																●	●	●			
com–, con–																●	●				
un–																	●	●			
dis–, im–																			●		
up–, down–, out–, over–, under–																			●		

Vocabulary

Lesson	1	2	3	4	5	6	7	8	9	10	11	12	13	14	15	16	17	18	19	20	R1
1. Learn unfamiliar vocabulary	●	●	●	●	●	●	●	●	●	●	●	●	●	●	●	●	●	●	●	●	●
2. Infer word meanings from context clues	●	●	●	●	●	●	●	●	●	●	●	●	●	●	●	●	●	●	●	●	●
3. Identify definitions/descriptions of terms	■	■	■	■			■	■		■		■	■		■	■		■	■	■	■
4. Identify synonyms				●	●						●										
5. Identify antonyms						●						●									
6. Distinguish between synonyms and antonyms								●						●							
7. Complete analogies							●										●				
8. Complete word associations									●	●			■								

Comprehension

Lesson	1	2	3	4	5	6	7	8	9	10	11	12	13	14	15	16	17	18	19	20	R
1. Follow written directions	●	●	●	●	●	●	●	●	●	●	●	●	●	●	●	●	●	●	●	●	●
2. Identify words using context clues	●	●	●	●	●	●	●	●	●	●	●	●	●	●	●	●	●	●	●	●	●
3. Read stories independently	●	●	●	●	●	●	■	■	●	●	●	●	●	●	■	●	●	●	●	■	●
4. Complete exercises independently	●	●	●	■	●	●	■	●	●	●	●	●	●	●	■	●	●	●	●	●	
5. Improve listening comprehension	■	■	●	■	●	●	■	●	●	●	●	●	●	●	■	●	●	●	●	●	■
6. Group words appropriately when reading orally	■	●	●	■	●	●	■	●					●		■			●		●	
7. Interpret punctuation correctly when reading orally	●	●	●	■	●	●	■	●					●		■			●		●	
8. Develop literal comprehension skills:																					
– Recall details	●	●	●	●	●	●	●	●	●	●	●	●	●	●	●	●	●	●	●	●	●
– Locate specific information	●	●	●	●	●	●	●	●	●	●	●	●	●	●	●	●	●	●	●	●	●
9. Develop inferential comprehension skills:																					
– Infer word meanings from context clues	●	●	●	●	●	●	●	●	●	●	●	●	●	●	●	●	●	●	●	●	●
– Infer information from the story	●	●	●	●	●	●	●	●	●	●	●	●	●	●	●	●	●	●	●	●	
– Use context clues to predict correct responses	●	●	●	●														●		●	●
– Summarize the story																					
– Draw conclusions based on story			■	■	■							■	■	■				■		■	
– Predict outcomes				■										■							
– Classify words under topic headings											■							■			

KEY: ● = Primary emphasis   ■ = Secondary emphasis   ▲ = Integrated with other skills

Comprehension, cont.

Lesson	1	2	3	4	5	6	7	8	9	10	11	12	13	14	15	16	17	18	19	20	R
10. Develop applied comprehension skills:																					
– Relate reading to personal experience				■				■	■	■	■			■	■	■	■				
– Draw conclusions based on personal experience			■	■	■	■	■	■	■	■	■	■	■	■	■	■	■	■	■		
11. Learn/review basic factual information																		■	■	■	■
12. Relate story to illustrations	■	■	■	■	■	■	■	■	■	■	■	■	■	■	■	■	■	■	■	■	■

Literary understanding

Lesson	1	2	3	4	5	6	7	8	9	10	11	12	13	14	15	16	17	18	19	20	R
1. Distinguish between fiction and nonfiction	●	▲	▲	▲	▲	▲	▲	▲	▲	▲	▲	▲	▲	▲	▲	▲	▲	▲	▲	▲	▲
2. Identify/interpret characters' actions, motivations, and feelings	●	●	●	●	●	●	●	●	●	●	●	●	●	●	●	●	●	●	●	●	●
3. Identify/interpret plot	●	●	●	●	●	●	●	●	●	●	●	●	●	●	●	●	●	●	●	●	●
4. Relate title to content of story					●	●	●	●					●								
5. Identify/interpret setting (place)																	■				

Writing

Lesson	1	2	3	4	5	6	7	8	9	10	11	12	13	14	15	16	17	18	19	20	R
1. Write legibly	▲	▲	▲	▲	▲	▲	▲	▲	▲	▲	▲	▲	▲	▲	▲	▲	▲	▲	▲	▲	▲
2. Copy words accurately	●	●	●	●	●	●	●	●	●	●	●	●	●	●	●	●	●	●	●	●	●
3. Capitalize words appropriately	●	●	●	●	●	●	●	●	●	●	●	●	●	●	●	●	●	●	●	●	●
4. Spell words with greater accuracy	●	●	●	●	●	●	●	●	●	●	●	●	●	●	●	●	●	●	●	●	●
5. Form new words by adding the ending:	■																				
–ing		■																			
–est			■																		
–y						■															
–ly				■																	
–ful, –less							■	■													
6. Change the y to i before adding –er, –est										■								■			
7. Unscramble words																					
8. Write sentence answers to questions	●	●	●	●	●	●	●	●	●	●	●	●	●	●	●	●	●	●	●	●	●

Note: Specific suggestions for additional writing assignments appear in the individual lesson notes for Book 3 and in Chapter 3 of this manual.

Study Skills

Lesson	1	2	3	4	5	6	7	8	9	10	11	12	13	14	15	16	17	18	19	20	R
1. Increase concentration	●	●	●	●	●	●	●	●	●	●	●	●	●	●	●	●	●	●	●	●	●
2. Skim story to locate information	●	●	●	●	●	●	●	●	●	●	●	●	●	●	●	●	●	●	●	●	●
3. Complete exercises:																					
reading comprehension questions	▲	▲	▲	▲	▲	▲	▲	▲	▲	▲	▲	▲	▲	▲	▲	▲	▲	▲	▲	▲	▲
fill-in-the-blank	▲	▲	▲	▲	▲	▲	▲	▲	▲	▲	▲	▲	▲	▲	▲	▲	▲	▲	▲	▲	▲
matching	▲	▲	▲	▲	▲	▲	▲	▲	▲	▲			▲	▲	▲	▲	▲	▲	▲		
multiple choice																■					
4. Apply reasoning skills to exercises:	●	●	●	●	●	●	●	●	●	●	●	●	●	●	●	●	●	●	●	●	●
context clues	●	●	●	●	●	●	●	●	●	●	●	●	●	●	●	●	●	●	●	●	●
process of elimination	●	●	●	●	●	●	●	●	●	●	●	●	●	●	●	●	●	●	●	●	●

KEY: ● = Primary emphasis   ■ = Secondary emphasis   ▲ = Integrated with other skills

SCOPE AND SEQUENCE: Challenger Writing 3

Lesson	STRAND 5 Put These Sentences in Order	STRAND 6 What Do You Think? (sentence completion)	STRAND 6 What Do You Think? (questions w/starters)	STRAND 6 What Do You Think? (questions w/o starters)	STRAND 8 Combine the Sentences (2 sentences)	STRAND 8 Combine the Sentences (3 sentences)	STRAND 9 Use These Words in Sentences	STRAND 10 Complete These Paragraphs	STRAND 10 Write a Paragraph (guided)	STRAND 10 Write a Paragraph (open-ended)
1		X			X		X	X		
2	X	X					X	X		
3		X			X		X	X		
4	X		X				X	X		
5			X		X		X	X		
6	X		X				X	X		
7				X		X	X		X	
8	X			X			X		X	
9				X		X	X		X	
10	X			X			X		X	
11				X		X	X		X	
12	X			X			X		X	
13				X		X	X		X	
14	X			X			X		X	
15				X		X	X		X	
16				X		X	X			X
17	X			X			X			X
18				X		X	X			X
19	X			X		X	X			X
20				X			X			X
Review	X			X		X				X

SCOPE AND SEQUENCE: Student Book 4

Phonics / Lesson	1	2	3	4	5	R	6	7	8	9	10	R	11	12	13	14	15	R	16	17	18	19	20	R
1. Use phonic skills to decode unknown words	●	●	●	●	●	●	●	●	●	●	●	●	●	●	●	●	●	●	●	●	●	●	●	●
2. Identify long and short vowel sounds	■	■		■												■								
3. Recognize sound for -le												■												
4. Identify silent letters													■											
5. Distinguish sounds for g														■										

Word Analysis / Lesson	1	2	3	4	5	R	6	7	8	9	10	R	11	12	13	14	15	R	16	17	18	19	20	R
1. Use syllabication to decode words	●	●	●	●	●	●	●	●	●	●	●	●	●	●	●	●	●	●	●	●	●	●	●	●
2. Divide words into syllables	■	■	■	■	■			■							●	■	■	■	●					■
3. Combine syllables to form words						■						■												
4. Recognize common word endings: -er	■		■																					
-y					▲																			
-ing						■																		
-est, -ness, -ship, -ment													■											
-ful											■													
-less														■										
5. Recognize common word beginnings													■											
6. Form compound words								■								●								
7. Recognize singular and plural forms									●								■			■				

Vocabulary / Lesson	1	2	3	4	5	R	6	7	8	9	10	R	11	12	13	14	15	R	16	17	18	19	20	R
1. Learn unfamiliar vocabulary	●	●	●	●	●	●	●	●	●	●	●	●	●	●	●	●	●	●	●	●	●	●	●	●
2. Infer word meanings from context clues	●	●	●	●	●	●	●	●	●	●	●	●	●	●	●	●	●	●	●	●	●	●	●	●
3. Identify definitions/descriptions of terms	●	●	●	●				■		●					●	●	●	●						
4. Produce definitions/descriptions of terms				●															▲					
5. Learn/review idiomatic expressions/common sayings	●																			●				
6. Identify synonyms		●				●							●	●										
7. Identify antonyms		●				●							●	●										
8. Distinguish between synonyms and antonyms																								
9. Complete word associations		●								●											●			
10. Complete analogies				●				●																
11. Complete double acrostic													■							●				
12. Learn/review multiple meanings and pronunciations											■													
13. Learn/review abbreviations																		■						■

KEY: ● = Primary emphasis   ■ = Secondary emphasis   ▲ = Integrated with other skills

Comprehension

Lesson	1	2	3	4	5	R	6	7	8	9	10	R	11	12	13	14	15	R	16	17	18	19	20	R
1. Identify words using context clues	●	●	●	●	●	●	●	●	●	●	●	●	●	●	●	●	●	●	●	●	●	●	●	●
2. Read selections independently	●	●	●	●	●	●	●	●	●	●	●	●	●	●	●	●	●	●	●	●	●	●	●	●
3. Complete exercises independently	●	●	●	●	●	●	●	●	●	●	●	●	●	●	●	●	●	●	●	●	●	●	●	●
4. Improve listening comprehension	■	■	■	■	■	●	■	●	●	●	■	●	■	■	■	■	●	●	■	●	●	●	■	■
5. Group words appropriately when reading orally	■	■	■	■	■	●	■		●	■			■	●	●	■			■	●	●	■	■	●
6. Interpret punctuation correctly when reading orally	■	●		■	■	●	■			■			■	●	●	■			■	●	■	■	■	
7. Develop literal comprehension skills:																								
- Recall details	●	●	●	●		●	●	●			●		●	●	●	●			●	●	●	●	●	●
- Locate specific information	●	●		●		●	●	●				●	●	●		●		●	●	●	●	●	●	
- Sequence events																						●		
8. Develop inferential comprehension skills:																								
- Infer word meanings from context clues	●	●	●	●	●	●	●	●		●	●		●	●	●	●	●	●	●	●	●	●	●	●
- Infer information from the reading	●	●	●	●	●		●	●	●	●	●	●	●	●	●	●	●	●	●	●	●	●	●	
- Draw conclusions based on reading		●	●	●	●			●								●								
- Use context clues to predict correct responses			●		●		●		●		●		●	●	●			●	●	●	●	●	●	●
- Determine topic headings for words											●													
- Classify words under topic headings							●					●			●									
- Determine cause and effect relationships										●												●		
9. Develop applied comprehension skills:																								
- Draw conclusions based on personal experience	●		●	●	●		●	●	●	●	●		●	●	●	●	●		●	●			●	
- Relate reading to personal experience		●	●	●	●	●	●	●	●	●	●	●	●	●	●		●	●	●	●	●	●	●	●
- Sequence events					●				●	●														
10. Learn/review basic factual information	●	●	●	●	●	●	●	▲	●	■	●	●	▲	▲	●	●	●	●			▲			●
11. Locate/infer information from a menu or other list																				●		●	●	
12. Locate/infer information from an illustration or diagram				■					■	■														
13. Relate reading to illustrations	■	■	■	■	■		■	■	■	■	■		■	■	■	■	■		■	■	■	■	■	■

Writing

Lesson	1	2	3	4	5	R	6	7	8	9	10	R	11	12	13	14	15	R	16	17	18	19	20	R
1. Write legibly	▲	▲	▲	▲	▲	▲	▲	▲	▲	▲	▲	▲	▲	▲	▲	▲	▲	▲	▲	▲	▲	▲	▲	▲
2. Copy words accurately	●	●	●	●	●	●	●	●	●	●	●	●	●	●	●	●	●	●	●	●	●	●	●	●
3. Capitalize words appropriately	●	●	●	●	●	●	●	●	●	●	●	●	●	●	●	●	●	●	●	●	●	●	●	●
4. Spell words with greater accuracy	■	●	●	●	●	●	●	●	●	●	●	●	●	●	●	●	●	●	●	●	●	●	●	●
5. Form new words by adding the endings: -er	■	■																						
-y			■	■																				
-ing							■			■														
-ly								■	■															
6. Change f to v to form plurals																								

KEY: ● = Primary emphasis   ■ = Secondary emphasis   ▲ = Integrated with other skills

Writing, cont.

Lesson	1	2	3	4	5	R	6	7	8	9	10	R	11	12	13	14	15	R	16	17	18	19	20	R
7. Change the *y* to *i* before adding: *-er, -est, -ness*													■						■					
-ly											■							■						
8. Unscramble words																							●	
9. Write sentence or paragraph answers to questions	●	●	●	●	●		●	●	●	●	●	●	●	●	●	●				●				

Note: Specific suggestions for additional writing assignments appear in the individual lesson notes for Book 4 and in Chapter 3 of this manual.

Study Skills

Lesson	1	2	3	4	5	R	6	7	8	9	10	R	11	12	13	14	15	R	16	17	18	19	20	R
1. Increase concentration	●	●	●	●	●	●	●	●	●	●	●	●	●	●	●	●	●	●	●	●	●	●	●	●
2. Skim passage to locate information	●	●	●	●	●	●	●	●	●	●	●	●	●	●	●	●	●	●	●	●	●	●	●	●
3. Apply reasoning skills to exercises: context clues	●	●	●	●	●	●	●	●	●	●	●	●	●	●	●	●	●	●	●	●	●	●	●	●
process of elimination				●	●	●	●	●	●	●	●	●	●	●	●	●	●	●	●	●	●	●	●	●
"intelligent guessing"	●									●	●	●	●											
4. Use a dictionary to look up word meanings		▲		▲	▲	▲	▲	▲	▲	▲	▲	▲	▲	▲	▲	▲	▲	▲	▲	▲	▲	▲	▲	▲
5. Use a world map or atlas															▲									

KEY: ● = Primary emphasis   ■ = Secondary emphasis   ▲ = Integrated with other skills

Lesson	STRAND 5 Put These Sentences in Order	STRAND 6 What Do You Think? (questions w/o starters)	STRAND 8 Combine the Sentences (2 or 3 sentences)	STRAND 8 Combine the Sentences (4 sentences)	STRAND 9 Use These Words in Sentences	STRAND 10 Write a Paragraph (open-ended)	STRAND 10 Write a 3 Paragraph Summary (guided)	STRAND 10 Write Paragraphs (3 guided paragraphs)
1	X	X			X	X		
2		X	X		X	X		
3	X	X			X	X		
4		X	X		X	X		
5	X	X			X	X		
6		X		X	X	X		
7	X	X			X		X	
8		X		X	X		X	
9		X	X		X		X	
10		X	X		X		X	
11	X	X		X	X		X	
12		X		X	X		X	
13	X	X			X			X
14		X		X	X			X
15	X	X			X			X
16		X		X	X			X
17	X	X			X			X
18		X		X	X			X
19	X	X			X			X
20		X		X	X			X
Review		X				X		X

Chapter 1. Preparing to Teach

These suggestions are offered to help you prepare to teach using this program. We hope that you will find these suggestions helpful. Some of them may need to be modified to fit your particular situation.

Scheduling Considerations

Most beginning readers progress best when you meet with them for one hour five times a week at a regularly scheduled time. A schedule in which learners meet only two or three times a week or at different times each week can work, but often progress is slower than for learners who work with a teacher at the same time each day.

In volunteer programs, meeting daily is often impossible. In this setting, try to schedule at least two sessions a week. If only one session a week is possible, encourage learners to set aside some time each day to read. Emphasize that daily practice will be essential for progress in developing reading skills.

The Lesson Components

Each lesson in *Challenger* has three basic components: word study, a reading selection, and skill-building exercises.

1. **Word Study.** In Books 1 and 3, word study includes a chart with words that contain specific phonetic elements, plus words for study—words being used in the lesson for the first time in the series. Lessons in Books 2 and 4 do not have word charts, but they do have words for study.

2. **The Reading Selection.** Books 1 and 3 contain pieces of short fiction. Books 2 and 4 have informational nonfiction reading selections.

3. **The Exercises.** Each lesson has several exercises designed to develop decoding, vocabulary, comprehension, and reasoning skills. The first exercise in Books 2–4 is a comprehension exercise based on the reading selection. Suggested questions that can be used in oral discussion to assess comprehension are included in the lesson notes for Book 1.

Because *Challenger* is a very flexible program, there are several ways to handle the lesson material when working with your students. With students beginning in Book 1, you may cover one lesson in each session. Or you may briefly review the preceding lesson, then spend the bulk of the session on the new lesson. Particularly with students working in Books 2–4, you may spend part of the session on material addressing student-specific goals or needs. Another option is to spend the first part of the

session discussing the reading selection and exercises done for homework and the second part of the session introducing the reading selection and previewing the exercises for the next lesson.

It will take a few sessions to determine the pace and procedures that work best for your students. Keep in mind, however, that following a consistent procedure helps learners because they tend to work much better when they have a sense of routine.

Planning the Lessons

It is important to prepare thoroughly to teach each lesson. The following steps should help you prepare for teaching a lesson.

1. Read the lesson notes found in this manual for suggestions to help you teach a particular lesson. Go over the answers in the Answer Key found in the back of the student book. Decide what you want to emphasize (your objectives), list activities, and prepare any materials you will need.

2. Plan pre-reading activities to introduce the reading selection. Try to anticipate questions students may have about the exercises.

3. Decide what you want to emphasize (reading comprehension, spelling rules, etc.), and plan how you will do it.

4. Look over any notes you made after the preceding class to see if there is anything that students need to review.

5. Plan a writing activity based on suggestions in Chapter 3 of this manual or in the lesson notes. Also consider using the separate writing books for more formal instruction in writing.

6. Decide upon any reinforcement activities you may want to use, and complete any preparation needed. (Suggestions for reinforcement activities are given in Chapter 4.)

7. After the session, make notes about approaches and strategies that worked well and areas that need reinforcement for individual learners and for the group as a whole.

Try to allow a few minutes before students arrive to prepare yourself mentally and emotionally for the session. As the teacher, your main function is to serve as a bridge between the student and the lesson material. How well the session goes is often determined by how relaxed and focused you are on the work.

The Teacher-Student Relationship

Establishing a good teacher-student relationship is absolutely essential for students' progress. Mature students rely heavily on teachers' support and encouragement to bolster their self-confidence and reinforce their motivation, particularly in periods of extreme frustration.

Completing the lessons takes a lot of work. Encourage students to view their time with you and their homework assignments as daily workouts or practice sessions. Sports and music, which require daily practice, are helpful analogies. No matter how much progress is being made, most learners experience a sense of frustration at one time or another. Your encouragement will help them to get through those periods when they feel like giving up.

Above all, these lessons should be seen as opportunities for learners to move smoothly toward their reading goals. They do not have to demonstrate mastery of the material in one lesson in order to go on to the next lesson. Mastery comes with consistent practice. It is crucial for you to think in terms of improvement rather than mastery and to regard mistakes as natural and helpful. Some learners will be very sensitive to mistakes in their work. They will need continual reinforcement of the concept that we all learn from our mistakes.

Finally, remember that reading comprehension depends to a large extent on the background information a student has. As you come to know your students better, you can identify gaps in background knowledge that you can help to fill through reinforcement activities, discussion, and pleasure reading or other supplemental reading. Plan the sessions with the students' personal goals and needs in mind.

Building a Good Working Relationship

- Avoid treating learners with either condescension or pity. Remember that adult learners have a wealth of experience to draw upon.
- Greet students pleasantly, and spend a few minutes talking before you begin the session. You might discuss what has happened in your students' lives or in your life, what they have read that they found particularly interesting, or how their homework went. Then use a phrase such as "Shall we get started?" to indicate that it is time to begin the session.
- In a tutorial or small-group situation, work from the learner's book rather than your own. This practice conveys a "we're in this together" spirit.
- Use positive reinforcement during the sessions. Remind learners of the progress they are making. When they are particularly discouraged, do this in a

concrete way by showing them how many pages they have completed or how their writing has improved.

Supplies

GENERAL SUPPLIES

- An alphabet chart with uppercase and lowercase letters is helpful for beginning readers and writers.
- Have a dictionary available and, if possible, access to the Internet. These valuable resources provide additional information about many of the words, people, events, and other things mentioned in *Challenger*.
- A map or an atlas will enable learners to find the geographical location of places mentioned in the lessons.

Be prepared to teach students how to use these resources. Encourage them to do research as often as their interest, abilities, and time permit.

TEACHER SUPPLIES

You will need:

- your copies of the *Challenger* student book and teacher's manual and the writing book if you are using the correlated writing program
- your lesson plan
- blank paper for making notes during the session
- a pen or pencil for making marginal notes and marking corrections in the students' books. (Avoid red ink as it may be associated by some students with bad memories of school.) Colored highlighters are also helpful for marking troublesome words.

STUDENT SUPPLIES

For each class, students need:

- their *Challenger* books and their copies of the writing book, if the class is using the correlated writing program
- pens or pencils
- their writing notebooks. We recommend using a loose-leaf binder with wide-lined paper for writing assignments and reinforcement activities.

A Summary of *Dos*

- Do schedule as many sessions each week as possible.
- Do develop a consistent lesson format.
- Do take time to decide the pace that works best for your learners.
- Do prepare for each class.
- Do take a few moments to relax before each class.
- Do develop a good working relationship with your students because it is essential to their reading progress.
- Do make sure that the environment in which you teach is as conducive to good learning as possible.

Chapter 2. Teaching the Lessons

How you teach the lessons in Challenger *will depend on a number of issues. Whether you are tutoring a single student or working with a small group, what book your students are working in, the number of times you meet with them each week, and various other concerns will have to be taken into consideration.*

Sample Teaching Session Formats

Because of its flexibility, *Challenger* lends itself to a variety of teaching session possibilities. The following sample format outlines a procedure that can be used with a small group of students who all are working on the same lesson in *Challenger 2–4*.

THE CURRENT LESSON

1. **Homework Review.** For most lessons, read aloud some or all of the reading selection assigned for homework. Go over the Exercise 1 comprehension questions and discuss the reading selection. Suggestions for discussion are given in the individual lesson notes. Go over the other exercises, paying particular attention to any new material introduced in the lesson.
2. **Summarizing.** Have students summarize what they learned from the lesson.
3. **Writing Activity.** Use the writing book for the lesson. Suggestions for writing activities are also given in Chapter 3 of this manual and in the individual lesson notes.
4. **Reinforcement Activity.** If time permits, give students additional practice in an area of difficulty.

THE NEW LESSON

1. **Word Study.** Introduce or review the phonics principles, and have students read words from the word chart (for Book 3).
2. **The Reading Selection.** Have students read the Words for Study. Introduce the reading in the new lesson using one or more pre-reading activities. Assign the reading of the selection for homework, or read the selection orally and assign a second reading of the selection for homework.
3. **Preview Homework Exercises.** Preview the exercises in the new lesson with students to be sure they understand how to do them. Teach any new principles or rules pertaining to the exercises. Suggest topics for a writing activity, or assign the exercises for this lesson in the writing book.

Whenever possible, try to reserve the last segment of each session for pleasure reading. In the beginning,

you may read a story, poem, or article of interest to your students. As students' confidence increases, you might take turns reading "just for fun" material. Select material that deals with students' hobbies, work, or specific goals. For instance, if a student has mentioned wanting to read to his children, bring in age-level appropriate stories, and help the student practice reading them. If a student loves to cook, help him or her to read recipes from a cookbook.

Do not expect to know in the beginning how much time to allot for each segment of the lesson. All students are different, and understanding how to pace the lessons takes time. By observing students' responses and rates of accuracy and improvement, you will become able to predict how much time a given segment of the lesson should take.

Particularly for students working in Book 1, it may be preferable to spend two class sessions on one lesson. That way, the first session begins with the word study, followed by pre-reading activities. Next you and your student read the story orally and discuss it. The exercises can then be previewed for homework, or the student can complete them during the session. In the next class session, you can go over the exercises, have the student summarize what was learned in the lesson, and do writing and reinforcement activities.

Specific suggestions for teaching students working in Book 1 are included in the Introduction to Book 1, which begins on page 46.

Below are suggestions for teaching the main components of each lesson in *Challenger*. These components include word study, the reading selection, and the exercises. Dealing with writing assignments and suggestions for reinforcement activities are discussed in Chapters 3 and 4.

Word Study

The *Challenger* series places significant emphasis on word recognition skills, since a major obstacle to reading improvement is a poor sight vocabulary. New words are introduced in the odd-numbered books through the word charts and in all books in the Words for Study section preceding each reading selection.

THE WORD CHARTS

In Books 1 and 3, word charts appear at the beginning of each lesson. The words in the chart illustrate particular phonics principles being introduced or reviewed in the lesson. Many of the chart words are also used in the story and the exercises.

The phonics approach to decoding used throughout *Challenger* is based on learning to recognize the following:

- basic sound-letter relationships
- common letter combinations regularly found in English words
- common syllable patterns that indicate how words are pronounced

The chart on pages 8–10 lists the main sound-symbol relationships, plus letter combinations and syllable patterns that influence decoding.

The phonics approach provides an organizing principle for introducing new words in this controlled-vocabulary series. By learning some basic phonics principles, students develop the necessary tools for sounding out new words, reviewing forgotten words, and handling increasingly difficult material. Since the phonics method is based on a problem-solving approach to decoding, the tendency to blurt out the first word that comes to mind gives way to a more reasoned discovery of how to decode words.

The following procedure is suggested for working with the word charts.

1. Students say the guide sound for the first group of words.
2. Students sound out the words containing the guide sound. Use your judgment in deciding how many words students should read. They don't have to read all the words in any given chart. They can sound out the remaining words as they encounter them in the readings or the exercises.
3. When students have completed the chart, do a brief review of the words they have read. You can point to words at random and have students read them. Or you may say a word and have students locate it.
4. You may want students to practice writing some of the chart words. Writing selected words reinforces both the letter patterns and word recognition.

Particularly for word charts that focus on vowel sounds, we recommend that you have students begin with the vowel sound when sounding out words. Starting with the vowel sound helps students to develop the problem-solving approach. Many beginning readers identify the initial sound in the word and then guess the rest. Often it is a wrong guess. By emphasizing the vowel sound, adding the ending sounds, and then working on the initial sounds, students decode with much greater accuracy. The following example is based on Lesson 2 of Book 1.

1. Students say the guide sound for the first row in the chart, /ā/.
2. They cover up the *d, t,* and *e* of the word *date* and say the vowel sound, /ā/.

3. They uncover the letters to the right of the vowel, *te,* and say the vowel sound plus the consonant, /āt/.
4. Then students uncover the *d* and say /dāt/.
5. If necessary, review the function of the silent *e*.

Beginning students sometimes have difficulty putting the sounds together. Assist them by modeling the pronunciation of the words and having students repeat them.

Some students can sight-read many of the chart words in the early lessons of Books 1 and 3. These students may resist learning the phonics approach. Assure them that they will not have to sound out words they can sight-read, but that this method will give them a way to attack new words. Use the following steps when working on word charts with students who have a basic sight vocabulary.

1. Have students read the words in the order in which they appear. Point out the letter and syllable patterns of the words they already know how to decode.
2. When students miss a word, teach the guide sound, and have them sound out the word, beginning with the vowel sound when the chart focuses on vowel sounds.
3. During the random review, have students review all the sounds whether or not they had difficulty with them.
4. Provide reinforcement activities that focus on the sounds and words that gave students difficulty.

When working on the word charts, concentrate on developing word attack skills. Since students probably know the meanings of most of the chart words, avoid spending a lot of time on definitions. There are opportunities for developing vocabulary skills in context later in the lessons. If students ask for the definition of a chart word, state the meaning, and use the word in a sentence.

THE WORDS FOR STUDY

The Words for Study section contains words that appear in the story and exercises for the first time in this controlled-vocabulary series. They are listed in the order and form in which they appear in the lesson.

Students may be able to sight-read some of these words. As students progress, they may be able to sound out the unfamiliar words that adhere to phonics principles they have studied. If students cannot sight-read or sound out a word, say the word and have students repeat it a few times. Either state the meaning, or ask students to try to figure out the meaning as the word is used in context in the lesson.

Since Words for Study are listed in the form in which they appear in the lesson, some of them have endings such as *-s, -ed,* or *-ing*. Make sure students notice and read the endings on words that have them.

Sometimes a student's pronunciation of a word will differ from yours. Offer the standard pronunciation only if the student asks for it. Mispronunciation becomes important if it interferes with a student's reading comprehension or spelling. In these instances, encourage students to use the standard pronunciation.

USING KEY WORDS

Students can use words they already know as key words to help them sound out and remember new words. A key word is a familiar word that helps students remember a specific sound/symbol relationship. Key words should be short, common words the student can read easily. Students should usually select the key words themselves.

Key words are especially helpful for the following phonics elements: *r*-controlled vowels, *l*-controlled vowels, silent letter combinations, and vowel combinations, particularly combinations that spell more than one sound. For instance, in Lesson 12 of Book 1, the vowel combination *ea* is shown with two lists of words. You might suggest that students select one word from each list, such as *eat* and *head,* to use as key words. When students encounter the words *deal* and *least* in Lesson 14, they can write their key word *eat* in the margin to remind them that those words have the long *e* sound.

The Reading Selections

The stories in Book 1 are designed to be read aloud in class and then discussed orally. Specific instructions for handling the readings in Book 1 can be found in the Introduction to Book 1, beginning on page 46.

The readings in Books 2–4 may be handled in a number of ways, depending on your students' needs and the amount of time you have with them. It is a good idea to provide for two readings of each selection, one for fluency and one for comprehension. The readings can be both oral and silent, with one done in class and the other done for homework. Tell students that even experienced readers often have to read things more than once, particularly instructions, textbooks, forms, and so forth.

Each reading selection should be introduced with appropriate pre-reading activities and followed with post-reading activities.

PRE-READING ACTIVITIES

It is important to introduce each reading selection using one or more pre-reading activities. The type of pre-reading activities you select will depend upon whether students are reading the fiction in Books 1 and 3 or the informational readings in Books 2 and 4. Pre-reading activities for individual lessons are suggested in the lesson notes.

Pre-reading activities should accomplish one or more of the following objectives.

- to stimulate students' interest by drawing on their prior experience or understanding of the subject
- to give students a purpose for reading
- to provide essential background information

The first pre-reading activities usually will be to have students read the Words for Study and the selection's title and then predict what the reading will be about or tell what they think the title means.

You can link the subject of the reading to students' personal experiences by asking, "Have you ever done/ been/thought/felt . . .?" questions. You can give students a purpose for reading by setting a task for them as they read. For instance, in Lesson 5 of Book 3 you might say, "As you read, think about what kind of person Ginger is." For Lesson 9, Book 4 you could say, "What are some questions about Internet dating that the story might answer?"

Students will better understand some of the readings in Books 2 and 4 if pertinent historical or geographical background is provided. For example, a discussion of Hitler's attempt to destroy Europe's Jewish population during World War II should precede the reading of the excerpts from Anne Frank's diary in Lessons 12 and 13 of Book 4.

READING THE SELECTION

There are a variety of ways to handle the reading selections, and the procedure used should vary from lesson to lesson, particularly for students working in Books 1 and 2. The following methods have proved effective with beginning readers.

- Read to the students. By reading aloud while students follow along in the text, you model good oral reading and facilitate comprehension.
- Read one sentence aloud while your student follows along. Then have your student read the sentence aloud. This method is sometimes called "echo reading."
- You and your student read the selection aloud together ("duet reading").
- A group of students reads a selection aloud together.
- Alternate reading aloud sentences or short paragraphs with a student.

When the first reading is done as homework, you may want to introduce some of the selections by reading aloud the first paragraph or two. Tell the students that you will read only the beginning of the story while they follow along in the book. Then ask one or two questions to make sure students have understood what you read. By reading aloud, you can create interest in the reading at the same time you are modeling good reading.

POST-READING ACTIVITIES

1. **Oral Reading.** Have students in Books 1 and 2 read the selection aloud before starting to discuss it. This gives you an opportunity to note their strengths and weaknesses and also to help them develop good oral reading habits. Students in Books 3 and 4 should also read at least part of the selection aloud for most lessons. How often you do this and how much of the selection is read aloud depend upon time and the needs of your students.

2. **Summarize.** Have students summarize the reading by identifying and stating the main points. Discuss any predictions they made about the reading based on the Words for Study and the title.

3. **Exercise 1.** For students working in Books 2–4, go over their responses to the reading comprehension questions in Exercise 1.

4. **Discuss the Reading.** Have a general discussion of the reading to make sure students have understood what they have read and to give them practice in developing listening and speaking skills. Ask literal-, inferential-, and applied-level questions to assess students' comprehension. Suggested questions are given in the lesson notes for each lesson.

Literal-level Questions. These questions deal with the most basic kind of comprehension, that is, remembering what the author said. In answering literal questions, students do not need to infer information or apply what they have read to prior knowledge. Answers to literal questions can be found in the reading selection, and you should encourage students to look back at the reading for the answers.

Start with a general question such as, "What does this sentence tell you?" or "What happened in this paragraph?" Then move on to questions about specific details. Literal questions about the stories in Books 1 and 3 can deal with characters, events, settings, or other details. Examples of detail-specific questions are: "Where does this story take place?" "What are the characters' names?" "What did Kate do with the cake?"

Literal questions about the readings in Books 2 and 4 also can deal with specific details. You might ask, "Why do skunks spray their liquid?" or "How did Black Bart get started holding up stagecoaches?"

Inferential-level Questions. These questions require students to use information in the reading to draw conclusions that are not actually stated. Examples of inferential questions pertaining to the story in Lesson 9 of Book 1 are: "Why didn't Eddie want Kate to bake the cake for the party?" "Do you think Bob will think it's funny that they bought him toys for his birthday?"

Inferential questions for the informational reading in Lesson 9 of Book 2 are: "Why didn't John Sutter want people to know gold had been found on his land?" "Explain what 'made a strike' means in this story."

Applied-level Questions. These questions help students relate what they have read to their own experiences. Examples of applied questions are: "Do you know people like the characters in this story? Describe them." "Tell about a similar experience you have had." "What would you do if you were in this situation?"

Applied questions for the informational readings might be: "How would your life be different if Edison hadn't invented the lightbulb?" "Describe an ad that made you want to buy or do something."

Literal-, inferential-, and applied-level questions help students respond to the reading selections and develop critical reading skills. With practice, students learn to use information from their reading to support their own thoughts. They also begin to see connections between the situations in the readings and their own life experiences. When they make such connections, reading becomes an enjoyable activity that helps them to think more clearly and that motivates them to learn more.

FACILITATING GROUP DISCUSSION

To create an atmosphere in which the reading selections and students' reactions to them can be discussed freely and openly, consider these suggestions.

- Plan questions to get the discussion started, but be flexible in order to take advantage of students' interests and curiosity.
- Make sure students understand two basic ground rules: that one person speaks at a time and that they treat each other's opinions with respect.
- Encourage participation, but don't force it.
- Keep the discussion focused.
- Avoid asking questions that can be answered with *yes* and *no*.
- Allow students to react to each other's opinions and comments. Avoid dominating the discussion yourself.

View discussions as you view the students' other work—in terms of improvement, or growth, instead of mastery. It takes time to develop a good discussion group in which participants really listen to each other and gain the necessary confidence to express themselves genuinely. It also takes time for students to learn the kinds of questions to ask and the types of information to contribute. You can help them by modeling appropriate questions and responses during the early sessions, then making fewer and fewer contributions as students become more skillful.

When tutoring an individual student, discussion of the reading is just as essential. It is important for the learner to develop speaking and listening skills and to be able to express his thoughts about and reactions to what he has read. It may be harder to get an individual student to participate at first, but as you learn more about his interests and abilities, you can prompt the discussion with these in mind.

The Exercises

In addition to reading comprehension exercises, there are other exercises in the lessons that build decoding, vocabulary, and comprehension skills. Many of these other exercises help learners to develop their reasoning abilities by requiring them to think and infer, to use context clues, to practice the process of elimination, and to apply what they already know to new situations.

PREVIEWING THE EXERCISES

Generally, the exercises are assigned as homework. Allow enough time at the end of the session to preview the exercises so that students understand how to do them. Since exercise formats are repeated frequently, you should only have to explain the directions for any given format the first few times it occurs. When introducing a new exercise format, you may want students to complete the first one or two items to be sure they understand what to do.

When an exercise is based on phonics principles or spelling rules, an example may be given. When previewing this type of exercise, ask questions about the example to make sure students understand the process being illustrated.

For example, in Lesson 5 of Book 1, Exercise 1 deals with adding -ed to words. When previewing this exercise, have students look at the examples and ask: "Were any letters dropped or added to the root word when -ed was added?" When they have studied the examples and answered the question, tell them, "When adding -ed to words that end in silent e, drop the silent e before adding -ed. If a word has one syllable, one vowel, and one final consonant, double the final consonant before adding -ed."

Students may want to write these spelling rules in their writing notebooks.

DOING THE HOMEWORK

Homework is the learners' responsibility. They must understand and accept the concept that regular practice outside of class time is essential for them to improve their reading skills. You may want to review the importance of practice by comparing homework with practicing a sport or musical instrument.

Adult learners often profit by doing their homework with someone else who is working in the same book. They can help each other sort out any difficulties that may arise. Discussing problems and giving explanations reinforce understanding and recall of the material for both learners.

Sometimes adult learners try to do their homework right after a full day of work, while trying to make dinner, or just before going to bed.

Encourage them to schedule a definite study time in quiet surroundings when they will not be exhausted or distracted by other activities or responsibilities.

If once in a while a student doesn't complete the homework exercises, don't be concerned. If a student generally neglects the homework, however, you can suggest alternative plans for getting it done and help the student find a workable study time and place. Occasionally, an adult learner simply can't do any work outside the class session. If this is the case, both you and the student must recognize and accept the fact that progress will be slow.

The following reminders may be helpful from time to time.

- Students should complete all homework items to the best of their ability. Leaving an item blank is not nearly so helpful as guessing wrong and correcting an answer in class.
- Items in a given exercise do not always have to be done in order. Teach students how to use the process of elimination. For appropriate exercises, tell students to do the items they are sure of first, checking off answers as they use them. Then, for questions they are unsure of, they can select the most logical answers from the choices that are left.
- Students should check over their homework after finishing all the exercises to be sure they haven't skipped any answers.

GOING OVER THE HOMEWORK

It is important to go over all work that students do. They need feedback in order to correct mistakes and to build good reading and writing habits. They also need to know that their efforts are important enough for you to spend time on.

Going over the homework provides the opportunity to review and reinforce concepts introduced and practiced in the exercises. When a student misses several items in an exercise, it is a signal that additional reinforcement is necessary.

If you are tutoring an individual student, have him or her read his answers aloud. If you work with a group, the whole group can go over most of the exercises together.

Have students take turns reading their answers aloud. They should read whole sentences in exercises that have them. Tell students to correct their own work.

When going over students' work, be careful not to concentrate on their mistakes to the extent that you overlook their overall progress. Positive reinforcement is particularly important during this time.

Take your time and enjoy this part of the lesson. Take advantage of any opportunities that arise to link items in the exercises to students' own experiences or to previous discussions. It is always helpful for students to see the relationship between their reading and their lives beyond the classroom.

THE LESSON SUMMARY

Have students summarize the lesson. This helps to facilitate learning and remembering. Ask them to say what the lesson was about in their own words. Then ask, "What did you learn from this lesson? What was hard for you?" Review any important concepts that they left out.

Some Final Thoughts

GIVING EXPLANATIONS

It is important to respond as promptly and clearly as possible to questions that students raise in class. When questions arise, give explanations that are brief and to the point. Don't be afraid to say, "I don't know, but I'll find out" when you don't have the answer to a specific question. For instance, if a student asks why some words have a silent *gh,* you can respond, "I don't know, but I think it has to do with their origins. If you're interested, we can check that in the dictionary later."

THE NEED FOR POSITIVE REINFORCEMENT

It is important to remember the value of positive reinforcement in all work that students do. Develop the habit of saying "good" or "right" after each correct response. Even if students make an error, there is usually something positive you can say. For example, you can say, "You've almost got it, but let's read the second sentence again."

Stress the notion of progress, since students are progressing as they complete each lesson. From time to time, you may want to suggest that they look back to the work they did in earlier lessons in the book or compare the writing they are doing now with what they did earlier in their writing notebooks.

THE IMPORTANCE OF OBSERVATION

It is important to pay close attention to how well students are progressing through the lessons in order to provide reinforcement activities when necessary and to adapt procedures as students become ready for greater challenges. Keep the following questions in mind to help you assess students' progress.

- Can students sound out or sight-read more words with less help?
- Are students correcting more of their own mistakes?
- Are students more adept at discussing the readings?
- Do students answer more questions correctly?
- Are students' writing skills gradually improving?

As you become attuned to students' progress, it will become easier to predict the areas that will need special reinforcement as well as those that students will probably grasp easily. You will thus be able to adapt the pace and procedures of the lessons to students' developing skills.

A Summary of *Dos*

- Do have a general discussion of the reading to assess students' comprehension, and ask literal-, inferential-, and applied-level questions.
- Do make sure students understand how phonics helps them to improve their word attack skills.
- Do make sure students know why they need to do homework.
- Do make sure students know exactly how to do the homework exercises.
- Do help students to develop good study habits.
- Do maximize learning by having students correct their own work.
- Do take time to review homework without rushing.
- Do give explanations when students request them.
- Do provide positive reinforcement regularly and naturally.
- Do consciously monitor students' progress.

Chapter 3. Writing

The Challenger *series emphasizes helping students to develop their reading skills. Opportunities for sustained writing in the student books are necessarily limited. This chapter gives suggestions for integrating more writing practice into the lessons on a regular basis. To provide additional writing practice, you may wish to include the correlated* Challenger Writing *student workbooks as part of your* Challenger *curriculum. More information on the correlated* Challenger *writing books is given on pages 37–38 of this teacher's manual.*

Providing Opportunities for Writing

Generally, basic reading students progress more rapidly if they have a writing activity as part of each lesson. There are several purposes for including writing practice.

- Writing is part of literacy. Writing reinforces and enhances reading skills.

- Writing helps students to formulate and express their thoughts more precisely. It also helps to develop reasoning skills as students learn to monitor whether or not their writing makes sense.

- The writing that students do in their lessons can help them with other writing, such as for letters, reports, job applications, and resumés.

- Through sustained writing, students can develop and polish their writing skills.

Even students with severely limited writing skills can begin to write from their very first lesson. Provide opportunities for free writing that doesn't have to be polished. Encourage students to get used to expressing their thoughts in writing. Students who write on a regular basis will come to understand that the purpose of both reading and writing is to communicate ideas.

Students working in Book 1 can keep dialogue journals and dictate language experience stories. Dialogue journals act as written conversations between you and the student. Since the journals are kept confidential, students can write anything they want to. Because you do not correct or change anything they write, they are freed from the fear of making mistakes. In your responses to students' journal entries, you can model correct written English while showing an interest in what students are telling you. Students gradually come to see writing as a means of communicating their ideas rather than as a chore.

Language experience activities, based on topics the students are interested in, use material and vocabulary familiar to the students. In a language experience activity,

beginning students name a topic and dictate a story. You write down the story, and they can later read it. Somewhat more advanced students can dictate several words or phrases related to a topic, and you can create a word map for the topic from the dictated words. The students can write stories based on the word maps. Then the students can read the stories they have written.

In addition to the above activities, students with limited writing skills can write brief notes, grocery lists, reminders for appointments, instructions to family members, and so forth. The individual lesson notes include suggestions for writing activities to supplement the lessons. Other topics of interest to the students, such as personal letters or current events, are also appropriate writing activities. Also consider using the writing book to provide a step-by-step approach to developing writing skills. As students progress through the *Challenger* books, writing activities can be longer, more polished, and more complex.

Students should keep their writing assignments in a writing notebook. A loose-leaf binder with wide-lined notebook paper works well. They should keep all drafts of a given activity in their notebooks. Have them date their work so that they can see how their writing improves over time.

PRE-WRITING ACTIVITIES

Selecting a Topic. Choosing a topic depends upon the type and purpose of the activity. The topic may be linked directly to the current lesson, but it doesn't have to be. In any case, the topic should be something the writer is interested in and knows something about.

Defining the Purpose and Audience. It is extremely important, particularly for inexperienced writers, to have a clear understanding of the purpose of the writing activity and the audience for whom it is intended. Understanding the purpose of the writing helps the writer to generate ideas and clarify the topic. Keeping the audience in mind helps to avoid one of the most common mistakes inexperienced writers make: leaving out important information that the reader needs to know.

Generating and Organizing Ideas. Brainstorming and idea mapping are useful techniques for generating and organizing ideas relating to the topic. Working in pairs or small groups, students can discuss the topic, jotting down ideas as they are mentioned. They can map their ideas by circling the main ideas and clustering around them the details that support those ideas. Then they can plan the order in which they want to present the main ideas. It often helps new writers to do this by developing a brief outline from the idea map.

Clarifying the Topic. The writer needs to clarify the topic by writing a complete sentence that expresses the main theme or concept that he or she wants to communicate. This can be done either before or after the brainstorming and idea-mapping steps. If it is done before, the writer should reread the statement after the idea-mapping process and, if necessary, revise it to include any new ideas that arose.

WRITING AND REVISING

First drafts of any writing activity that will be revised and edited should be double-spaced to allow ample room for editing. In a tutoring situation, you will want to read and react to the first draft so that you can guide the student in the revision process. If you have a group of students, they can share their work with each other. Working in pairs or small groups, writers can read their drafts aloud to one another and react to each other's writing on the basis of content and organization. The Writing Revision Checklist on page 39 can serve as a guide for this process. You can adapt the checklist to the needs and abilities of your students and to the requirements of specific writing assignments.

When writers have revised their first drafts, they can then exchange papers and act as editors, checking for mechanical problems such as missing words, spelling, capitalization, and punctuation. The Editing Checklist on page 40 can be used as a guide or adapted to your students' abilities. Give writers the opportunity to make changes before collecting the edited version.

Evaluating and Remediating Student Writing

When responding to student writing, be sure to make positive comments before noting areas for improvement. Your reactions should be based more on the content, style, and organization of the writing than on the mechanical aspects. You can use the Teacher's Evaluation Guide on page 41 or adapt it to suit your needs.

Have a short conference with each student individually to discuss written assignments. Begin by stressing the good points, giving positive feedback and reinforcement. Select one weakness for the writer to work on in the next writing activity. The most helpful areas will be those that will significantly improve the student's writing when mastered.

Deal with each student's mechanical problems as they occur in the student's writing. Provide additional practice for the student that addresses a specific problem. If most of your students have a particular mechanical problem, you can teach a mini-lesson about it.

The following are a few general suggestions for helping students with mechanical problems.

SPELLING DIFFICULTIES

When students misspell words they have studied in *Challenger,* have them look up the correct spelling in the Word Index found in the back of their student books. If students misspell a word they haven't studied, point out any parts of the word that are correctly spelled, and praise the logic of any phonetically reasonable misspellings.

For instance, if a student spells *friend* as *frend,* point out that the spelling represents the way the word sounds, but that there is a silent letter in *friend.* Help the student to find the correct spelling in the Word Index or the dictionary, and have him or her practice writing it correctly a few times. Suggest that students keep a list of words that they find hard to spell in a special section of their writing notebooks or on index cards. Help students learn how to use a dictionary when they are ready. This is an important skill for them to have.

Students who misspell a great many words will probably need remedial spelling help in addition to their work in *Challenger.* One approach is to ask an adult learner which words he or she most wants to learn to spell. These will usually be high-utility words for that learner. Learning to spell these often-used words will improve the learner's spelling rapidly.

Students who can spell very few words correctly should still be given regular and varied opportunities to write. Accept their level of competence, which may include many invented spellings, and do not make them correct every misspelled word. Instead, look for general patterns of misspellings, and try to correct those one at a time. Tackling a general problem helps students to spell correctly all the words that fall into that category rather than learning to spell one word at a time. *Patterns in Spelling*, a program published by New Readers Press, may be very helpful for these students.

GRAMMATICAL ERRORS

Grammatical errors occur because of the way the student has learned the language. For instance, students who say "he don't" or "they was" will also write that way. Bad grammatical habits take a lot of oral and written practice to replace. You can provide additional practice for these students, as well as modeling correct grammar in the classroom.

SHORT SENTENCES

Students who write short, choppy sentences may need help in thinking of more information to add in order to make their writing more interesting. When working in pairs, one student can ask questions of the other about the information contained in a first draft. By discussing the topic, the student can come up with additional details or descriptive information to add to the next draft.

RUN-ON SENTENCES AND FRAGMENTS

Run-on sentences usually sound all right to the students who have written them, so you will need to help them see that, by using commas and periods where necessary, readers can follow the thoughts more easily. To illustrate how punctuation helps the reader, have the student read the sentences aloud, pausing only at commas and taking a breath only at a period. If you prefer, you can demonstrate by reading aloud the same way. When students understand the function of punctuation marks, have them revise the run-on sentences as necessary.

Have students read sentence fragments aloud also, and then ask, "Is that a complete thought?" Help them to fill in the missing information orally and then rewrite the fragment as a complete sentence.

OMITTED WORDS

All writers omit words occasionally because the mind thinks faster than the hand can write. Often, students notice a missing word when reading their writing aloud. Sometimes, however, a student will read a word that's not there without realizing that it is missing. In this case, you can point to each word in the sentence as the student reads it. Encourage students to reread their writing after they have written a draft. Students who often omit words should point to each word as they reread what they have written.

CONFUSING SENTENCES

When a student writes a confusing sentence, say, "I don't know what this means. Can you explain it to me?" Once you understand the intent, start a more coherent version of the sentence, and have the student finish it and read the revision. Ask if it now says what the student intended to say. If not, work on the sentence until the revision accurately expresses the student's original idea.

Other Considerations

Writing, like reading, should be evaluated in terms of improvement rather than mastery. Most students read far better than they write. Allow them to develop from their own starting points, making them aware of their strengths as well as patiently helping them to work on their weaknesses.

Here are a few other suggestions to consider in helping students with their writing.

- As often as possible, have writers read their writing aloud. Students usually enjoy doing this, and it gives them a chance to hear whether or not their writing makes sense. Insist on honest but courteous reactions from the other students.
- With the writers' permission, use writing from previous or present students as models to demonstrate a specific

writing activity. Seeing the work of their peers helps students understand how the activity is to be done.

- Compile worksheets of sentences or paragraphs that illustrate common problems. For extra practice, students can work together to correct the errors and better understand how to avoid common writing problems.
- Provide the opportunity for students to publicly display or occasionally publish their final drafts.

A Summary of *Dos* and *Don'ts*

- Do provide regular opportunities for writing activities appropriate for students' levels of ability.
- Do have students keep writing notebooks for all their writing assignments.
- Do allow students to get used to expressing themselves in writing through free-writing activities that don't have to be polished.
- Do have students occasionally revise and edit their writing.
- Do be sure students understand the purpose of each writing activity and keep the audience in mind as they write.
- Do have students work together in pairs or small groups to generate ideas and to react to each other's writing.
- Do find something to praise in each piece of writing.
- Do base your responses primarily on content, style, and organization.
- Don't overemphasize mechanical errors.
- Do select a specific area for each student to work on to improve writing skills.
- Do provide opportunities periodically for students to display or publish their writing assignments.

Correlated Writing Books

The eight *Challenger Writing* workbooks have been developed to provide additional writing practice for students at each level of the *Challenger* reading series. Each of the eight writing books contains two pages of exercises for each lesson in the corresponding *Challenger* student book. Comprehension of the reading selections is aided by doing exercises in the writing books. Students are asked to write about personal opinions and experiences related to the readings. Thus, reading comprehension and vocabulary building are reinforced while writing and thinking skills are being developed.

Challenger Writing is designed to systematically develop the skills necessary for writing sentences, paragraphs, and more. Writing skills are developed sequentially throughout the eight writing books, as exercise formats become familiar while increasing in difficulty and sophistication.

Related strands of exercises also become more difficult as the series levels progress.

These strands include the following:

- filling in missing words
- putting sentences in order
- completing sentences and paragraphs
- writing guided open-ended paragraphs

As well as helping to develop writing skills, the exercises in the correlated *Challenger* writing books also develop and reinforce critical thinking skills. Questions about time order help develop sequencing skills. Exercises that ask for a reason why an incident in a story may have happened reinforce the concept of cause and effect. Learners develop basic skills in logic and reasoning as they write coherent sentences and responses to questions.

And because *Challenger* is a controlled-vocabulary reading series, the vocabulary in the student writing books is also controlled. Words used at each level of the writing books are those that have been introduced in the corresponding level of the student book.

Writing Revision Checklist

(to be used to react to early drafts)

	Author		Reader	
	Yes	**Needs Work**	**Yes**	**Needs Work**
Is the topic clearly stated?				
Does each paragraph have a sentence that tells clearly what the paragraph is about?				
Are there enough supporting details, examples, or reasons?				
Are all ideas related to the topic?				
Have all the important questions that readers might ask been answered?				
Is there a beginning, a middle, and an end?				
Are all ideas arranged in a logical order?				
Does the writing seem complete?				
Are there connecting words to help readers relate the ideas to each other?				
Are there some long, medium, and short sentences?				
Are there different kinds of sentences (for instance, questions or commands)?				
Have interesting, colorful, and appropriate words been chosen?				
Rather than some words being used again and again, have different words been used to express the same idea?				

Editing Checklist
(to be used to guide the final draft)

	Author		Reader	
	Yes	Needs Work	Yes	Needs Work
Is the topic clearly stated?				
Do all the ideas relate to the topic?				
Do added ideas make the author's meaning clearer?				
Does any new order of sentences or paragraphs improve the writing?				
Is the revised draft easier to understand?				
Is the revised draft more convincing?				
Are all words spelled correctly?				
Are all sentences punctuated correctly?				
Are capital letters used whenever necessary?				
Is each sentence a complete thought?				
Have all run-on sentences been fixed?				
Do pronouns refer clearly to someone or something?				
Are all action words used correctly?				

Teacher's Evaluation Guide

1. **Purpose**
   - Is the main theme of the composition clearly stated?

   - Does the writing reflect a clear sense of the intended audience?

2. **Content and Ideas**
   - Are there clearly stated main ideas supporting the main theme?

   - Are main ideas supported by reasons, examples, and other details?

   - Are main ideas and supporting material related to the main theme?

   - Is content appropriate to the theme and the audience?

3. **Organization and Development**
   - Does each paragraph have a single main idea plus supporting material?

   - Are main ideas and supporting material in a logical order?

   - Are transitions used when appropriate?

   - Is there an introduction and a conclusion, if appropriate?

4. **Sentence Structure**
   - Are all sentences complete thoughts?

   - Is there a variety of sentence structures?

5. **Language**
   - Are the words accurate and appropriate to the theme and audience?

   - Is the language clear, concrete, and concise?

6. **Check Mechanical Problems**

— Spelling	— Sentence fragments
— Punctuation	— Run-on sentences
— Capitalization	— Verb tense usage
— Subject-verb agreement	— Pronoun usage

7. **Positive Reinforcement**
   - What are the best things about this composition?

8. **For Next Time**
   - What one thing should the writer concentrate on improving in the next writing activity?

Chapter 4 Reinforcement Activities

These activities reinforce students' understanding and retention of the lesson material and give further practice in areas of weakness. When planning reinforcement activities, keep in mind that they should be fun. Select activities that students can enjoy, and avoid those that might cause frustration. Be sure to keep a record of activities you develop that work well.

Word Index Activities

After every four or five lessons in each book, there are word indexes of all the words introduced up to that point. Activities based on these word lists can reinforce word recognition skills and review meanings. Some activities based on the word indexes require little or no preparation. Others require some preparation on your part, but students appreciate your taking time to design activities specifically for them.

WORD REVIEW

Have a student pick any column in the word index that directly precedes the current lesson and read all the words. Students should mark words they can't sight-read or sound out with relative ease. After they have read the entire column, review the troublesome words. A note of caution: Students with certain learning disabilities have great trouble reading words in isolation and may need to review words in context.

GUESS THE WORD

Have a student pick a column of words. Then select a word from that column, and give a clue for the word. Have the student find the word in the column and read it. Try to give clues that relate to the student's environment or experience, since this association makes retention easier. A variation on this is for you to pick a column of words, then have the student select individual words and give clues.

SPELLING BEES

Oral spelling bees can be particularly helpful when a specific pattern or principle is emphasized. For instance, all the words might contain the same consonant blend or have doubled consonants before an ending. Spelling bees should be spontaneous, brief—10 words is usually sufficient—and informally presented. They should not resemble quizzes.

FLASH CARD ACTIVITIES

Flash cards can be made by printing words on 3 x 5 index cards. The following are examples of activities to do with flash cards.

Beat the Clock. Having a student read a series of related words on flash cards is a good way to reinforce specific phonics skills and to develop sight vocabulary. Students often enjoy flash card activities using a timer. They like to see how many correct answers they can produce before the time runs out.

Phonics Review. If a student has trouble mastering a particular sound-symbol relationship or phonics principle that has been introduced and studied, this activity can be very helpful. Select 15 or 20 words that demonstrate a phonics principle, such as *r*-controlled vowels, the silent *e*, or vowel pairs. You can use the word charts in Books 1 and 3 as a source for words, as well as the word indexes. Continue to use the phonics flash cards until the student can sight-read the words automatically.

Categories. You will need 15 flash cards for this activity. Refer to the appropriate word index to make sure you use words the student has studied. Think of three categories, and then select five words the student can associate with each category. For instance, the three categories might be people, parts of the body, and things to eat.

To begin, lay out the 15 cards in three columns of five cards each. Have the student read the words on all the cards first. Then name the first category. You might say, "I want you to put all the words that pertain to people in the first column." When this has been done correctly, name the second category. After this category has been completed, have the student try to figure out the category for the remaining words.

Concentration. This game provides word recognition reinforcement for students who have trouble differentiating between similar words. It is based on the card game of the same name and can be played by two to four people. You will need duplicate sets of flash cards to give you two cards for each word being reviewed. The cards should be laid out facedown. Players take turns turning up two cards at a time. If the cards match, the player removes the pair from the playing area. If the cards do not match, they are turned facedown again. When all the cards have been matched, the player with the most pairs wins. The level of difficulty can be increased by using pairs of similar words such as *dairy* and *diary*.

Make a Sentence. In this activity, each flash card contains a single word. All the words together are used to form a sentence. Be sure to include words the student finds troublesome. Include capitalization and punctuation signals on the flash cards so the student can use these clues to figure out the correct arrangement. As the student's skills improve, increase the complexity of the sentences.

Reading and Writing Activities

The following activities can help to build reading, comprehension, and writing skills. These skills include sequencing, recognizing cause and effect, summarizing, sentence combining and expanding, and comparing and contrasting ideas.

WHAT'S THE ORDER?

For this sequencing activity, entire sentences are printed on index cards. The sentences need to be carefully worded so that they will make sense when placed in an appropriate order. Lay out the cards in random order, and have students read each sentence. Then they should put the sentences in an order that makes sense. Have them read all the sentences aloud in the order they have selected. Below is a set of sentences that illustrate sequencing in chronological order.

I rode a bus to the park. (4)
I had so much fun that I got home very late. (5)
I phoned a friend to see if he wanted to go. (2)
My friend refused to go. (3)
I wanted to go to the park. (1)

Occasionally, there may be more than one way the sentences can be arranged to make sense. Any sequence that a student can justify should be considered acceptable.

MATCHING

This activity can help develop awareness of cause-and-effect relationships. It requires five sentences and 10 index cards. Write the sentence beginnings on five cards and the sentence endings on the remaining cards. After students have arranged the cards to form five complete sentences, they should read them aloud. Below is a set of sentence beginnings and endings to illustrate this activity.

1. Andy wanted to celebrate because (C)
2. Jack always put on a hat when he went out because (A)
3. Mack really needed to take time and relax more because (D)
4. Joan wasn't asked to go to the party because (E)
5. Linda wanted to take a course at the high school because (B)

A. he was starting to lose his hair.
B. she wanted to learn more about reading.
C. he had just won a new television set.
D. he was always losing his temper.
E. her friends knew she was out of town.

When preparing your own sentences, be sure there is only one sensible ending for each sentence beginning. Each example above starts with an effect. This activity can also be done by starting the sentences with causes and having students match the effects. Below is an example.

1. Andy had just won a new television set, so
A. he wanted to celebrate.

KEY WORDS

This activity can help students to write summary statements of the main ideas in paragraphs or reading selections. Select four or five key words in the reading, and write them on an index card or the chalkboard. Ask students to write a sentence about the reading, using all the key words. The following example is based on Lesson 15 of Book 2.

Key words: hobby barbed wire people collect

An appropriate response would be: "Some people collect different kinds of barbed wire as a hobby."

SENTENCE COMBINING

Making one sentence out of several short sentences is good practice for students who tend to write short, choppy sentences. Prepare a set of short sentences, each containing one idea. Have students combine them into a single longer sentence. Compare results, keeping in mind that there are usually several different acceptable responses. The following example is based on Lesson 2 of Book 3.

Jerome walked into the room.
Jerome saw Steven.
Steven had his shirt on.
Steven had his shorts on.
He was standing on his head.

Appropriate responses would be: "Steven, who had his shirt and shorts on, was standing on his head when Jerome walked into the room." Or: "When Jerome walked into the room, he saw Steven, wearing his shirt and shorts, standing on his head."

This activity can be done orally or by students writing their responses and then reading them aloud.

SENTENCE EXPANDING

This is another activity to help students write longer, more complex sentences. Write a kernel sentence on the board or on chart paper, and have students add descriptive words and phrases to expand the basic idea. The kernel sentence can be related to the reading selection in the current lesson, such as "People have hobbies." Or it can be something learners can relate to easily, such as "The car was damaged." Suggest that students add details that answer such questions as how, why, which ones, and when.

COMPARE AND CONTRAST

Some reading selections lend themselves to comparison and contrast activities. Students might list the differences between the eating habits of Diamond Jim Brady and those of a regular man after reading the selection on Brady in Lesson 17, Book 4. Or, they might list similarities and differences between two characters in the stories in Books 1 and 3.

Puzzles and Games

PUZZLES

Word puzzles are an excellent way to reinforce both meaning and spelling. Online puzzles that correspond to *Challenger Books* are available from New Readers Press. Also, puzzles and other activities can be found in magazines sold in drugstores and supermarkets. You can create similar puzzles with vocabulary from past and current word indexes.

WORD AND INFORMATION GAMES

Students often enjoy games modeled after television shows such as "Jeopardy" and "Wheel of Fortune." These games take some time to prepare but are a great way to reinforce vocabulary and information.

Students can create their own "Jeopardy" games by preparing sets of questions and answers based on the reading selections. They can also create categories of vocabulary words. For example, all the answers in a category might begin with the letters *st.* Other categories might include people's names, things to eat, places to visit, and compound words.

A game based on "Wheel of Fortune" can be played using words and phrases from the lessons. On a piece of paper, draw boxes representing each letter in a phrase. In place of spinning a wheel, "contestants" draw from a stack of cards on which dollar values are written. Be sure to include some "lose a turn" and "extra turn" cards, as well as a "bankrupt" card. As students guess letters correctly, write the letters in the boxes. This type of activity is an excellent way for students to become more aware of letter patterns in English words.

Student-requested Activities

From time to time, students may need help with specific personal needs, such as filling out application forms or reading a letter or brochure. These are excellent reinforcement activities because they help students to apply the skills they are building and they remind students of the relevance of reading and writing to their daily lives.

Encourage students to let you know in advance, whenever possible, if they plan to bring in this type of material. In that way, you can plan the lesson to allow time for helping students complete the task. Sometimes the activity will be something, such as filling out a form, that all of the students in the group can benefit from. Often, however, you will need to plan time to meet with the individual student who needs the help.

A Summary of *Dos*

- Do plan reinforcement activities to build comprehension skills and to give extra practice in areas of weakness.
- Do keep a record of activities that work well.
- Do encourage students to develop some of the activities.
- Do encourage students to bring in material they need your help with and to let you know in advance that they will do so.

Chapter 5 Using the Lesson Notes

The sections that follow contain suggestions for teaching the material in each lesson. Keep in mind that the lesson notes are only suggestions. If you try one of the ideas a few times and find it doesn't work with your students, disregard it.

Primary and Secondary Emphases

In most cases, the items listed under the "Primary emphasis" heading receive the greatest emphasis in the lesson and require the most teaching. Except for the early lessons in Book 1, reading comprehension and vocabulary development receive primary emphasis in most lessons. The first time a particular principle, task, or skill is introduced, it is also listed under "Primary emphasis." Items listed under "Secondary emphasis" often are skills that have been introduced previously and are now being reinforced.

The Reading Selections

The lesson notes contain suggestions for pre-reading and post-reading activities. It is a good idea to vary the methods used for presenting the reading selections and assessing comprehension. Carefully monitoring your students' progress will help you to develop sound procedures for improving reading and comprehension skills.

Developing Your Lesson Plan

As you prepare for a teaching session, refer to the notes for the lesson or lessons you will be working on, and decide which suggestions you want to incorporate into your lesson plan. It is a good idea to write down the specific ideas and suggestions you plan to use. List the objectives you hope to achieve for your students, and decide how to handle each segment of the lesson. Plan the activities you will use to reach the objectives, and gather any materials you may need. Note particularly how you plan to teach any new concepts presented in the lesson. Also make note of any suggestions that might be helpful to the students when they are doing their homework.

Jot down any remarks or reminders about particular difficulties students may have had with the lesson. Also note specific words or skills for which you may want to develop reinforcement activities. Be sure to keep notes of any procedures and techniques that seem to work well so that you can use them again.

Book 1 Introduction

Challenger 1 is designed for adult and adolescent students reading at or above a 2.0 reading level as determined by standardized reading inventories. Students beginning in this book should know how to blend sounds together to form words, have a basic understanding of sound-symbol relationships, and be able to discriminate between short and long vowel sounds. They should also be able to read some words by sight. Book 1 is appropriate for students who test at level 1 or 2 on the *Challenger Placement Tool*.

Book 1 emphasizes learning to recognize phonics elements and principles, developing phonetic decoding and reading comprehension skills, and building vocabulary. Book 1 lessons include the following significant features.

- New vocabulary is introduced in each lesson by means of word charts organized on the basis of phonics principles. The phonics principles provide students with an important tool for decoding words, enabling them to progress more rapidly than a random introduction of unrelated words would allow.
- Words are reviewed throughout the lessons so students learn to sight-read them or sound them out with minimal difficulty.
- Oral reading of stories helps to establish accurate, fluent reading.
- Stories gradually increase in length and complexity.
- Oral discussion of stories is used to aid and assess comprehension.
- Exercises give students practice in skills such as adding endings, distinguishing between similar words, and identifying synonyms and antonyms.

Scheduling Considerations

At least for the early lessons, Book 1 works best in a tutorial setting. This allows you to give your undivided attention to the student and pace the work according to the student's needs.

Students working in Book 1 usually need 1½ hours of time to complete each lesson. If your sessions are an hour long, you can plan two sessions per lesson, allowing time for writing activities, such as dialogue journal writing and language experience activities, as well as reinforcement activities that provide extra practice to develop skills.

As students progress beyond the midpoint of Book 1, a group setting with three to five students may work well if such a setting is possible. This way, students receive support and stimulation from one another, making learning a more enjoyable activity.

Suggestions for Teaching the Lessons

Each of the 20 lessons in Book 1 includes a word chart, a story, and reading and writing exercises. Many of the chart words are reviewed in the story and exercises in a lesson. The stories, which describe happenings in the lives of a group of friends, give students experience with reading lighthearted fiction. Most adults are familiar with the story form and should be able to relate to many of the incidents they read about.

THE WORD CHARTS

Each lesson begins with a word chart containing new words that illustrate specific phonics principles. For each lesson, you should explain the phonics principles being introduced or reviewed in the chart. Pages 8–10, Common Phonics Elements and Principles in English Words, may be a helpful reference for you. Have students sound out the words following the procedures recommended in Chapter 2 of this manual. Then do a random review of the words before proceeding to the story segment of the lesson.

THE WORDS FOR STUDY

Point out that the Words for Study are new words that appear in the story or in the exercises that follow. Have students sight-read as many of these words as possible. If a student can't sound out or sight-read one of the words listed, simply say it, and have the student repeat it a few times while looking at the word. Most students should be able to sound out the majority of phonetically regular words by the middle of the book.

READING THE STORY

Pre-reading suggestions are given in the lesson notes for Book 1. As part of the pre-reading activities, have students predict what the story will be about based on the Words for Study, the title, and the art. Students can also make predictions about what other vocabulary words they might expect to find in the story. You may also give a brief introduction to the story or ask a question that provides the student with a purpose for reading.

Oral reading is stressed in Book 1 in order to develop good reading patterns. Second readings of the stories should be assigned for homework. The following are some suggestions for handling the oral readings and discussions of the stories. It's a good idea to vary your procedure from lesson to lesson to avoid boredom or frustration. It may take awhile to find the procedures with which your student feels comfortable.

- Read aloud the first paragraph of the story. Ask a question or two to determine if students have understood what you read. Have students read the next sentence aloud. Continue taking turns reading sentences until the end of the story. Help students to sound out words or use context clues when necessary. Discuss what is happening at good breaking points in the story. At the end, briefly summarize the story with students, and then discuss it. Questions for discussion are suggested in the individual lesson notes.

- As students become more proficient, you can alternate reading whole paragraphs. Again, discuss what is happening at good breaking points in the story.

- If students have a great deal of trouble reading aloud, you might try echo reading. In this procedure, you read aloud one sentence while students follow along in the book. Students then read aloud the same sentence. Continue in this manner until the story is finished, stopping to discuss what is happening at appropriate points in the story.

- You can also help your students build fluency and confidence by reading aloud together. With this method, be sure to note words the students have trouble with, so you can reinforce recognition of them after you have read and discussed the story together.

- Have students with weak decoding skills read a paragraph twice, once for accurate decoding and once for meaning. Discuss content only after the second reading. After discussing the whole story, ask students to reread one or two sentences that were troublesome.

As students become better at decoding and hear you model good oral reading, their fluency improves. Then they can read more of the story themselves. For students whose comprehension skills need to be developed, continue to ask questions at good breaking points in the stories.

ASSESSING COMPREHENSION

Comprehension is assessed through oral discussion in Book 1. Brief informal discussions about the stories are far less threatening than having to give written answers to comprehension questions. Lead the discussion by asking literal-, inferential-, and applied-level questions as described in Chapter 2. Suggestions for all three types of questions are given in the individual lesson notes.

Encourage students to give precise answers and to see relationships that are developed across sentence or paragraph boundaries. The following dialogue, based on Lesson 1, illustrates how you can do this.

Teacher:	What happened in the first paragraph?
Student:	Some guy overslept.
Teacher:	Good. What's his name?
Student:	Bob.
Teacher:	So what happened to Bob because he overslept?
Student:	He was late for work.
Teacher:	Right. Bob was late for work because he overslept.

In this dialogue, the teacher models a precise answer for the student and draws attention to the cause- and effect-relationship in the content of the story. Through dialogues such as this, you can assess comprehension, help students develop precision in their answers, and build awareness that the purpose of reading is to obtain meaning.

DEALING WITH ORAL READING DIFFICULTIES

It is important that students develop good reading habits from the beginning. The most important habit for students to develop is that of monitoring their reading for meaning. While they read, students should continually ask themselves if what they have read makes sense. Since fluency is also very important, avoid interrupting students' reading unnecessarily. Whenever possible, allow students to read through a whole passage, and then have them reread certain sentences in which they misread words. The following are some suggestions for dealing with typical oral reading problems that beginning readers have.

Decoding Problems. There are two common types of decoding problems: incorrectly decoding and not recognizing a word. When an incorrectly decoded word interferes with meaning, ask, "Does that make sense?" If students substitute a word with a similar meaning, such as reading "riding the bus" for "taking the bus," simply ignore the substitution. If students don't recognize a word from a word chart, help them to sound it out using the word chart procedure. If they don't recognize a word listed under Words for Study, simply pronounce it for them. Make a note of words or sounds that give students frequent trouble, and emphasize these words in reinforcement activities.

Skipping Words. When students occasionally skip words, make a mental note of it. When they finish the first reading, have them reread a sentence or two to see if they read the skipped words the second time through. If they do not, point out the skipped words, and have them read the sentence again. Check to be sure they understand the passage.

Misreading Little Words. Short words often give the most trouble. Students need to learn that comprehension is affected when they misread words such as *in* for *on* and *form* for *from.* Again, you can have students reread a sentence when they finish the story to see if they read the words correctly. If a student consistently makes many errors of this type, particularly errors involving letter reversals, it may signal a learning disability. In that case, the student should be tested for that possibility.

Ignoring Punctuation Marks. In oral reading, the most important punctuation marks are the comma, the period, and the question mark. If students ignore these marks, explain how they function, and model how the voice responds to these marks.

Ignoring Word Endings. Note any endings, such as *-ed* or *-ing,* that students fail to read in the story, and have them reread words with those endings after they have finished the story. Students who drop endings in their everyday speech may need extra practice and reinforcement to overcome this problem.

THE EXERCISES

Generally, the exercises should be previewed during the class session and completed for homework. Book 1 students are not responsible for reading the directions that precede each exercise. The directions are for your benefit. Students who are capable of reading the directions, however, should do so during the homework preview.

Explain in your own words how to do each exercise. If there is a column of answer words, have students read the words. When an item has been done as an example, have the students read it. Explain, or have the students explain, how it was done. In the early lessons, have students complete one item in each exercise to be sure they know how to do it. When all of the exercises have been previewed, have students explain briefly what they are supposed to do in each one.

Remind students that they are to answer all questions. If students have a tendency to skip items they don't know, explain that they should make "intelligent guesses." Show

them how the use of context clues and the process of elimination are strategies for selecting correct answers.

Go over all the homework exercises during the next class session. Have students correct all wrong answers. For the first 10 lessons, 70 percent accuracy is acceptable. Eighty percent accuracy is a reasonable expectation for the last 10 lessons. If students score below these levels more often than not, divide each lesson over more class sessions, and increase the number of reinforcement activities.

Writing Activities

Providing writing opportunities on a regular basis is important for beginning readers. Dialogue journals and language experience stories are appropriate writing activities for students in Book 1. Both types of activities are discussed in Chapter 3 of this manual. In addition, the lesson notes suggest topics related to the lesson material that students might write about. Writing Book 1 also provides writing activities to extend the lesson content and to help students develop and practice their writing skills.

The Lesson Segments

The procedure for each session should be as consistent as possible. Most sessions will have the following segments. You may want to vary the order to suit your particular situation.

1. **Homework Review.** Go over the exercises in the previous lesson that were done as homework.
2. **Word Study.** Introduce the new lesson, and explain the phonics principles presented in the word chart. Have the student read some or all of the chart words and then the Words for Study.
3. **Reading the Story.** Do one or more pre-reading activities to introduce the story in the new lesson. Have the student read the story aloud and then discuss it.
4. **Writing Activity.** Have the student do some free writing, or work with the student on a pre-writing activity such as using idea mapping or dictating a language experience story.
5. **Reinforcement Activity.** When time permits, focus on an area of difficulty in a way that is fun for the student. See Chapter 4 for suggestions.
6. **Homework Preview.** Go over the exercises to be done for homework to be sure the student knows how to do them.

Individual Lesson Notes

The individual lesson notes, which begin on page 49, contain suggestions and procedures for teaching the lessons in Book 1.

LESSON 1
The Long and Short Vowels

Primary emphasis
- Long and short vowel patterns
- Single consonant sounds
- Oral and silent reading comprehension
- The silent *e* rule

Secondary emphasis
- Accurate, legible writing
- Context clues
- Distinguishing between similar words
- Writing and study skills

Word Chart

Note: V = any vowel, C = any consonant

1. Long vowel patterns introduced:
   - The silent *e* (VCe): *name, time, woke, rule*
   - Open syllables (CV and V): *be, I, go*
   - Double vowel (VV): *see, need*
2. Short vowel pattern introduced:
   - Closed syllables (VC, CVC): *at, yes, is, Bob, but*
3. Special notes:
   - The word *a* is usually pronounced /ə/.
   - There are two pronunciations of long *u*: /oo/ and /yoo/.
   - Help students sound out *Eddie,* since *ie* hasn't been introduced yet.

Words for Study
1. Most of the words here are not phonetically regular. Pronounce those that students don't recognize, and have them repeat each word several times while looking at it.
2. Point out the apostrophe in *o'clock* and the abbreviation *Mr.*

Pre-reading Activities
Ask or say to students:
1. Have you ever been late because you overslept? What happened?
2. Read this story to find out why Bob is late for work and what happens to him.

Post-reading Activities
Ask or say:
1. Tell what happened to Bob after he overslept.

2. How did Bob get to work?
3. Why did Bob stay in a job he hated?
4. About what age do you think Bob and Eddie are? Why do you think so?
5. What do you think Bob will do now? Why?
6. Do you know anyone who has recently lost a job? What did that person do?
7. Do you think someone should be fired for being late to work?

Language Experience or Writing Activity
Complete one of these sentences.
> I agree that Bob should be fired because . . .
> I disagree that Bob should be fired because . . .

Additional Activities
1. Read to your students for pleasure at the end of each lesson, beginning with this lesson. Suggested material: short stories, articles of interest to students, poems, news stories, etc.
2. Make folders for storing language experience stories and students' writings.

Exercises

1 READ AND WRITE
Students should copy the sentences accurately, paying special attention to capitalization and punctuation.

2 READ AND WRITE
- Have students read the words on the left. Some are words students haven't studied yet. Review the long vowel silent *e* rule.
- Suggest that students read each sentence, saying "blank" for each line. Read the first sentence: "*Blank* did not have *blank* to go to the park." Then have students read the sentence with *Tim* and *time* filled in, and write the words on the correct lines. Assign the rest of the exercise for homework, or have the students finish it with your help.

Summarizing the Lesson
Help students to reflect on what they have learned. Ask, "What were the most important things you learned in the lesson?"

LESSON 2
More Work with Long and Short Vowels

Primary emphasis
- Long and short vowel patterns
- Single consonant sounds
- Oral and silent reading comprehension
- The silent *e* rule

Secondary emphasis
- Legible, accurate copying
- Distinguishing between similar words
- Context clues
- Writing and study skills

Word Chart
1. Long vowel patterns reviewed: the silent *e* (VCe), double vowel (CVVC)
2. Short vowel patterns reviewed: closed syllables (VC and CVC)
3. Short vowel pattern introduced: one vowel, two consonants (CVCC): *which*
4. Special notes:
   - Long *u* is pronounced /oo/ and /yoo/.
   - Help students sound out *when* and *which,* since the digraphs *wh* and *ch* are new.

Words for Study
1. Pronounce the words that students don't recognize and can't sound out. Have them repeat each word several times.
2. Point out the *-ed* ending on *relaxed* and the apostrophe in *let's.* Ask if students know what two words make up *let's.* If they don't, tell them *let's* is another way to say *let us.* Have them write *let us* and compare with *let's* to find the difference. Explain that the apostrophe stands for the missing *u* in *let's.*

Pre-reading Activities
Ask or say:
1. What do you remember about Bob and Eddie from Lesson 1?
2. In this story, Bob has a job interview. Have you ever had a job interview? How did you feel before the interview? Read this story to find out how Bob feels before his interview.

Post-reading Activities
Ask or say:
1. Tell what happened in this story.
2. Where did Dan Rose live?
3. What did Bob tell his dad he would do if Mr. Rose offered him the job?
4. Do you think Bob and Eddie have been friends for a long time? Why or why not?
5. What did Eddie do to help Bob relax before the job interview? Did it help?
6. Who do you think arranged the appointment between Bob and Dan Rose?
7. Do you think Bob should take a job he does not know how to do? How might he learn how to do it?
8. What are some of the questions Dan Rose might ask when interviewing Bob for a job to fix bikes?

Language Experience or Writing Activities
1. Dictate a language experience story about finding a job.
2. Tell about a job or task you like or do not like to do.

Additional Activities
1. Obtain job application forms for students to practice filling out. Help students to prepare the form, and suggest that they keep it for future reference.
2. Discuss what to expect at a typical job interview. Help students prepare answers for the types of questions usually asked at job interviews.

Exercises

2 READ AND WRITE
During your preview of this exercise, have students read all the words in the column on the left. Some are new words. Review the long vowel silent *e* rule. Remind students to read the first sentence as "Mom needed a *blank* box for the roses."

Summarizing the Lesson
Discuss with students what they learned from the lesson. Do a random review of chart words and the Words for Study.

LESSON 3

More Work with Long and Short Vowels

Primary emphasis

- Long and short vowel patterns
- Single consonant sounds
- Oral and silent reading comprehension
- The silent *e* rule

Secondary emphasis

- Distinguishing among similar words
- Context clues
- Writing and study skills

Word Chart

1. Long vowel patterns reviewed: VCe, CVVC
2. Short vowel pattern reviewed: CVC

Pre-reading Activities

Ask or say:

1. What do you remember about Eddie from the stories in Lessons 1 and 2? Allow students to reread the sections of those stories that mention Eddie. Help students scan the stories to find Eddie's name.
2. As you read, decide if you think Bob spends a lot of time with Kate.

Post-reading Activities

Ask or say:

1. Tell how Kate and Eddie met.
2. Where did Kate work?
3. How often does Eddie see Kate?
4. Was Eddie driving the jeep when he saw Kate at the lake? How do you know?
5. Who are the most important characters in this story?
6. What are some things you learned about Eddie, Kate, and Dave?

7. Do you think it was wise for Kate to ride off with Eddie when she had just met him? Why or why not?

Language Experience or Writing Activities

1. Tell about what you like to do with your friends.
2. Tell about a special day you remember.

Additional Activities

1. Ask students to describe how they imagine the location of this story. Ask, "What time of year do you think it was? What kind of weather? What were people wearing?"
2. Introduce the use of dialogue journals. See Chapter 3 for details.

Exercises

1 READ AND WRITE

During the homework preview, explain the long, short, and silent vowel marks. Tell students to read each word and listen for the vowel sounds before marking them.

2 READ AND WRITE

Each of these sentences has three blanks. The words to be filled in are similar and could easily be confused. During the homework preview, have students read the words in each group to be sure they can distinguish among them. Then have students complete the first two sentences to be sure they understand what to do.

Summarizing the Lesson

Discuss with students the most important things they learned from this lesson. Review difficult words or concepts.

LESSON 4
Changing the First Consonant Sound

Primary emphasis
- Long and short vowel patterns
- Single consonant sounds
- Oral and silent reading comprehension
- The silent *e* rule

Secondary emphasis
- Distinguishing among similar words
- Context clues
- Writing and study skills

Word Chart
1. Have students read down each column of three rhyming words, so they will recognize the similarities in sound and spelling and begin to develop an awareness of word patterns.
2. Long vowel patterns reviewed: VCe, CVVC, CV
3. Short vowel patterns reviewed: CVC, CVCC
4. Make sure students know that *qu* is pronounced /kw/ in *quite* and *quit* and that *ph* is pronounced /f/ in *phone.*

Words for Study
1. The name *Louise* is difficult for many students. Have students repeat it several times while looking at it.
2. Review the word *apostrophe,* and ask if students know what two words make up *didn't.* If they don't, tell them that *didn't* is another way of saying *did not.* Have them write *did not.* Compare *didn't* with *did not* to find the difference. Explain that the apostrophe stands for the missing *o* in *didn't.*

Pre-reading Activity
Ask or say:

Do you remember making something that turned out so bad that you were embarrassed someone would see it? In this story, Kate tries to bake a cake for the first time. Read to find out what happens to Kate's cake.

Post-reading Activities
Ask or say:
1. Tell what happened in this story.
2. Why do you think Kate refused Aunt Louise's help in baking the cake?
3. Compare how Kate felt about accepting help at the beginning of the story with how she felt at the end.
4. Do you think Kate will try to bake another cake soon? Why or why not?
5. The next time Kate decides to bake a cake, what do you think she will do differently?
6. Do you think Kate will laugh about this someday?
7. Can you remember a time when you refused help because you wanted to do something yourself? How did it turn out?

Language Experience or Writing Activities
1. Tell about an experience similar to Kate's. Think about the first time you cooked, sewed, painted, or fixed something.
2. Do you have any funny stories about cooking? What did you do with the food that was made?

Additional Activity
Read the last sentence in the first paragraph of the story. What does the exclamation mark tell you? How should this sentence be read aloud?

Exercises

1 READ AND WRITE
Some words in the left column are new. Have students read all the words during the homework preview.

2 YES OR NO
These lighthearted questions are for reading practice. There are no "correct" answers.

Summarizing the Lesson
Discuss with students the most important things they learned in this lesson. Ask students to summarize what they have learned so far about words with long and short vowels. Review the word pattern concept.

LESSON 5
Changing the End Consonant Sound

Primary emphasis
- Long and short vowel patterns
- Single consonant sounds
- Oral and silent reading comprehension
- Distinguishing among similar words

Secondary emphasis
- The ending -ed
- Context clues
- Writing and study skills

Word Chart
1. Have students read down each long vowel column to get a sense of the changes in the final consonant sounds. Then do the same for the short vowel columns.
2. Long vowel patterns reviewed: VCe, CVVC
3. Short vowel patterns reviewed: CVC, CVCC

Words for Study
1. Use the procedure outlined in Lessons 2 and 4 to teach the contractions *it's* and *don't.* Stress that *it's* is the contraction for *it is,* not the possessive form for *it* (*its*).
2. Be sure students know the abbreviations for *Mrs.* and *Ms.* Review *Mr.* from Lesson 1.

Pre-reading Activity
Ask or say:

To whom do you go for help and advice? In this story, Bob asks Aunt Louise about a small problem. As you read the story, think about what kind of person Aunt Louise is.

Post-reading Activities
Ask or say:
1. What are two things the story mentions about Aunt Louise?
2. What was Aunt Louise doing when Bob arrived?
3. Where was Bob just before he visited Aunt Louise?
4. What time of day did Bob visit Aunt Louise? How do you know?
5. Bob said he had a problem at work and needed help. What did Aunt Louise think the problem was?
6. What are some things you learned about Aunt Louise in the story?
7. Do you think Aunt Louise is a good listener? Why or why not?
8. Does the story tell us what advice Aunt Louise gives Bob? If the story continued, what advice would you expect her to give him? What advice would you give him?

Language Experience or Writing Activity
Can you think of someone in your life like Aunt Louise? Write or tell about why you like this person or about an incident when this person listened to you and gave you advice. Did you follow the advice? What happened?

Exercises

1 READ AND WRITE
During the homework preview, tell students that they are going to practice adding -ed to words they have studied. Go over the examples, helping students to discover the spelling patterns. For each example, ask, "Were any letters added, dropped, or changed when -ed was added?" When students have discovered the pattern for each column, state the patterns as follows:
- For column 1 words, simply add -ed to the base word.
- For column 2 words, drop the silent e before adding -ed.
- For column 3 words, double the final consonant before adding -ed.

Have students do item 2 in each column. Then have students read the remaining words in each column with the -ed added to be sure they understand how to do the exercise.

Summarizing the Lesson
Discuss what students learned from the lesson. Review the patterns for adding -ed that were introduced.

LESSON 6
Ending Consonant Blends

Primary emphasis
- Ending consonant blends *nd, nt, ck, mp*
- Short and long vowel patterns
- Oral and silent reading comprehension

Secondary emphasis
- The ending *-ed*
- Distinguishing among similar words
- Context clues
- Writing and study skills

Word Chart
1. Explain that each consonant can be heard in a consonant blend. Have students read down the columns of rhyming words, concentrating on the sounds of the blends.
2. The **CVCC** words in this chart all have short vowel sounds except the *ind* words, which have a long vowel sound. Be sure to point this out to students.
3. Ask students what missing letters the apostrophes stand for in *can't, don't,* and *won't.*

Pre-reading Activities
1. Review what students learned about Eddie in Lessons 1–3.
2. Ask: Have you ever bet on the horses or played the lottery or bingo? Have you ever played cards at an online casino? In this story, Eddie has good luck playing cards online. Read to find out if he stops betting before his luck runs out.

Post-reading Activities
Ask or say:
1. Tell what happened in this story.
2. Why does Eddie have only a little money at the beginning of the story?
3. Find a sentence in the story that tells what Eddie's friends think about betting on cards.

4. When Eddie first starts to play, what does he want to do with the money he thinks he'll win?
5. What does Eddie plan to do with his money after he wins six hands?
6. What happens after Eddie wins the first six hands?
7. Why do you think that Eddie keeps playing until he loses?
8. Find a sentence in the story that shows that Eddie hasn't learned anything from losing his money.
9. Do you think that Eddie made a good decision to play cards online?
10. Would you have done anything differently?

Language Experience or Writing Activities
1. Does Eddie believe in luck? Do you believe in luck? Write or tell about a time you felt lucky.
2. Discuss and list gifts people give that are not purchased at a store (suggestions: time, help, support, friendship, volunteer work, blood). Complete one of the following sentences.
   I want to give the gift of . . .
   I give the gift of . . .
3. How do you feel about gambling?

Additional Activity
Read an excerpt from an article about online betting—by either playing cards or betting on horses—with or to your students.

Exercises

1 READ AND WRITE
Review the three patterns for adding *-ed* introduced in Lesson 5.

Summarizing the Lesson
After discussing what students learned from the lesson, review the ending consonant blends and the patterns for adding *-ed.*

More Work with Ending Consonant Blends

Primary emphasis
- Ending blends *ng* and *nk*
- Oral and silent reading comprehension
- Short vowel pattern (**CVCC**)

Secondary emphasis
- The ending *-ing*
- Distinguishing among similar words
- Context clues
- Writing and study skills

Word Chart
1. The *ng* and *nk* endings may be difficult for students to pronounce.
2. Students may need help sounding out the *th* in *thing, thank,* and *think,* since this unvoiced *th* has not been introduced yet.
3. Point out that the *w* in *wrong* is silent.

Pre-reading Activities
Ask or say:
1. Do you know what "getting up on the wrong side of the bed" means? How do you feel when you get up on the wrong side of the bed?
2. As you read this story, look for things that happen to Dave that make him decide he has gotten up on the wrong side of the bed.

Post-reading Activities
Ask or say:
1. In your own words, retell the story starting with the ringing alarm clock.
2. What do you think *funk* means in this sentence: "The clock rang, and Dave *woke up* in a funk"?
3. How did Dave get to work after he junked his jeep? What does "junked his jeep" mean?
4. List the things that made Dave decide he had gotten up on the wrong side of the bed.

5. In what room did the cat cause the trouble? Was Dave in that room when the cat broke the jam pot? How do you know?
6. Do you think Dave lives alone with his cat? Why or why not?
7. Is Dave a neat person? What information from the story did you use in deciding your answer?
8. Do you think Dave made the right decision? What would you do in the same situation?

Language Experience or Writing Activities
1. What kinds of things make you angry in the morning?
2. Write or tell about a time when you got up on the wrong side of the bed.
3. Write or tell about how you like to spend your days off.

Additional Activity
Ask: What if Dave had gotten up on the right side of the bed? Have students retell the story from this point of view.

Exercises

1 READ AND WRITE
Review the rules for adding the *-ed* ending, and tell students that they apply them to adding *-ing* as well. Point out *fix* in the first column. Tell students that although it looks like the words in column 3 (**CVC** words), *x* is not doubled before adding the ending.

Summarizing the Lesson
Discuss with students the most important things they learned in the lesson. Review rules for adding endings that begin with a vowel.

LESSON 8
Review of Vowels and Consonants

Primary emphasis
- Long and short vowel patterns
- Single consonant sounds
- Oral and silent reading comprehension

Secondary emphasis
- Distinguishing among similar words
- Context clues
- Synonyms
- Writing and study skills

Word Chart
1. Have students read down the columns of rhyming words.
2. Long vowel patterns reviewed: **VCe, VVC**
3. Short vowel patterns reviewed: **CVC, CVCC**

Words for Study
Have students tell the differences in spelling and pronunciation between *were* and *where*. Point out that *here* represents a third pronunciation of *-ere*. Provide practice in sentences if students confuse these words.

Pre-reading Activities
Ask or say:
1. Have you been to an amusement park? What was it like?
2. In this story, Aunt Louise and Jack go to an amusement park. As you read, decide if you think Jack and Aunt Louise have known each other for a long time.

Post-reading Activities
Ask or say:
1. Was Aunt Louise sensitive about her age? How do you know?
2. When Jack noticed that Aunt Louise was getting mad, what did he do?
3. What are some of the things Jack and Aunt Louise did at the amusement park?
4. Why did Jack say it was time to go home?
5. Aunt Louise said, "It seems as if we just got here!" When people say this, what does it usually mean?

Language Experience or Writing Activities
1. Complete the following sentence. Something *I have always* wanted to do is . . .
2. When does time seem to go by very slowly for you? Very quickly? Write about an experience you remember.

Exercises

2 READ AND WRITE
Teach when to use *a* and when to use *an* during the homework preview by giving examples such as, "Eddie ate *an* apple, but Bob ate *a* banana."

3 READ AND WRITE
Review the long, short, and silent vowel marks.

4 READ AND WRITE
During the homework preview, introduce this matching exercise by going over the example. Point out the check mark (✓) before *huge*. Then have students do item 2. Make sure they understand that they are to match words having the same meaning. Remind them to check off each word they use.

Explain the process of elimination. Tell students they don't have to do the items in order. They can do the ones they know first, skipping those they are not sure of. Then they can go back and do the skipped ones when fewer choices remain.

5 READ AND WRITE
Although students will be composing complete sentences, most of the words they will need to use are in the questions to be answered. Teach or review the use of initial capital letters and end punctuation for sentences.

Summarizing the Lesson
Discuss with students what they learned from the lesson. Review the uses of *a* and *an* and the concept of forming words by changing the initial consonants.

LESSON 9
Vowel Sounds for -y

Primary emphasis
- Vowel sounds for *y*: *y, ay, ey, oy, uy*
- *-y* as a suffix
- Words that end in *-ly*
- Oral and silent reading comprehension

Secondary emphasis
- Context clues
- Synonyms
- Writing and study skills

Word Chart
1. The letter *y* as /ī/ and the vowel combinations *ay, ey, oy,* and *uy* are introduced.
2. Explain that days of the week are capitalized.
3. Point out that *y* is considered a consonant at the beginning of such words as *yesterday*.

Words for Study
Tell students that *what's* is the contraction for both *what is* and *what has*.

Pre-reading Activities
Ask or say:
1. Do you remember the story in Lesson 4 about Kate's attempt to bake a cake? Find a reference to that episode in this story.
2. In this story, read to find out how Bob's friends plan to celebrate his birthday.

Post-reading Activities
Ask or say:
1. Retell this story in your own words.
2. Two people offer to bake a cake for the party. Who are they?
3. Why do you think Eddie wanted Aunt Louise to bake the cake instead of Kate?
4. Is knowing how to bake a cake important to Kate? Why do you think so?
5. Did everyone agree on what to buy Bob? Who did not agree? Why?

6. Find the place in the story that suggests that everyone went along on the shopping trip.
7. How do you think Bob will feel when he opens his gifts?

Language Experience or Writing Activities
1. What is the strangest birthday gift you ever received?
2. Write about a birthday you remember.
3. Complete the following sentence: If I could spend my birthday doing anything I wanted, I would . . .

Additional Activities
1. Introduce abbreviations for the days of the week.
2. Bring a calendar to class. Help students figure out which day of the week their birthdays fall on and write sentences using this information.
3. List ideas for celebrating birthdays that don't cost much money.

Exercises

1 READ AND WRITE
Point out that the *y* in these words sounds like long *e*. Have students explain what to do when adding *-y* to the words in each column. If necessary, review what they learned about adding *-ed* and *-ing* in earlier lessons.

2 READ AND WRITE
During the homework preview, have students read the words that end in *-ly* in the box.

3 READ AND WRITE
During the homework preview, introduce the rule for changing *y* to *i* before adding any ending unless the ending starts with *i*.

4 READ AND WRITE
Review the process of elimination during the homework preview. Have students complete any two items to make sure they remember how to do this type of exercise.

Summarizing the Lesson
Have students reflect on what they learned in the lesson. Ask them to state the spelling rules about adding endings that start with a vowel and about changing *y* to *i* before adding an ending.

LESSON 10
Silent Letters

Primary emphasis
- Silent letters *kn, wr, mb, ight, tch*
- Oral and silent reading comprehension

Secondary emphasis
- Distinguishing among similar words
- Context clues
- Antonyms
- Word associations
- Writing and study skills

Word Chart
1. Have students identify the silent letters in each cluster. They may want to draw a line through each silent letter.
2. Point out that *ight* spells /īt/ in many common words.
3. Tell students that *tch* is a common spelling for /ch/ at the end of a syllable with a short vowel.

Words for Study
Tell students that *I'll* is the contraction for *I will.*

Pre-reading Activities
Ask or say:
1. In this story, Eddie acts foolishly and gets hurt. Read to find out what happens to Eddie and why it happens.
2. As you read, find a place in the story where Kate shows that she cares about Eddie.

Post-reading Activities
Ask or say:
1. Where is Eddie supposed to be at six o'clock?
2. Why is Eddie late?
3. Why was Eddie worried about being late?
4. How did the accident happen?
5. Where does Eddie's car end up?
6. What happens to the car in the accident?
7. What shape is Eddie in after the accident?
8. What does Kate say when Eddie says he's been in an accident?
9. Compare the night out that Eddie had planned with what really happens.
10. If Eddie hadn't had the accident, would he still have been late?

11. Did Eddie make a good decision when he tried to drive fast instead of calling Kate? What would you have done if you were Eddie?

Language Experience or Writing Activities
1. Write or tell about a time when things did not turn out as you expected.
2. What are some things to do after a car accident?
3. Continue the story. What happens after Eddie calls Kate?

Additional Activities
1. Discuss cause and effect. Then read the fourth paragraph in the story to find a cause and effect. You could also explain that the whole story is about cause and effect. Ask what is the cause and what is the effect.
2. If passing the driver's license test is a goal of any of your students, begin to use a driver's manual in your lessons. Start with the pages on traffic signs. (*Studying for a Driver's License,* a book available from New Readers Press, is designed to help low-level readers pass the oral or written driver's test.)

Exercises

2 OPPOSITES
This matching exercise should be done the same way as the synonym matching exercises in Lessons 8 and 9. But be sure students understand they are to match *opposites* this time. If necessary, review the process of elimination during the preview.

3 WORD STUDY
During the homework preview, explain that in each row of words, there is one word that does not fit with the rest. Have students read the example and explain why *yesterday* is the right answer. Have them do the second item and, if necessary, the third item.

Summarizing the Lesson
Discuss with students what they learned from the lesson. Do a random review of words that contain silent letters.

LESSON 11
The *r*-Controlled Vowels

Primary emphasis
- The *r*-controlled vowels in *ar, are, or, er, eer, ir, ur*
- The endings *-er* and *-ier*
- Oral and silent reading comprehension
- Spelling (changing *y* to *i*)

Secondary emphasis
- Context clues
- Writing and study skills

Word Chart
Explain that when the letter *r* follows a vowel, the sound of the vowel is somewhat affected. Also point out that *er, ir,* and *ur* are pronounced the same way.

Words for Study
Teach the contraction *I've* using the same procedure as in earlier lessons.

Pre-reading Activities
Ask or say:

1. Have you ever been to a fortune-teller? What was it like?
2. Do you know anyone who has ever been to a fortune-teller? Who was the person, and what did he or she think about the experience?
3. As you read, look for a sentence that describes how Kate feels about going to the fortune-teller.

Post-reading Activities
Ask or say:

1. What does Kate show Aunt Louise?
2. Why does Kate ask Aunt Louise to go to the fortune-teller?
3. What does Aunt Louise say about fortune-telling?
4. What does Kate say Eddie would do if he knew she was going to a fortune-teller?
5. Why does Kate stop outside the fortune-teller's shop instead of going in?
6. What are the three ways that Mary says she tells fortunes?
7. If a fortune-teller reads a palm, what does he or she look at?
8. Why does Kate laugh at what the fortune-teller says?
9. If the story continued, what else do you think the fortune-teller would say to Kate?
10. Do you think that the fortune-teller really sees Kate's future, or is she telling Kate what she wants to hear?

Language Experience or Writing Activities
1. Does anyone in your life remind you of Aunt Louise? Write or tell about why this person reminds you of her.
2. Complete the following sentence: I like/do not like to try something new because . . .

Exercises

1 READ AND WRITE
Review the silent *e* and doubling rules used when adding endings. Point out *box* in the first set. Explain that *x* is not doubled. This is also true for *w* in words like *few.*

3 READ AND WRITE
During the homework preview, go over both parts of this exercise thoroughly. If necessary, review the *y* to *i* conversion introduced in Lesson 9. Then have students write *handier.*

Next, explain that when students have written all the *-ier* words, they should fill in the blank in each sentence below with the *-ier* word that fits best. Have them find the sentence in which *handier* fits best. They should write *handier* in the blank in sentence 6.

Summarizing the Lesson
Discuss with students the most important things they learned from this lesson. Ask them to explain the procedures for adding endings that start with a vowel and for adding endings to words that end in a consonant plus *y.*

LESSON 12
Vowel Combinations

Primary emphasis
- Vowel combinations *ai, ea, ie, oa, ue, oi, oo, ou*
- Context clues
- Oral and silent reading comprehension

Secondary emphasis
- Distinguishing between similar words
- Writing sentences
- Writing and study skills

Word Chart
1. The upper section contains long vowel combinations except for the second column of *ea* words. Point out that the first vowel is long in the long vowel pairs and the second vowel is silent. Encourage students to select key words such as *eat* and *head* for both *ea* sounds.
2. The lower section contains some of the more troublesome vowel combinations. Encourage students to pick key words for both *oo* sounds and for this pronunciation of *ou*.

Words for Study
Teach the three contractions following the usual procedure.

Pre-reading Activities
Ask or say:
1. Have you ever picked a fight with someone just because you were in a bad mood?
2. In this story, Kate is in a bad mood. Read to find out how Eddie changed her mood.

Post-reading Activities
Ask or say:
1. Tell the story in your own words.
2. Find the paragraph that mentions three reasons why Kate was in a bad mood. What are the three reasons?
3. What did Kate do before she shouted? Why? Did it help?

4. What is Eddie's good news?
5. How did Eddie change Kate's mood?
6. Was Kate excited about Eddie's new job? How do you know?
7. If Kate had been in a better mood, what do you think she would have done differently?
8. What could Kate have said or done to prevent the fight? What could Eddie have said or done to prevent the fight?

Language Experience or Writing Activities
1. What are some things that put you in a bad mood?
2. Write or tell about a time when you heard some good news that cheered you up.
3. List and discuss Kate's problems in terms of problems she can solve and problems beyond her control.

Exercises

1 READ AND WRITE
During the homework preview, have students read the words in the box. Tell them to use these words to complete this little story. Have them complete the first sentence, checking off the words at the left as they use them. Note that in the third paragraph it doesn't matter whether they write *soap* and *water* or *water* and *soap*.

3 READ AND WRITE
This exercise is like Exercise 5 of Lesson 8. Appropriate answers can be, "I like it better when the sun is out" or "I like it better when the moon is out." Also appropriate would be, "I never go to the movies; I rent DVDs instead." Accept all reasonable responses.

Summarizing the Lesson
Discuss with students what they learned from the lesson. Do a random review of words from the chart. Make note of vowel combinations that give students trouble, and plan reinforcement activities for extra practice.

LESSON 13
The *r*-Controlled Vowel Combinations

Primary emphasis

- The *r*-controlled vowel combinations *air, ear, oar, oor, our*
- Oral and silent reading comprehension
- Context clues

Secondary emphasis

- Distinguishing among similar words
- Word associations
- The *-er* ending
- Reviewing factual information
- Writing and study skills

Word Chart

1. There are two pronunciations for both *ear* and *our*. Encourage students to choose and learn a key word for each sound.
2. In "A Review of Sounds," keep in mind that even though the sounds are being reviewed, many of these words are new. Vowels followed by the letter *w* have not been formally studied. However, the student has studied *saw* and *now,* so the words listed under these key words should cause no difficulty.
3. The consonant blends *sm* and *sch* haven't been studied yet. If necessary, help students to sound out *smart* and *school.*

Pre-reading Activities

Ask or say:

1. In this story, Dave is tired of the routine in his life. Do you ever get tired of the routine in your life?
2. As you read this story, notice how Dave's opinion of his artwork changes.
3. Read this story to find out why Dave thinks night school is going to be a lot of fun.

Post-reading Activities

Ask or say:

1. Before he began night school, how did Dave spend his evenings?
2. What are some reasons Dave decided to go to night school?
3. What did Dave think his picture looked like? What did he think Joan's picture looked like?

4. What did Dave lie about? Why do you think he lied?
5. Compare how Dave feels about his social life at the beginning of the story with how you think he feels about it at the end.
6. Dave is tired of watching TV. Do you watch TV? Do you get tired of it also? What are some things you like to do instead?
7. Did Dave's opinion of his painting change after talking to Joan? Do you think people form opinions about themselves as well as their work from what other people say?

Language Experience or Writing Activities

1. In this story we learned the reasons Dave went back to night school. There are many reasons people go back to school. Tell about why you or someone you know decided to go back to school.
2. Dave's picture of a pear did not look good to him at first. He wanted to tear it up and quit. Have you had similar feelings when you attempted something new? Did you quit or stay with it? Did your feelings about what you were doing change?

Exercises

1 READ AND WRITE

Explain that the words in the boxes are to be used for the sentences directly to the right. Have students do the first set during the preview.

2 READ AND WRITE

Have students read the words in the box. Explain that one of the meanings of the ending *-er* is "a person who does something." This exercise illustrates that meaning.

3 WORD STUDY

Remind students to pick out the word that doesn't fit with the other words.

Summarizing the Lesson

Discuss with students what they learned from the lesson. Encourage students to include in their summaries bits of information they might have learned from the sentences in Exercise 1 or the questions in Exercise 2.

L E S S O N   1 4
Vowels Followed by the Letter *l*

Primary emphasis
- Vowels followed by *l, al, el, il, ild, ol, ul, ull*
- Context clues
- Oral and silent reading comprehension

Secondary emphasis
- The endings *-ful* and *-less*
- Synonyms and antonyms
- Common expressions
- Writing and study skills

Word Chart
1. When the letter *l* follows a vowel, the sound of the vowel often is affected. Have students choose and learn key words for any of these combinations that cause difficulty.
2. Students can remember the sounds for *ild* and *ol* better if they mark the vowels long.

Pre-reading Activities
Ask or say:
1. In this story, we learn that paying bills is a job Jack hates. Do you hate to pay bills? Why or why not?
2. As you read, compare how Jack and Eddie feel about paying bills.

Post-reading Activities
Ask or say:
1. Where does this story take place?
2. How did Eddie feel toward Jack? What information from the story did you use to decide?
3. Why did Eddie think Jack was laughing? Was he right?
4. Why did Jack laugh while paying his bills?
5. Compare Jack's and Eddie's attitudes toward paying bills.
6. Why do you think Jack and Eddie thought a 10-cent phone bill was funny?
7. Do you think Jack expects to hear from the phone company about the mistake in the bill? Why or why not?

8. If you were in the same situation as Jack, would you do the same thing? Why?
9. What if the telephone company had overcharged Jack instead of undercharging him? How do you think Jack's reaction would have been different?

Language Experience or Writing Activities
1. Complete the following sentence: My attitude toward paying bills is . . .
2. Bring to class a few sample bills. Discuss important things to remember when paying bills such as the due date, keeping records, and the interest on the balance. Then discuss terms such as *balance, charges, finance, remit, interest rate,* and *grace period.*

Exercises

1 READ AND WRITE
Point to *-ful* in the directions, and have students read it. Then have them read the words in the box with the ending *-ful* added. Explain that when they have written all the words with *-ful* added, they should use those words in the sentences. Have them read the example sentence. If they are confused, have them complete an item on their own.

2 READ AND WRITE
Preview this exercise in the same way as Exercise 1. During the homework review, ask students to explain the difference between *harmful* and *harmless.* Then ask them the difference between *careful* and *careless* and between *helpful* and *helpless.* Point out that endings often change the meanings of words.

5 READ AND WRITE
Have students use a word from column A and one from column B to complete each sentence. Have students check off words in both columns as they use them, and remind students to use the process of elimination as they do the exercise.

Summarizing the Lesson
Discuss what students learned from the lesson. Do a random review of the chart words.

LESSON 15
Digraphs and Consonant Blends

Primary emphasis

- Digraphs and consonant blends *ch, sh, st, sk*
- The endings *-est* and *-iest*
- Oral and silent reading comprehension
- Context clues

Secondary emphasis

- Distinguishing among similar words
- Synonyms
- Writing and study skills

Word Chart

1. Have students pronounce the digraphs and consonant blends before they sound out the words.
2. Note that these digraphs and blends are found at both the beginning and end of words.

Words for Study

Teach *couldn't* as you have other contractions.

Pre-reading Activities

Ask or say:

1. Have you ever shopped on the Internet or used an online auction? Was it easy or hard? Read the story and see what Kate buys without meaning to.
2. While reading the story, decide if you think Eddie was thoughtless to laugh and if Kate was right to get angry.

Post-reading Activities

Ask or say:

1. Retell the story in your own words.
2. What does Kate want to buy online?
3. What does Eddie tell her about shopping online?
4. What things would Kate like to buy if she had the money?
5. At what point in the story should Kate and Eddie have stopped surfing the Internet?
6. What shocks Kate when she reads the list of things that people are selling?
7. Why does Eddie laugh the first time?
8. Why does Kate get angry at what she sees on the Internet?
9. How does Kate end up buying the piece of toast shaped like Elvis?
10. Why does Eddie laugh the second time?
11. Do you think Eddie is thoughtless to laugh at Kate?
12. What would you tell Kate and Eddie about how they are acting?

Language Experience or Writing Activities

1. Ask students if they have ever bought anything on the Internet. Ask how the experience affected their understanding of the story. Have them write about one experience.
2. Ask students to think about shopping in stores and then complete one of the following sentences:
   I like to shop in stores for . . .
   I do not like to shop in stores for . . .
3. Do you think that Kate is angry at herself, at Eddie, or at Eddie and herself? Why?

Exercises

1 READ AND WRITE

Review the *-er* ending introduced in Lesson 11. Point out the relationship between *-er* meaning "more" and *-est* meaning "most." If necessary, review the rules for adding endings that start with a vowel.

2 READ AND WRITE

Review the *y* to *i* conversion if necessary.

Summarizing the Lesson

Discuss what students learned from the lesson. Review the digraphs and consonant blends introduced in the word chart.

LESSON 16
Consonant Blends

Primary emphasis
- Consonant blends *bl, cl, fl, gl, pl, sl*
- Oral and silent reading comprehension
- Compound words
- Context clues

Secondary emphasis
- Distinguishing among similar words
- Writing sentences
- Writing and study skills

Word Chart
Have students pronounce the consonant blends before they sound out the words. Point out that these blends are at the beginning of words.

Words for Study
1. Be sure students know that the abbreviation *Dr.* stands for *doctor* and that the first letter should be capitalized.
2. Teach the contraction *haven't* following the usual procedure.

Pre-reading Activities
Ask or say:
1. Have you ever been hurt because you were rushing? In this story, Bob is rushing to work and slams his hand in the car door.
2. As you read this story, look for two reasons Bob felt as if he were going to faint.

Post-reading Activities
Ask or say:
1. Explain how Bob's accident happened.
2. In what two places does this story take place?
3. Did Bob see the doctor?
4. The story mentions two reasons why Bob felt like fainting. What are the two reasons?
5. Do you think June does a good job of nursing Bob's hand in this story? Explain.
6. Do you agree with Aunt Louise's saying "Bad times can turn into good times a lot more often than people think"? What was the bad time for Bob? What was the good time?

7. Do you think Bob did the right thing after his accident? What would you do differently?

Language Experience or Writing Activities
1. Has rushing ever caused you trouble? Explain.
2. Tell about a time when you met an old friend after many years.

Additional Activities
1. Aunt Louise's friends are always quoting her. Read some sayings or proverbs in class. Discuss the meaning of each.
2. Ask if students ever had to deal with a first-aid emergency. Discuss first aid for bleeding and other emergencies. You might want to get a first-aid manual or brochures from the American Red Cross. The American Red Cross can also provide other information about first aid.

Exercises

1 READ AND WRITE
Remind students that they did a similar exercise in Lesson 13.

2 READ AND WRITE
During the preview, review the concept of compound words. List several compound words that students have encountered such as *girlfriend, birthday, herself, payday,* and *something.*

Explain that students will choose words from **A** and add words from **B** to them to form compound words. Then they will use the compound words to fill in the blanks in the sentences.

Have students read the example sentence and note that *pay* and *check* are joined to form the compound word. Have them complete items 2 and 3 to make sure they understand how to do this exercise. Tell students to check off words as they use them and to use the process of elimination.

Summarizing the Lesson
Discuss what students learned from the lesson. Point out that when compound words are formed, the spelling of the words does not change as sometimes happens when adding endings.

LESSON 17
More Consonant Blends

Primary emphasis
- Consonant blends *br, cr, dr, fr, gr, pr, tr, str*
- Classifying words
- Oral and silent reading comprehension
- Context clues

Secondary emphasis
- Distinguishing among similar words
- Reviewing factual information
- Writing and study skills

Word Chart
Have students pronounce these initial consonant blends before sounding out the words.

Words for Study
1. Review compound words by having students identify the two words in *upset* and *anywhere*.
2. Teach the contraction *hadn't* following the usual procedure.

Pre-reading Activities
Ask or say:
1. Review the stories in Lessons 1 and 2. In this story, we learn how Bob has been doing in his new job.
2. In this story, Bob carefully plans his date with June. Read to find out what Bob forgot to plan.
3. What does it mean to "freeze in your tracks"? Read this story to find out what caused Bob to freeze in his tracks.

Post-reading Activities
Ask or say:
1. Tell what happened in the story.
2. It was Saturday morning, and Bob thought the night would never come. Does he want the night to come? What does this sentence tell you about how Bob is feeling?
3. Dan Rose yelled at Bob for five minutes. Was Bob worried about losing his job? Explain your answer.
4. Find a sentence that shows that Bob is doing well in his job repairing bikes.

5. What were some of the decisions Bob had to make as he prepared for his date?
6. Find a place in the story that shows Bob is a considerate person.
7. What caused Bob to freeze in his tracks?
8. At the end of the story, Bob has an important date with June and no money. What do you think he will do next?

Language Experience or Writing Activities
1. List some ideas for solving Bob's problem.
2. Do you remember a day when time seemed to pass quickly or slowly? Describe it.
3. Even when he was at work, Bob took pride in how he looked. Do you think how a person dresses for a job matters? Think of some jobs where it does matter and some jobs where it does not matter.

Exercises

2 READ AND WRITE
Have students read the headings for the three categories and the words in the box. Explain that they should decide under which heading each word in the box fits best. Have them explain why *barn* is listed under "Farm." Then have them read *bus stops* and note that it could go under either "Town" or "School." Suggest that they should therefore skip it for now and go on to the next item. Students should have no difficulty seeing that *churches* should be listed under "Town."

3 READ AND WRITE
Explain that this exercise calls for students' own opinions. Tell them to write what they like best on the lines at the left of each group. Then they should write what they like least on the lines at the right. There are no right or wrong answers.

Summarizing the Lesson
Discuss with students the variety of things they learned from this lesson.

More Digraphs and Consonant Blends

Primary emphasis
- Digraphs and consonant blends *wh, th, thr, tw, sm, sn, sp, sw*
- The words for numbers 1 through 20
- Oral and silent reading comprehension
- Context clues

Secondary emphasis
- Distinguishing among similar words
- Compound words
- Reviewing factual information
- Writing and study skills

Word Chart
1. Some people pronounce the *wh* digraph as /w/; others pronounce it as /hw/. Either way is acceptable.
2. Note that the words in the first *th* row have the voiced *th* sound. Words in the other two rows have the soft, or unvoiced, *th* sound.

Words for Study
Review compound words by having students identify the two words in *afternoon, everybody,* and *nothing.*

Pre-reading Activities
Ask or say:
1. The title of this story is "A Way with Kids." What does it mean to have a way with kids? Do you think you have a way with kids? Why or why not?
2. As you read this story, think about how Jack solves his problem with Billy. Think about what you would say or do if you were in Jack's place.

Post-reading Activities
Ask or say:
1. Summarize the story in your own words.
2. Why was Jack taking care of Billy?
3. What two things did Billy do to Jack as soon as the family left?
4. Where does this story take place? How do you know?

5. Do you think Mary's mother had trouble with Billy? Why or why not?
6. What advice did Mary's mother give Jack before she left? In your opinion, was this useful advice?
7. Have you ever been in a situation similar to Jack's? What did you learn about children from your experience?
8. Do you think Jack will be asked to watch Billy again? Do you think he would accept? Why or why not?

Language Experience or Writing Activity
Jack needed to make a decision when things got difficult. He chose to use self-control and not lose his temper. Write or tell about a time when you used self-control or when you should have used self-control but didn't.

Additional Activity
Have the class discuss the subject of children's behavior problems. List what they find works and what doesn't work to curb bad behavior.

Exercises

2 NUMBERS
Have students read the words for the numbers 1 through 20. Then do a random review by writing several of the words for them to read without the figures. Make sure students write the word rather than the figure when they do the exercise.

3 READ AND WRITE
Remind students to add words from **B** to the words in **A** to form compound words and then use the compound words to fill in the blanks in the sentences.

Summarizing the Lesson
After discussing what students learned from the lesson, do a random review of the chart words and of the words for 1 through 20.

LESSON 19
Still More Consonant Blends

Primary emphasis

- Consonant blends *sc, scr, shr, spl, spr, squ, str, chr*
- The prefixes *un-* and *re-*
- Oral and silent reading comprehension
- Context clues

Secondary emphasis

- Distinguishing among similar words
- Word associations
- Reviewing factual information
- Writing and study skills

Word Chart

These consonant blends can be troublesome. Spend as much time as necessary for students to feel confident in recognizing and pronouncing them.

Words for Study

Teach that the prefix *un-* means "not" and the prefix *re-* means "again."

Pre-reading Activities

Ask or say:

1. Have you ever broken something in a store and had to pay for it? Share how you felt.
2. As you read this story, look for the points at which the story could have turned out differently if Kate and Bob had acted differently.

Post-reading Activities

Ask or say:

1. Tell what happened in the story.
2. Why does Kate go to Dan's?
3. What does Kate see that she likes but cannot afford?
4. What is the first thing that Kate does when Bob says she can take the scooter for a ride? What does Kate do next? What is the third thing that Kate does?
5. What does Bob tell Kate besides to be careful?
6. What scares Kate about the scooter?
7. What three things does Kate do when she sees the squirrel?

8. How has Kate hurt herself in the accident?
9. What happened to the scooter in the accident?
10. Does Bob seem to care more about the scooter or Kate?
11. Does Kate seem to care more about the cost of the scooter or the squirrel?
12. Would you have swerved so that you didn't hit the squirrel? Do you think that Kate would really have hit the squirrel?

Language Experience or Writing Activities

1. Bob let Kate ride the scooter even though she did not have enough money to buy it. Was it a good idea for Bob to let Kate ride it? Was it a good idea for Kate to agree to ride it? Write what Kate might have said when Bob said she could ride it.
2. Sometimes people have bumper stickers on their cars that say such things as "I brake for turtles" or "I brake for deer." Explain what these mean.
3. Write a list of important things to remember to do when dealing with an emergency.

Exercises

3 READ AND WRITE

Remind students to choose the word that doesn't fit with the rest of the words in each row.

4 AND 5 READ AND WRITE

Students should write words on all the lines at the top before using them in the sentences. Point out that there are no spelling changes when *un-* and *re-* are added to the beginnings of words. Discuss how adding *un-* and *re-* changed the meanings of words during the homework review.

Summarizing the Lesson

After students summarize what they learned in the lesson, do a random review of the words with consonant blends. Make note of any blends that students have difficulty producing and develop reinforcement activities for extra practice.

LESSON 20
Sounds for *c* and *g*

Primary emphasis
- The sounds for hard and soft *c* and *g*
- The sound for *dge*
- Oral and silent reading comprehension
- Context clues

Secondary emphasis
- Distinguishing among similar words
- Classifying words
- Reviewing factual information
- Writing and study skills

Word Chart
1. Sounds for *c* introduced:
   - *c* followed by *a, o,* or *u* sounds like /k/
   - *c* followed by *e* or *i* sounds like /s/
2. Sounds for *g* introduced:
   - *g* followed by *a, u,* and sometimes *i* sounds like /g/
   - *g* at the end of a word sounds like /g/
   - *g* followed by *e* or *i* often sounds like /j/
3. *dge* at the end of a word sounds like /j/
4. Special note: There are many common exceptions to the soft *g* rule such as *get, give, gift, giggle,* and *girl.*

Pre-reading Activities
1. Review the story in Lesson 17 briefly.
2. Ask: Have you ever made plans to do something, only to find you didn't have enough money to do it? What did you do?
3. Bob has no money. He must call June about their date. What do you think will happen?

Post-reading Activities
Ask or say:
1. Tell the story in your own words. Start with why Bob didn't have any money (from Lesson 17).
2. Do you think it was difficult for Bob to ask Aunt Louise for money? Find a place in the story that supports your answer.
3. Was Aunt Louise the only person Bob considered borrowing money from for his date? How do you know?
4. Do you think Aunt Louise wanted to help Bob by lending him money? Why?

5. Aunt Louise didn't give Bob money. What did she give him? Was it valuable to Bob?
6. How did Aunt Louise and June know something was wrong when Bob called them?
7. What would you have done in Bob's place?

Language Experience or Writing Activities
1. Tell about something you have done that didn't cost much money but was fun.
2. Both women in the story knew something was wrong because of Bob's voice on the phone. What are some other ways you can tell how someone is feeling?
3. List recreational activities in your community that are inexpensive, for example, going to parades, parks, nature centers, street festivals, and community centers.

Exercises

1 READ AND WRITE
Explain that for some items students will use all the choices, while for other items they will choose only one word depending on the number of blanks in the sentences.

2 READ AND WRITE
Review the procedures for Exercise 2 in Lesson 17 if necessary.

3 TWELVE QUESTIONS
This exercise is primarily for word review. Students are not expected to know all the answers. Explain that if students don't know an answer, they should make an intelligent guess. If reference materials are available, they could work in pairs and look up answers. During the homework review, take some time to explain items students didn't know.

Note: Either *true* or *false* is correct for item 4. According to some sources, both deer and bears can run at a speed of 30 miles per hour. Other sources claim that deer can run 40 miles per hour.

Summarizing the Lesson
Since this is the final lesson in *Challenger 1,* spend some time discussing what students have learned from working in this book.

First Review and Second Review

These reviews give students an opportunity to work with many of the words and concepts they have studied in this book one more time before beginning Book 2. An accuracy rate of 85 percent or better indicates that a student is ready to go on to Book 2.

The reviews can be either completed in class or assigned as homework. Preview the exercises as you have been doing for the lesson work. For the sake of variety and exposure to new formats, three new types of exercises appear in the reviews: multiple-choice questions, analogies, and word pairs. Preview these exercises as follows.

1 READ AND WRITE

Explain that students should select from the four choices the word that best fits in the sentence and write the word in the blank.

3 READ AND WRITE

For each question, have students choose a word from the box that means the opposite. Have students write the word on the line.

4 READ AND WRITE

Have students use *a* or *an* in these sentences.

After going over the second review, some sort of celebration is in order. Take some time to discuss what students have accomplished. Provide a treat, if possible. They've earned it, and so have you!

Book 2 Introduction

Challenger 2 is generally used by students who have completed *Challenger 1*. The primary purpose of Book 2 is to reinforce phonics skills, vocabulary, and reasoning skills introduced in Book 1. Book 2 differs from Book 1 in several respects. The 20 lessons in Book 2 contain brief nonfiction reading selections on a wide variety of topics rather than the short fiction that appears in Book 1. First readings of the selections are usually silent and done as homework to develop reading independence. Written comprehension questions follow each reading selection.

Book 2 is an appropriate starting place for students who can read at the 2.0–3.0 reading levels and need the skills practice that this book provides. Book 2 is also an appropriate starting place for students who test at level 2 on the online *Challenger Placement Tool* and who prefer reading nonfiction to fiction.

Few new words are introduced in Book 2 in order to give students an opportunity to review thoroughly the vocabulary they have learned so far. In addition, there are reviews after every five lessons in Book 2 that provide additional opportunities to review words and reinforce concepts. The word indexes at the end of each review can be used when planning reinforcement activities.

Scheduling Considerations

One-hour sessions are appropriate for students in Book 2. This time frame allows students to do some oral reading, discuss the reading selection, go over the homework exercises, work on writing and/or reinforcement activities, and preview the next lesson.

Book 2 works well in three types of instructional settings. All types have both advantages and disadvantages that you should consider in preparing the lessons.

ONE-TO-ONE TUTORIAL SETTING

The advantage of working with only one student is that you can offer him or her your undivided attention. The student usually progresses rapidly because you can pace the work and plan reinforcement activities exclusively tailored to his or her needs.

The disadvantage is that the student is deprived of the support and stimulation that can best be provided by other students. For example, the discussions about the reading passages are more interesting when other students participate.

CLASSROOM SETTING

The advantage of this setting is that students receive support and stimulation from one another, making learning a more enjoyable activity. You can divide a larger class into small groups to work on specific activities. More advanced students can assume much of the responsibility for giving explanations and leading reinforcement activities. This, in turn, reinforces their own skills. Less advanced students usually benefit from peer instruction, provided you are available for any clarifications that need to be made.

The disadvantage of this setting is that you cannot usually be so thorough in addressing each student's needs as you could be working one-to-one.

GROUP TUTORIAL SETTING

In this setting, each student works at his or her own pace. Students working at the same level can often team up. More advanced students can help those having trouble with the material. This type of learning environment suits students who don't work well in groups on a consistent basis.

One disadvantage of this setting can be that some students begin to see the lessons more as a competition than as an opportunity to improve their reading. You may have to remind students that they are competing with their own past performance rather than competing with each other.

A second disadvantage is that this type of setting makes incredible demands on you. Not only must you be familiar with many lessons simultaneously, but also you must be able to sustain a high level of concentration and stamina in order to work individually with several students during each session.

Suggestions for Teaching the Lessons

It is important for you to read the material in the first five chapters of this manual if you have not already done so. These chapters discuss concepts and procedures upon which *Challenger* is based and give general suggestions for using the series. The following are specific suggestions applicable to Book 2.

WORDS FOR STUDY

Words that appear for the first time in this controlled-vocabulary series are listed before the reading passage in each lesson. Words appear in the same form in which they initially appear in the reading selection or exercises. This gives students additional practice in reading word endings. Many students, especially those who start their reading program in Book 2, can sight-read most of these words. Have students sound out any words they don't know with as little help from you as possible. After students have read all the words, do a brief random review.

The following are some suggestions to help students sound out unfamiliar words. The examples used are all from Lesson 1.

- Have students sound out one-syllable words according to the methods used in Book 1. For students starting this series in Book 2, teach any sounds they do not know in the unfamiliar word. The material on pages 8–10, Common Phonics Elements and Principles in English Words, may be helpful.
- Students working in Book 2 may have difficulty sounding out words of more than one syllable. Have them sound out such words as *recorded* one syllable at a time. Begin by covering every syllable except *re.* After they sound out *re,* have them uncover and sound out *cord,* and then have them say *record.* Then have them sound out *ed* and say *recorded.*
- Key words and vowel markings also help students to sound out unfamiliar words. If a student working on the word *Clark* has forgotten the sound for *ar,* write *car* in the margin, and underline *ar.* Also, most students have no difficulty sounding out *touch* if you draw a line through the *o* to indicate that it is silent.
- Combining phonics methods with verbal and context clues can help students remember new words. For example, after a student has sounded out *Pin* in *Pinocchio,* he or she may be able to complete the word if you ask, "Have you heard the story of the little boy whose nose grew longer every time he told a lie?" If he or she knows the name, point out the unusual *cch* spelling for the /k/ sound, and explain that it comes from Italian. If students don't know the story of Pinocchio, briefly summarize it for them. Be alert to these opportunities to broaden students' background knowledge.

THE READING SELECTIONS

Pre-reading and post-reading activities are discussed in Chapter 2. Specific suggestions are given in individual lesson notes. Explain to students that the selections in Book 2 are not stories; they are brief articles about a variety of subjects. The following ideas may be helpful in your planning.

- After Lesson 1, first readings should be done for homework, so students can develop silent reading skills. Have students read the passage orally during the homework review. For students starting in Book 2, see suggestions for developing oral reading skills in the Introduction to Book 1 on page 46–48.
- Follow-up discussions of the reading selections help students to understand and enjoy the readings. For suggestions on conducting these discussions, see Chapter 2. Some questions for discussion are given in the individual lesson notes.
- You may need to remind students that they do not have to agree with the point of view presented in any selection. Some beginning readers have a tendency to believe that because something is in print, it is necessarily true. Discuss students' opinions and points of view freely and objectively.

THE EXERCISES

Preview the exercises during the class session, and have students complete them for homework. Make sure students know how to do each exercise. Book 2 students should be able to read the directions themselves. A few deliberately difficult items are included in most of the exercises to challenge the students' reasoning abilities. Keep the following points in mind as you work with students on the exercises.

- Exercise 1 is always a reading comprehension exercise. Encourage students to refer to the reading selection when necessary. Some students consider this "cheating." Point out that even experienced readers often have to read some things more than once.
- Explain that a long line beneath a question indicates that the answer should be written as a complete sentence. Review sentence capitalization and punctuation if necessary.
- Remind students to answer all questions. Explain that they should make intelligent guesses if they don't know an answer. Show them how the use of context clues and the process of elimination can be strategies for selecting correct answers. Remind students also that mistakes are valuable because they can learn from them.

- Students should correct all exercises during the homework review. Any grading required should be done on corrected work. Consider an overall average of 80 percent or better an excellent score.
- Common American expressions and idioms appear in many exercises. Students often appreciate learning more about these expressions, so take a few moments to explain them whenever the situation calls for it.

Suggestions for specific exercises are given in the individual lesson notes beginning on page 73.

Writing Activities

Writing activities are discussed in Chapter 3 of this manual. Suggested topics can be found in the individual lesson notes. Use these suggestions in planning writing assignments. Students working in Book 2 should do an extended writing activity at least once a week. Personal letters and short compositions about discussion topics that interest students are appropriate writing activities. Let students pick topics from a list of suggestions you provide. Draw from discussions about the reading selections, student comments and interests, and current issues for appropriate topics. Some activities should involve formal writing that is corrected and revised. Writing Book 2 also provides writing activities to extend the lesson content and to help students develop and practice their writing skills.

The Lesson Segments

After the session in which Lesson 1 is completed and Lesson 2 is previewed for homework, the procedure for each session should be as consistent as possible. Most sessions will have the following segments. You may want to vary the order to suit your particular situation.

1. **Homework Review.** Have students read aloud at least some of the reading selection in the lesson studied for homework. Have them summarize the selection, go over their answers to the comprehension questions in Exercise 1, and discuss the selection. Then go over the rest of the exercises, and have students make any necessary corrections.

2. **Writing Activity.** Students may work in groups or singly on the current writing activity, depending on what it is.

3. **Reinforcement Activity.** When time permits, focus on an area of difficulty in a way that is fun for the students. See Chapter 4 of this manual for suggestions.

4. **Homework Preview.** Preview the next lesson, which students will complete for homework. Have them read the Words for Study and title of the selection and then predict what they think the selection will be about. Do one or more pre-reading activities. Also have them read the directions for the exercises and do one item in any exercise that might be confusing.

Individual Lesson Notes

The individual lesson notes that begin on page 73 contain specific suggestions and procedures for Book 2 lessons.

LESSON 1
Sneezing

Primary emphasis
- Silent and oral reading comprehension
- Phonics skills
- New vocabulary
- Consonants, blends, and digraphs

Secondary emphasis
- Context clues
- Long and short vowel sounds
- Learning/reviewing factual information
- Homonyms
- Writing and study skills

Words for Study
1. Many of these words are not phonetically regular. Pronounce those that students don't recognize, and have them repeat each word several times while looking at it.
2. When introducing *Pinocchio,* ask if students are familiar with the story of the puppet who became a real boy. Tell them that the *cch* spelling for /k/ comes from Italian.

Pre-reading Activities
1. Have students read the title of the selection and share some things they know about sneezing. Ask students what things make them sneeze. Make a list of their responses.
2. Ask students if they get a warning before they are going to sneeze, and if so, what it is. If anyone is successful at stopping sneezes, ask how they do it.

Post-reading Activities
1. Discuss the answers to the questions in Exercise 1. Ask or say:
2. What are some things Donna Griffiths probably could not do during the six months she was sneezing?
3. How do you think people probably treated Donna Griffiths during the time she was sneezing? Consider both family members and strangers.
4. Besides "God bless you," what else might people say when someone sneezes?

5. Name some of the illnesses that people can catch from germs spread by sneezing.
6. What are some other ways germs are spread besides sneezing? Discuss some preventive measures that people can take to reduce the spread of infections.

Writing Activities
1. Complete the following sentences: When I am just about to sneeze, I feel . . . After I sneeze, I feel . . .
2. Discuss and then write about some things people can do to maintain good health.

Exercises

1 ABOUT THE READING
Explain that answers to "What do you think?" questions are not found in the passage and that students should write their own opinions.

2 WORD SOUNDS
During the homework preview, have students read the directions aloud. Have them read the example (sentence 1) and explain what they are to do.

Have students do the second item. Tell them to read the entire sentence in order to fill in the blank correctly. Then tell them to reread the sentence after the blank has been filled in to make sure the sentence makes sense.

Students may prefer to write the three words in the left column first.

4 MARKING THE e'S
After students have read the directions, review the vowel markings, the long and short *e* sounds, and the function of the silent *e* (to make the preceding vowel long).

5 WORDS THAT SOUND THE SAME
Have students read the two words to be used in the first sentence. Then have them read the sentence filling in the words orally. Point out that while the words sound the same, they are spelled differently and have different meanings. The correct spelling of the word depends on its meaning in the sentence.

LESSON 2
Cats

Primary emphasis
- Silent and oral reading comprehension
- Phonics skills
- New vocabulary
- Consonants, blends, and digraphs
- Classifying information

Secondary emphasis
- Context clues
- Word sounds
- Homonyms
- Writing and study skills

Words for Study
Make sure students know why *United States* is capitalized.

Pre-reading Activities
1. Show students pictures of cats, and ask what students have observed about cats.
   Ask:
2. Have you ever seen a cat's eyes shine in the dark? (Part of a cat's eye reflects light to help the cat see when light is dim.)
   Say:
3. As you read this article, look for the answer to the question, "Why does it take more time to train a cat than a dog?"
4. Read a poem about cats, or play one or more of the songs from the musical *Cats* by Andrew Lloyd Webber, based on poems by T. S. Eliot.

Post-reading Activities
1. Discuss the answers to the questions in Exercise 1.
   Ask or say:
2. Why does the author say it takes more time to train a cat than a dog? Do you agree? Why?
3. How do you feel about the man on the West Coast leaving $415,000 to his cats?
4. What information from the article shows that cats are well suited to hunt at night? What are some other animals that see well at night? What is the reason some cats and other animals are equipped to see well at night?

5. What are some other kinds of cats besides house cats?
6. Discuss cats. What are some characteristics and behaviors common to members of the cat family?

Writing Activities
1. Complete one of the following sentences:
   I like cats because . . .
   I do not like cats because . . .
2. Write about a pet cat you have now or had in the past. If you never had a cat as a pet, write about one in your neighborhood.
3. Write one new thing you learned about cats from reading this selection.

Additional Activities
1. Find one or more comic strips with a cat character. Cut the comic into story sections, and use it to help students practice putting events in correct sequence.
2. Show an interesting picture of a cat. Write a group story by asking each person to contribute one sentence.
3. Students may need help reading large numbers such as $415,000. If students want help in learning how to read large numbers, explain place values and the use of commas.
4. Learn about some of the endangered cats of the world.

Additional Vocabulary Practice
carnivorous – referring to animals that eat meat
domestic – having to do with the home
endangered – in danger of becoming extinct
fact – something done, real, or true. Ask students to find a fact in this article.

Exercises

2 WORD SOUNDS
During the homework preview, remind students that they did a similar exercise in Lesson 1. If students find this exercise confusing, suggest that they write the three word choices on the lines provided before deciding which word completes the sentence.

4 WORDS THAT SOUND THE SAME
Remind students that the correct spelling depends upon the meaning of the word in the sentence.

LESSON 3
The Number Seven

Primary emphasis
- Silent and oral reading comprehension
- Phonics skills
- New vocabulary
- Consonants, blends, and digraphs

Secondary emphasis
- Context clues
- Contrasting word sounds
- Number words
- Writing and study skills

Pre-reading Activities
1. Write the number seven in different ways, for example *7, VII, seven, 1+6, 8–1.* Introduce the lesson by saying there are many ways to represent the number 7. Ask for additional suggestions.
2. Ask if students can think of anything significant about the number seven.
3. Ask: Do you have a lucky number? What is it? How did you decide on it? How do you use it?

Post-reading Activities
1. Discuss the answers to the questions in Exercise 1. Ask or say:
2. Does anyone know how to play the children's game *Seven-Up*? Explain the game to the class.
3. What are two examples of the number seven in the Bible?
4. Tell how the number seven is considered lucky by some people and unlucky by others.
5. What is another number that some people consider unlucky?

Writing Activities
1. List the seven days of the week and their abbreviations, and ask students to practice writing them. Point out that days of the week and months of the year are always capitalized. Suggest that students write the day of the week on their journal entries for spelling practice.
2. Complete one of the following sentences:
   People who are lucky . . .
   People who are unlucky . . .
3. Walking under a ladder is said to be bad luck. Think of a reason why this could turn into bad luck for someone.

Additional Activities
1. Ask students to write one sentence every day for the next seven days. The sentence should tell something about the day, and each should be different. Give students an opportunity to share what they wrote the following week.
2. Help students to use the Internet to look up the "Seven Wonders of the World."
3. Discuss the "seven deadly sins" (anger, covetousness, envy, pride, lust, gluttony, and sloth).
4. Help students to locate the world's oceans on a map or atlas.

Exercises

2 WORD SOUNDS
During the homework preview, make sure students understand how to do this exercise. Have students read aloud the list of words and then decide together where to write *blame* and *flame,* or *game* for number 1.

3 NUMBER WORDS
Explain that the answers to the "Do you know?" questions are different in different states. Encourage students to try to find out the correct answers if they don't already know them or to make an "intelligent guess." Students usually enjoy seeing if their "intelligent guesses" come close to the correct answers.

LESSON 4
Fun Food Facts

Primary emphasis
- Silent and oral reading comprehension
- Phonics skills
- New vocabulary
- Consonants, blends, and digraphs
- Antonyms

Secondary emphasis
- Oral reading
- Context clues
- Reviewing factual information
- Writing and study skills

Words for Study
Find Japan on a world map or atlas.

Pre-reading Activities
Ask or say:
1. Share some things that you already know about such foods as pizza, milk, popcorn, potatoes, and tomatoes before reading this article.
2. In this article you will learn some fun and interesting facts about the foods that you may eat regularly and some that may be new to you.

Post-reading Activities
1. Discuss the questions in Exercise 1.
   Ask or say:
2. The title of the article is "Fun Food Facts." What is a fact? How is it different from an opinion?
3. Compare the toppings for pizza in the United States and Japan.
4. About how many pounds of potatoes are eaten in the United States as French fries?
5. How do you think that popcorn would taste if you put sugar instead of salt on it and poured milk over it?
6. If you eat strawberries, do you add sugar or eat them without sugar?

Writing Activities
1. Write three facts from this article. Use sentences.
2. Compare popcorn and pretzels. Which do you like better? Explain why.

3. Each person eats about 22 pounds of tomatoes a year. Do you eat tomatoes? If so, how? Give some examples.

Additional Activities
1. Ask for a pizza fact from the article about both the United States and Japan.
2. Point out that *French* comes from *France,* the name of a country, and describes the people who are born there. Ask for other similar pairs of words (proper nouns and proper adjectives).
3. Help students write *3 billion* as a numeral. Ask why they think we usually write *millions, billions,* and *trillions* as words and numbers.
4. Study *cups, pints, quarts,* and *gallons* and their metric equivalents (milliliters and liters). Most dictionaries have metric equivalent tables. Bring to class any appropriate measuring cups or containers that would help students understand the conversions.

Exercises

3 WORD SOUNDS
During the homework preview, go over the example, and tell students to read through each sentence before filling in the blanks. Read the second sentence as follows: "Dave was so *blank* of the *blank* he drew in art class that he said *blank,* 'Hey everybody, look at my picture!'" Tell students to reread the sentences after the words are filled in to make sure they make sense.

5 WHICH WORD DOES NOT FIT?
During the homework preview, go over the example. Point out the answer *snack* in the first question. Then explain the process of elimination. Tell students they can cross out words they know are wrong to limit the choices.

LESSON 5
Love Letters

Primary emphasis
- Silent and oral reading comprehension
- Phonics skills
- New vocabulary
- Consonants, blends, and digraphs

Secondary emphasis
- Context clues
- Reviewing factual information
- Long and short vowels
- Homonyms
- Writing and study skills

Pre-reading Activities
1. Ask students if they like to write letters. Tell the class that this is the story of a very strange love letter.
2. Ask students if they know what a scribe is. Tell them that in this article they will find out what one scribe had to do.

Post-reading Activities
1. Discuss the questions in Exercise 1.
2. Ask students to summarize the selection.
   Ask or say:
3. Is this article about love letters or about *a* love letter? Suggest another title for the article.
4. Was the scribe paid for his work? How do you know?
5. Why do you think the painter did not write the letter himself?

6. Instead of "scribe," what are some titles for people who do similar work today? What tools do people today have that would make the work of a scribe easier?
7. What is the most boring job you ever had to do? What are some of the factors that make something interesting or boring to you?

Writing Activities
1. Have students write answers to these questions about the article: What is it about? Who is it about? Where did it take place? When did it happen? Why did it happen?
2. Discuss the kinds of letters or notes students need to write. Study the forms of a friendly letter and a business letter. Ask students to write a short note or letter to someone.

Additional Activities
1. Find France on a map or atlas.
2. Help students to read the number *1,875,000*.
3. Do you know anyone who did something unusual to demonstrate his or her love?
4. Discuss the fact that in former times many people didn't know how to write, so they hired scribes when they needed to have something written.

Exercise
5 MARKING THE VOWELS
Review the marks for long, short, and silent vowel sounds introduced in Lesson 1.

Review: Lessons 1–5

Explain to students that reviews appear after every five lessons. In addition to the review, you might also have students do a research and report activity in which students select one topic from the five lessons and find out more about it. Students can work singly, in pairs, or in groups and give oral and/or written reports.

Exercises

1 CHOOSING THE ANSWER
Tell students that the process of elimination is useful for multiple-choice questions. If students are not sure of the correct answer, they can eliminate the ones they know

are incorrect first. Have students complete the first item during the preview so that they understand what to do.

3 FACTS
If students don't recall this information, tell them to refer to Lesson 1.

Word Index
Mention to students that this list includes the words in Lessons 1 through 5 that had not been introduced in Book 1. The index can be used for word reviews, spelling checks, and reinforcement activities.

LESSON 6
Wigs

Primary emphasis
- Silent and oral reading comprehension
- Phonics skills
- New vocabulary
- Consonants, blends, and digraphs

Secondary emphasis
- Context clues
- Words that rhyme
- Word associations
- Sounds for *ea*
- Compound words

Words for Study
Explain *BC* (before Christ) and *AD* (anno Domini, in the year of the Lord) as used in dates. Find England and Egypt on a map or atlas.

Pre-reading Activities
1. Bring in pictures of people from historical periods when wigs were popular.
   Ask or say:
2. Have you ever worn a wig? What did you like or dislike about wearing a wig?
3. Read this selection about wigs to find out why some people in history wore wigs and how they kept wigs from sliding off their heads.

Post-reading Activities
1. Discuss the answers to the questions in Exercise 1.
   Ask or say:
2. Have people always worn wigs just to be in fashion?
3. Name one kind of animal and one kind of insect found in Egypt in 4000 BC.
4. How do you think the king of France got everybody to wear wigs?
5. Compare the wigs described in the reading to the wigs people wear today.
6. Why do people wear wigs today? (Examples: as theater costumes, for disguise, to cover bald spots, for fashion, after chemotherapy)

Writing Activities
1. Write a sentence using the word *bigwig*.
2. How has hair fashion changed during your lifetime?
3. What information in this article was the most interesting to you? Complete the following sentence: I thought the most interesting information about wigs was . . .

Additional Activities
1. How many years have passed since 4000 BC? Draw a time line to illustrate BC and AD. Figure out how many years have passed since 4000 BC. Then add AD 1624, 1702, and 2020 to the time line and any other dates that students would like to add.
2. In the first paragraph it states that in Egypt, "The bigger the wig was, the more important the person was." Discuss whether people still make judgments based on size today. (Examples: judgments about big homes, big cars, big paychecks)
3. Describe how you think it would feel to wear a wig made out of wool, animal hair, or gold. How heavy would it be? How would it feel on a hot summer day? Discuss other fashions that have been painful or uncomfortable. (Examples: corsets, bound feet, tight jeans, spike-heeled shoes)

Additional Vocabulary Practice
term – Look up the word *term* in the dictionary to see how many different meanings it has. Ask students what *term* means in the first paragraph.

toupee – a man's wig designed to cover a bald spot

Exercises

3 WHICH WORD DOES NOT FIT?
During the homework preview, go over the example, and have students explain why *month* is the word that doesn't fit. Then have students do the second item and explain their choices.

4 VOWEL SOUNDS
During the preview, have students read aloud the list of words to make sure they can pronounce all of the words correctly.

LESSON 7
Skunks

Primary emphasis
- Silent and oral reading comprehension
- Phonics skills
- New vocabulary
- Consonants, blends, and digraphs
- Synonyms and antonyms

Secondary emphasis
- Context clues
- Compound words
- Writing and study skills

Words for Study
Point out that *he's* is the contraction for both *he is* and *he has*.

Pre-reading Activities
Background information: Skunks have an unusual defense against danger. These black and white mammals can spray a liquid that can cause stinging and temporary blindness. Skunks can be found searching for mice, insects, eggs, and berries from sundown to sunup. They have few enemies aside from great horned owls and automobiles. Skunks are found in the Western Hemisphere from Hudson Bay, Canada, to the Strait of Magellan at the tip of South America.
1. Ask students to share any information they already know about skunks or any experiences they have had.
2. Ask if everyone is familiar with the smell of a skunk. If someone has not smelled a skunk, ask someone else to try to describe it. Discuss the difficulty of trying to describe a smell.

Post-reading Activities
1. Discuss the answers to the questions in Exercise 1. Ask or say:
2. How does a skunk show signs of being threatened? How would the skunk look if it were about to spray?
3. What causes a skunk to spray?
4. Do you think a skunk will spray without warning? What information in the article supports your answer?
5. If a skunk is stamping its forefeet and raising its tail, will it always spray?
6. What do you think you should do if you see a skunk? What should you probably not do?

Writing Activities
1. Write one or two sentences telling something new that you learned about skunks.
2. Write about what you would do or not do if you saw a skunk.

Additional Activities
1. Skunks will follow a sequence of steps when threatened. On slips of paper, write each of these steps. Ask students to work in pairs or individually to put them in correct order. When they are finished, have students check their work against the article.
2. Some skunks are striped and some are spotted, but they all are black and white. Ask students if a skunk's defense depends on hiding and escaping notice. Ask the class to list some animals that defend themselves by hiding. Pictures of animals that are camouflaged would illustrate this.
3. Make a list of animals, and discuss how they react to danger. Compare these responses to what skunks do. (Skunks usually move slowly and do not run if chased.) Next, discuss the terms *predator* and *prey,* and classify the listed animals accordingly.

Exercises

3 WORDS THAT MEAN THE SAME AND 4 WORD OPPOSITES
After students have read the directions and studied the examples, have them complete one item in each exercise during the homework preview. Remind them to use the process of elimination in completing these exercises.

5 SILLY VERSES
Students may be interested to know that this verse form is called a *limerick*. Both the rhyme scheme and the rhythm distinguish limericks from other verse forms. Ask if students have heard any other limericks.

LESSON 8
Eggs

Primary emphasis
- Silent and oral reading comprehension
- Phonics skills
- New vocabulary
- Context clues
- Word analogies

Secondary emphasis
- Compound words
- Writing and study skills

Pre-reading Activities
1. Ask how many are in a dozen. What other things besides eggs are sometimes sold by the dozen?
2. Have you ever tried to boil an egg in the microwave? Did it explode? Describe what it was like to clean the microwave. Read the article to find out why the egg exploded.

Post-reading Activities
1. Discuss the answers to the questions in Exercise 1. Ask or say:
2. How long does it take for a hen to make an egg?
3. What are two ways that the article says people eat eggs for breakfast? What are two other ways that people may eat eggs for breakfast?
4. Explain why trying to hard-boil an egg in the microwave is a bad idea.
5. Why should raw eggs always be kept cold?

Writing Activities
1. Eggs have a lot of food value but also a lot of cholesterol. Write something you know about cholesterol.
2. Did the information that eggshells have tiny holes surprise you? Write about something that surprised you.
3. Suppose the article had begun with a question: "What does the United States put out 87 billion of each year?" Would you have been more curious about what the article is about? Would you have been more interested in reading the article to find out the answer? Write about whether a question might be a good way to start a piece of writing and get a reader's attention.

Additional Activities
1. If possible, bring in cups, salt, teaspoons, water, and eggs that are several weeks old and ones that are newly bought, and conduct the fresh egg test described in the article. Have students describe their observations in writing. Explain that scientists conduct research like this to test their ideas.
2. Help students to research information that answers the following questions:
   - What kind of birds lay the largest and smallest eggs? (ostrich: 7" x 5"; hummingbird: size of a pea)
   - What other creatures besides birds lay eggs? (turtles, snakes, fish, insects, etc.)

Exercises

2 WORD SOUNDS
Discuss any information here that students are unfamiliar with.

3 WORD SOUNDS
During the homework preview, have students read aloud the list of words to be sure they can pronounce them correctly

4 WHICH WORD FITS BEST?
- Have students read the directions and the example and then explain why *glass* is the correct answer.
- Have students read the second item and explain the relationship between *ship* and *sea*. Then have them read the four choices and decide which choice goes with *plane* in the same way that *sea* goes with *ship*.
- Remind students that the process of elimination is helpful in selecting the correct answer.

LESSON 9
Gold

Primary emphasis
- Silent and oral reading comprehension
- Phonics skills
- Context clues
- New vocabulary
- Consonants, blends, and digraphs

Secondary emphasis
- Vowel sounds
- Matching definitions
- Writing and study skills

Words for Study
Point out that *isn't* is the contraction for *is not*. Locate California on a map or atlas.

Pre-reading Activities
1. Ask students how gold is used. (Examples: for jewelry, coins, repairing teeth, and in manufacturing)
2. Tell students that gold has been considered valuable worldwide since ancient times. It is beautiful, scarce, and very easily worked. Gold can be melted, drawn into fine wires, or pounded to be very thin. (Examples: gold foil and gold leaf)
3. Explain the process of panning for gold: Swirl a mixture of water and sediment from a river bottom in a pan rapidly enough to carry the water and most of the gravel and sand over the edge. Because gold weighs more than rock, any gold there is will remain on the bottom of the pan.

Post-reading Activities
1. Discuss the answers to the questions in Exercise 1. Ask or say:
2. Why didn't John Sutter want people to know gold had been found on his land?

3. Explain what "made a strike" means in the article. What can "a strike" mean in other contexts? (Examples: in bowling, baseball, labor disputes)
4. What do you think became of mining camps when the gold ran out? (Some mining camps became ghost towns while others grew into cities.)
5. Discuss the difference between "a lot of money" in 1848 and "a lot of money" now. Ask if students know how much such things as movie tickets and food items cost 20 or 30 years ago.

Writing Activity
Think of advantages and disadvantages of living during the period of the gold rush. Decide in which time you would rather live, and then complete one of the following sentences:
I would rather live during the gold rush because . . .
I would rather live today because . . .

Additional Activities
1. Ask students how they think people in the mid-1800s traveled to northern California. Follow the three routes that forty-niners took from the eastern United States:
   - by boat to Panama, across Panama, and then by boat to San Francisco (the closest port)
   - by boat around Cape Horn, South America
   - overland across the country
2. People also came to California from China, Australia, Latin America, and Europe. Find these places on a map or atlas, and trace possible routes to California.

Exercise

2 WORD SOUNDS
Discuss any information here that is unfamiliar to students.

Mother Goose

Primary emphasis
- Silent and oral reading comprehension
- Phonics skills
- Context clues
- New vocabulary
- Consonants, blends, and digraphs

Secondary emphasis
- Word associations
- Silent letters
- Homonyms
- Writing and study skills

Pre-reading Activities
1. Ask if students are familiar with Mother Goose rhymes. Recite or have students recite one or two.
2. Bring in a variety of Mother Goose books, and invite students who have young children to bring in books to share. Read aloud some of the rhymes. Ask which books people like the best and why.

Post-reading Activities
1. Discuss the answers to the questions in Exercise 1. Ask or say:
2. If there never was a real person named Mother Goose, who created these rhymes? (Like folk songs and folktales, they came from the people and were passed down orally.)
3. If many of these rhymes had been around for hundreds of years before 1760, where do you think they came from? (The colonists brought them from Europe.)
4. Do you think people who do not know the story behind "Hey diddle diddle" still enjoy the rhyme? Why?
5. Why did the queen never eat her soup without having one of her ladies-in-waiting taste it first? (Royalty often had servants taste food and drink to detect poisoning.)

Writing Activities
1. Visit a library, and select a number of children's books from a variety of cultures and countries. Look for books at the appropriate reading levels for your students. Read one or two stories aloud in class. Ask each student to choose a book, write about why a child might like it, and share it with the group. To help students begin writing, ask questions about what made their books interesting or why they think children would like their books.
2. Interested students could write children's poems. Students with artistic ability could illustrate the poems. The poems and art could then be compiled into a student book.

Additional Activities
Ask or say:
1. Figure out how many years have passed since 1760.
2. Compare Mother Goose rhymes to folk songs and stories. Explain that passing on information, stories, poems, and songs orally was common in days when few people could read or write.
3. Discuss and list reasons why students think it is important for adults to read to children often.

Exercises

2 WORD SOUNDS
During the homework review, students might enjoy reading the rhymes these lines came from.

4 SILENT LETTERS
During the preview, have students explain what was done in the example and complete the next item to make sure they understand what to do. Then have them read the 12 words to make sure they can decode them.

Review: Lessons 1–10

Encourage students to select one topic from Lessons 6 through 10 to research and report on. Students can work singly, in pairs, or in groups and give oral and/or written reports.

LESSON 11
Sleeping

Primary emphasis

- Silent and oral reading comprehension
- Phonics skills
- Context clues
- New vocabulary
- Consonants, blends, and digraphs

Secondary emphasis

- The sound for *aw*
- Long and short vowels
- Reordering words into sentences
- Writing and study skills

Pre-reading Activities

Ask or say:

1. Have you ever watched a child, cat, or dog while it was sleeping? What are some of the things you observed? Do you think you could tell when it was dreaming? How?

2. Do you think you or someone you know "sleeps like a log"? As you read this article about sleep, think about how much activity really occurs during the time people sleep.

Post-reading Activities

1. Discuss the answers to the questions in Exercise 1. Ask or say:

2. When people fall asleep, what are some changes in the body that can be measured?

3. Do you think sleep is necessary for good health? Why?

4. What happens when people do not get enough sleep? (A lack of sleep affects both physical and mental processes.)

5. What are some other needs that all humans have in common? (Examples: air, food, water, and shelter)

6. Name some jobs where it is very important that the workers have enough rest to do the job safely.

Writing Activities

Ask or say:

1. Write about a dream you remember.

2. About one-third of a person's life is spent in sleep. Write about what you would do with this extra time in your life if you did not have to spend it sleeping.

3. Discuss factors that affect sleep such as crossing time zones, working different shifts, stress, and uncomfortable surroundings. Ask students to choose one of these factors and write about their experience with it.

Additional Activities

1. Discuss how a paragraph is a series of sentences developing one idea or topic. As a group or in pairs, have students write brief topic headings for each paragraph in this article. (Examples: yawning, body changes, sleep stages, REM, and movement)

2. Read about Charles Lindbergh, who flew across the Atlantic alone, or someone else who went for a long time without sleep. Find out what the person did to stay awake.

Additional Vocabulary Practice

REM—Rapid Eye Movement—sleep is the fourth stage of sleep. It lasts from five to twenty minutes at a time. A person's eyes move rapidly even though his or her eyelids are closed.

Exercises

2 WORD SOUNDS

During the homework review, ask students to read these sentence pairs as couplets (two-line verses), emphasizing both the rhymes and the rhythms.

3 LONG AND SHORT VOWELS

Have students pronounce the words in the column at the left during the preview. Review the silent *e* rule that makes the preceding vowel sound long.

4 PUTTING WORDS IN ORDER

During the preview, remind students to capitalize the first word of each sentence and to use end punctuation. Note that there is more than one correct order for item 5: "The next day he was fired for sleeping on the job." "He was fired the next day for sleeping on the job." "He was fired for sleeping on the job the next day."

L E S S O N 1 2
Honeybees

Primary emphasis

- Silent and oral reading comprehension
- Phonics skills
- Context clues
- New vocabulary
- Consonants, blends, and digraphs

Secondary emphasis

- The endings -y and -ly
- Common sayings
- Writing and study skills

Words for Study

If students ask for any definitions, tell them to try to figure out the meanings from reading the selection. Tell them that the ability to figure out the meaning of a word from context clues is a skill proficient readers use regularly.

Pre-reading Activities

1. Tell students that this is an article with many interesting facts about bees. Ask the class what they already know about bees. Make a list, and add to it during the lesson. Review this list at the end of the class session.
2. Ask students if they like the taste of honey and if they use it in cooking.
3. Ask if anyone has ever been stung by a bee. If so, ask them to tell about it.

Post-reading Activities

1. Discuss the answers to the questions in Exercise 1. Ask or say:
2. Find the place in the article that explains how bees carry pollen as they move from flower to flower.
3. How many honeybees may live in one colony?
4. If 50 percent of the bees in a colony die, how many would be left?
5. The article says that pests may be the cause of the bees disappearing. What do you think the word *pests* means in this context? (insects)
6. How might chemicals used by beekeepers or farmers cause bees to die?

Writing Activities

1. Write three facts from this article about honeybees.
2. What was the most surprising fact to you about honeybees?
3. Write a paragraph to complete the following: I would like to know more about bees because . . .

Additional Activity

Help students find other facts about bees and honey. For instance, bees are insects that live throughout the world except near the North and South Poles. Honey differs in flavor and color, depending on the source of the nectar. (Examples: clover, wildflower, buckwheat) Bees' enemies include weed sprays, insecticides, bears, and skunks.

Additional Vocabulary Practice

pollinate – to spread pollen from one plant to another, to fertilize plants, to make plants able to produce

beeline – the shortest route. It comes from worker bees taking the shortest route back to the hive after they have gathered food.

Exercises

3 WORDS THAT END IN -y

Review the rules for adding endings that start with a vowel, and have students state the rule that applies to each column of words.

- For column 1 words, add -y to the base word.
- For column 2 words, drop the silent *e* before adding -y.
- For column 3 words, double the final consonant before adding -y.

If students don't know or remember the rules, ask, "Have any letters been added, dropped, or changed in the examples when -y was added?"

5 COMPOUND WORDS

Point out that these compound words are combined without a hyphen and are written as one word. Ask students for other compound words that they know that may have hyphens or are written as two words. (Examples: self-help, Native American, day care, soccer team)

L E S S O N   1 3
Handwriting

Primary emphasis
- Silent and oral reading comprehension
- Phonics skills
- Context clues
- New vocabulary
- Consonants, blends, and digraphs

Secondary emphasis
- Synonyms and antonyms
- *r*-controlled vowel sounds
- Writing and study skills

Pre-reading Activities
Ask or say:
1. Do you know that some people study the handwriting of others? Do you know why?
2. Read the following article to find out if people can learn anything about you by studying your handwriting. What kinds of things do you think they can learn?

Post-reading Activities
1. Discuss the answers to the questions in Exercise 1.
2. The first sentence in the article states, "Everything we do tells other people something about who we are." Ask students if they agree or disagree and to give examples.
   Ask or say:
3. Do handwriting specialists look at many aspects of a person's handwriting, or can a single feature give them enough information? How do you know?
4. What does "ruled by his head" mean? What would "ruled by his heart" mean?
5. What does "roll with the punches" mean? Do you think it is healthy to be able to do this? Why?
6. Studying handwriting is one way some people can learn about a person. What are other ways people can learn about each other?
7. Each person forms letters and words differently. What other distinctions or characteristics prove no two people are exactly alike? (Examples: fingerprints, voice, facial characteristics, genetic makeup)

8. In what kinds of police cases would a handwriting expert be called upon? (Examples: to examine a sample of writing and tell if it was written by a particular person; to tell something about the type of person who left a handwritten ransom note or warning)

Writing Activities
1. This lesson on handwriting provides a good opportunity to remind students to continue to write in their journals or to begin a journal. Say, "Each person's handwriting is unique. Each person is different and special. In your journal today, consider writing about something that is special about you."
2. Is "going by the rules" important in a community of people? Explain your answer. What can be done if a person disagrees with a rule?

Additional Activities
1. Make a list of the kinds of messages students might write by hand. (Examples: school notes, shopping lists, telephone messages, personal notes, letters) Briefly discuss each kind of message, and ask for suggestions, writing tips, or ideas from class members.
2. Discuss the importance of a signature in a court of law. Remind students never to sign a contract they do not fully understand or one that contains blank spaces. Stress that students should not allow themselves to be pressured into signing anything without carefully reading the entire document or getting help from someone they trust.

Exercise

4 VOWEL SOUNDS
After students have read the directions and the words in the box, have them fill in the first item for both the second and third columns (*bear* and *beer*). Point out that it is the vowel sound and not the spelling of the word that determines in which column each word belongs. During the review, point out the various spellings for each sound. You may want to use these words in a reinforcement activity or spelling quiz.

LESSON 14

Smoking

Primary emphasis
- Silent and oral reading comprehension
- Phonics skills
- Context clues
- New vocabulary
- Consonants, blends, and digraphs

Secondary emphasis
- Determining categories
- Adding -er to words
- Words that end in -er
- Sequencing events
- Writing and study skills

Words for Study
1. Point out that s at the end of years makes them plural the same way s does at the end of nouns. The date *1500s* means during the years from 1500 to 1599.
2. Review with students the meaning of BC and AD.

Pre-reading Activities
1. To build on background knowledge, ask students what they know about how smoking was introduced into the United States or into their home countries.
2. Ask students if they know anyone who has tried to stop smoking. Was it hard for that person? Did the person use any programs sponsored by state or local governments or the person's workplace? Did the person use any products such as nicotine patches or nicotine chewing gum to help?

Post-reading Activities
1. Discuss the answers to the questions in Exercise 1. Ask or say:
2. Where did tobacco first grow?
3. Why do you think that the explorers were given tobacco as a gift by native peoples?
4. How many years passed between the first article in England about the health effects of smoking and the TV ban on ads for smoking in the United States?
5. What does *mid-1960s* mean?

6. From the article, how do you know that banning smoking on planes didn't happen all at once?
7. How many years passed between the first state ban on smoking in public places and 2007 when 25 states had banned smoking?
8. Besides a ban on smoking at work and in restaurants and bars, where else is smoking banned? Name some places where you think smoking should be banned.

Writing Activities
1. Do you think that it is right for the government to ban smoking? Explain your reasons.
2. Have you ever tried to stop smoking? Write about the experience. If you did stop smoking, write about why you quit. If you never smoked, write about why you never started.

Additional Activities
1. Work out a dialogue that a student could use to present to a friend or adult relative about why that person should stop smoking.
2. Work out a dialogue that a student could use to present to a teenage son or daughter about why that person should stop smoking.
3. Bring in ads or pamphlets about the benefits of not smoking, and read them to your students or help them read them.
4. Help students research the costs of smoking in terms of money spent on tobacco products and the costs of medical care for people with smoking-related problems such as lung cancer, asthma, and heart attacks.

Exercises

3 WORKING WITH WORDS THAT RHYME
During the preview, remind students to read each sentence after they have filled in every blank to make sure that the sentence makes sense.

4 WORDS THAT END IN -er
During the preview, have students state the spelling rule illustrated in each of the three examples.

LESSON 15
A Very Strange Hobby

Primary emphasis
- Silent and oral reading comprehension
- Phonics skills
- Context clues
- New vocabulary
- Consonants, blends, and digraphs

Secondary emphasis
- Sequencing events
- Collective nouns
- Writing and study skills

Pre-reading Activities
Background information: When the western plains of the United States were being settled, conflicts arose between cattlemen and farmers over land rights. Many farmers needed fences to protect their fields from grazing sheep and cattle. Some cattlemen also wanted to build fences while others continued to allow their cattle to graze on open range. Wood and stone, fencing materials used in the East, were scarce in the West. The invention of barbed wire provided a means of fencing, but the fences resulted in range wars.

1. Ask students if they have seen barbed wire where they live. If so, for what purpose was it used?
2. Say: As you read the article, look for reasons people collect barbed wire, and find out some interesting things they do with it.

Post-reading Activities
1. Discuss the answers to the questions in Exercise 1. Ask or say:
2. What does a "link to this country's past" mean in the third paragraph of the reading?
3. Has a relative or friend ever given you something old and valued as a link to the past? If so, what was it?

4. What are some other hobbies that are "links to this country's past?" (Examples: coins, stamps, antique furniture, antique cars, model trains)
5. Why is it difficult for people to get a piece of each kind of barbed wire?
6. In what part of the United States would people most likely find old barbed wire?
7. What do you suppose the people of 1867 thought about barbed wire? Was it valued then for the same reasons that collectors value it today?
8. What kind of problems do you think the farmers were trying to avoid by fencing their property?
9. Why do you think people have hobbies?

Writing Activities
1. If you have been saving something old, write about what it is and why you are saving it.
2. Write about your hobby or one you would like to have.
3. Write about any strange hobbies you have heard about.

Additional Activities
1. Read an excerpt from the book *Shane* or some other western literature that illustrates the conflict between homesteaders and ranchers.
2. What does "won the West" mean in the third paragraph? What do you think "won the West" means from the viewpoint of a Native American?

Exercise

3 HOW DO YOU SAY IT?
During the preview, have students read the words in the box and complete one or two items below. Remind them to use the process of elimination and to make intelligent guesses for unfamiliar phrases.

Review: Lessons 1–15

During the preview, make sure students understand how to do Exercise 4. You may want them to complete one or two items as examples in class.

Encourage students to select one topic from Lessons 11 through 15 to research and report on. Students can work singly, in pairs, or in groups and give oral and/or written reports.

LESSON 16
Whales

Primary emphasis
- Silent and oral reading comprehension
- Context clues
- New vocabulary
- Consonants, blends, and digraphs
- Analogies

Secondary emphasis
- Phonics skills
- Change *y* to *i*
- Distinguishing similar words
- Writing and study skills

Pre-reading Activities
Background information: Whales can be found in all oceans of the world. Although they are mammals, whales have only a few bristles on their heads or are hairless. Some whales have teeth and some do not. The largest whales do not have teeth. They take in large amounts of water containing tiny animals and plants. Then they push the water out through their whalebone (baleen), which acts like a filter, and swallow the food that is left. Whales need to breathe air, but they can stay under water for as long as 50 minutes.

1. Ask students to tell what they already know about whales. Some students may be aware that whales are endangered.
   Say:
2. As you read the article, compare what you know about fish and what you are learning about whales. Think about how they are similar and how they are different.

Post-reading Activities
1. Discuss the answers to the questions in Exercise 1.
   Ask or say:
2. Find the comparison that the writer uses to help you understand the size of a blue whale.
3. Why did people in the 1800s hunt whales? (Whales were hunted for their oil and bones.)
4. When was the first effort made to try to cut back whale hunting?
5. How many years later did the United States pass a law banning whale hunting in its waters?

6. The United States continues to put new species on the Endangered Species List. What information in the reading proves this statement to be true?
7. About how many times shorter than the blue whale is the Beluga whale?
8. How do you think that pollution is a threat to whales? How are boats?
9. What example does the article give that the Endangered Species List works?

Writing Activities
1. Write three new facts that you learned from the article about whales.
2. What was the most interesting new information that you learned from about whales?
3. Summarize the information about California gray whales in three sentences.

Additional Activities
1. Bring to class information on international efforts to ban whaling. Discuss why some nations have opposed the ban.
2. Do you think the author of this article thinks whales are valuable and worth saving? If a whale hunter wrote an article about whales, in what ways might the article be different? In what ways might the article be the same?

Exercises

4 CHANGING THE *y* TO *i*
During the preview, have students study the example and ask, "What happens to the *y* when *-er* and *-est* are added?" During the review, state or have students state the spelling rule:
- When a words ends with a consonant plus *-y,* change the *y* to *i* before adding any ending that doesn't start with *i*.

6 WHICH WORD FITS BEST?
Remind students that they did a similar exercise in Lesson 8. Review the steps students should follow.

LESSON 17
Black Bart

Primary emphasis
- Silent and oral reading comprehension
- Phonics skills
- Context clues
- New vocabulary
- Synonyms and antonyms

Secondary emphasis
- Oral reading
- Consonants, blends, and digraphs
- The ending -*ful*
- Writing and study skills

Words for Study
- Point out that *he'd* is the contraction for both *he would* and *he had*. In this article, it is used for *he would*.
- Draw attention to the hyphens in *high-class* and *middle-aged*. Tell students that they are part of the correct spelling of these words.

Pre-reading Activities
Background information: This article is about a clever outlaw who called himself Black Bart the PO8 (poet). Here is a poem he left at the scene of one robbery:

> "here I lay me down to Sleep,
> to wait the coming Morrow,
> perhaps Success perhaps defeat,
> And everlasting Sorrow,
> let come what will Ill try it on,
> My condition can't be worse,
> And if theres money in that Box,
> Tis Munny in by purse"

Black Bart was an educated man. The spelling and punctuation mistakes were intentional.

1. Ask students if they have ever seen any movies with stagecoach robberies. If so, have them describe a typical western stagecoach robbery.
2. Tell students that Black Bart was an unusual outlaw. As a mask, he often wore a flour sack over his head with eye holes cut out. Ask students to look as they read the article for other ways Black Bart was different.

Post-reading Activities
1. Discuss the answers to the questions in Exercise 1. Ask or say:
2. According to this article, why did Black Bart first break the law? What was his reason for continuing?
3. Do you think Black Bart considered robbing stages serious business? Why or why not?
4. Name some ways that Black Bart was different from the usual robber.
5. Was Black Bart a violent man? What information in the reading supports your answer?
6. What does "riding shotgun" mean?
7. Why do you think Black Bart left a verse behind when he robbed a stage? Do you think it increased his chances of being caught? Why or why not?

Writing Activities
1. Write a class poem about Black Bart.
2. Write a class story. Decide where the story takes place, what year it is, who the people are, and what happens.
3. Write several reasons why people break the law and turn to a life of crime.

Additional Activities
1. It is thought that "PO8" was Black Bart's spelling of *poet*. Ask students for their interpretation of the PO8 signature.
2. Students may be interested to know that Black Bart lived in San Francisco, California. He was finally caught by tracing a laundry mark on a handkerchief he dropped during a holdup.
3. Suggest other stories about the Old West as supplementary reading for students who show a particular interest in this article.

Exercises

4 A VERSE FROM BLACK BART
During the homework review, help students to read this verse aloud. The meter is not regular and may be difficult for them at first.

5 THE ENDING -*ful*
Remind students to read the entire sentence before selecting the word that fits in the blank. During the review, discuss the meaning of the suffix -*ful*.

LESSON 18
Earth Day

Primary emphasis
- Silent and oral reading comprehension
- Phonics skills
- Context clues
- New vocabulary
- Consonants, blends, and digraphs

Secondary emphasis
- Sequencing events accurately
- The ending *-less*
- Reviewing *same* and *opposite*
- Spelling scrambled words
- Writing and study skills

Pre-reading Activities
1. To stimulate interest, show one or more pictures of Earth taken from outer space. Talk about how clean the oceans and land look from outer space. Ask students if they see something different when they look around. (Examples: polluted air and water, trash, bare land where forests once stood, garbage washed up on beaches, etc.)
2. Ask students if they have ever heard of or participated in Earth Day. If not, what do they think that it might be? Tell them to read the article to find out.

Post-reading Activities
1. Discuss the answers to the questions in Exercise 1. Ask or say:
2. What were cities and rivers like in 1970?
3. Why did Senator Gaylord Nelson want to have Earth Day in 1970?
4. What kind of choices do people learn how to make on Earth Day?
5. Find information in the article that explains what people can do in their own homes to save the planet.
6. How do you think that group walks can help people learn to protect the environment?
7. What kinds of things can businesses recycle?
8. How have laws helped to protect the environment?
9. Do you think that these laws were needed to make people protect the environment? Explain your opinion.
10. What reasons does the writer give for saying that "every day can be Earth Day"?

Writing Activities
1. Does your community celebrate Earth Day? If it does, what are some activities that it has on Earth Day? If it doesn't, how could you help start an Earth Day celebration?
2. We do a better job of protecting the environment now than we did in 1970, but we could do more. Write about one thing that you could do to help protect the environment.

Additional Activities
1. Go online to find pictures of the Chicago River or Lake Erie in the 1960s before the Clean Water Act was passed and pictures of those places today. Photos of cities with smog problems like Los Angeles could also be used to illustrate the difference that the Clean Air Act has made.
2. "Reduce, Reuse, Recycle" is the national slogan for helping to conserve our natural resources and protect the environment. Discuss what the slogan means. Ask for examples of each idea.

Exercises

2 WORD SOUNDS
The consonant blends emphasized in this exercise can be difficult. Have students read the words on the left during the preview. Point out that items 1 and 3 have more than one sentence. Remind students to read an entire item before filling in the blanks.

3 THE ENDING *-less*
During the review, discuss the meaning of the suffix *-less*, and contrast it with *-ful* (in Lesson 17).

4 SAME OR OPPOSITE?
During the homework preview, make sure students understand the difference between *same* and *opposite*.

5 SPELLING CHECK
Treat this as a game or puzzle rather than just another exercise. Remind students that it may help to cross out letters as they use them.

LESSON 19
Jails on the High Seas

Primary emphasis
- Silent and oral reading comprehension
- Phonics skills
- Context clues
- New vocabulary
- Consonants, blends, and digraphs

Secondary emphasis
- Homonyms
- Choosing the unrelated word
- Words that begin with *un-*
- Common sayings
- Writing and study skills

Pre-reading Activities
1. If possible, go online and print out a picture of a galley. Ask students to tell you anything they can about galleys from the picture. Prompt with such questions as: Does it look like a modern ship? What are some parts of the ship?
2. Read the title. Ask: Can you think of reasons why there would be jails at sea? Read the article to find a reason.

Post-reading Activities
1. Discuss the answers to the questions in Exercise 1. Ask or say:
2. What is meant by "the coming of steam" in the first sentence?
3. What do you think "inland sea" refers to? (the Mediterranean Sea)
4. Did the author say that a convict "was like an oar" or that a convict "was an oar"? Which is the more powerful statement? Why?
5. Do you think convicts preferred to be at sea or in port? Explain. Why do you think there were jails on the high seas?
6. Galleys were propelled by oars and sails. What advantages would there be to having two methods? What conditions may have determined which method was used? Would there be times when using both sails and oars would be necessary? (Galleys were used for war as well as trade.)
7. What do you think happened to galleys after steam was used to propel ships?

8. What do you think is the main idea of this article? What do you think the author really wants the reader to understand?
9. Besides steamships, what other forms of transportation used steam? (Examples: trains, cars, tractors)

Writing Activities
1. Summarize this article in two or three sentences.
2. Why would the speed of a ship be especially important during a war?
3. Compare the life of a convict today with that of a convict on a galley.
4. What is the difference between a convict and a slave? Do you think the convicts in this reading were treated more like slaves than prisoners? Why or why not?
5. What do you think is the most powerful statement in this article? Why?

Additional Activities
1. Find the Mediterranean Sea on a world map or atlas. Ask students what countries today border the Mediterranean Sea. Ask what continents border it.
2. Help interested students find information on the development of steamships and their impact on world trade.

Exercises
2 WORDS THAT SOUND THE SAME
Remind students that it is the meaning of the word in context that determines the correct spelling of homonyms.

3 WHICH WORD DOES NOT FIT?
All the words in most of these groups have some relationship to each other. Students will have to find the word that relates differently from the other words. You may want to have students do the first item during the preview.

4 WORDS THAT BEGIN WITH *un-*
Discuss the meaning of *un-* during the homework review.

5 COMMON SAYINGS
Discuss these sayings with students during the review. Explain any unfamiliar ones. Students may enjoy writing about what one of the sayings means or where they think it came from.

LESSON 20
The Father of Our Country

Primary emphasis

- Silent and oral reading comprehension
- Phonics skills
- Context clues
- New vocabulary
- Consonants, blends, and digraphs

Secondary emphasis

- Vowel sounds
- The ending -ly
- Compound words
- Common sayings
- Writing and study skills

Pre-reading Activity

Ask or say:

Why do you think George Washington is known as "the Father of Our Country?" Think about this question as you read.

Post-reading Activities

1. Discuss the answers to the question in Exercise 1.
   Ask or say:
2. What is George Washington known for besides being the first president? (Examples: He commanded the Continental Army in the Revolutionary War, and he was president of the convention that wrote the Constitution.)
3. What is the difference between *vice* as in *vice president* and *vice* as it is used in paragraph 3?
4. George Washington was against swearing, yet he allowed himself to be sworn in as first president. What is the difference?
5. Was George Washington a religious person? If you agree, why do you think so? If not, why?
6. What is the difference between a king and a president? Why do you suppose George Washington became upset when someone suggested he should be king?

7. Was Washington well liked and respected by everyone? Find information in the article to support your answer.

Writing Activities

1. Write one new thing you learned about George Washington.
2. During Washington's time, few people went to school. Washington went to school until he was 14 or 15. Write about whether or not you feel people need more education today than in Washington's time and why.
3. Do you think public executions "serve as a warning to others"? Why or why not?

Additional Activities

1. Students who enjoyed this article about George Washington may enjoy biographies about other presidents such as Abraham Lincoln.
2. Read to the class excerpts from the Constitution, and discuss them.
3. Since this is the last lesson in *Challenger 2,* ask students what their favorite reading selections were and why. You might guide students to supplementary reading books on similar subjects.

Exercises

3 COMPOUND WORDS

During the homework review, have students give the definition for *compound word*. Point out that when compound words are formed, the spelling and pronunciation of the two base words usually do not change.

5 MORE COMMON SAYINGS

Discuss these sayings, and encourage students to pick one to write about. Students may enjoy making up a story about how a given saying came to be.

Review: Lessons 1–20

Tell students to refer to the lessons for any of the items in Exercise 1, "Twenty Questions," that they don't remember. Students who complete this review with a score of 85 percent or more are ready to begin Book 3.

After going over the review, discuss what students have learned and accomplished while working in *Challenger 2.* Students may want to plan and prepare a celebration as well.

Book 3 Introduction

The format of *Challenger 3* corresponds to that of *Challenger 1*. Each of the 20 lessons begins with a word chart in which specific phonics principles are emphasized. The readings are short fictional pieces about a group of young adults. Comprehension and skill-building exercises provide opportunities to develop vocabulary, to use words in various contexts, and to improve analytical and reasoning skills.

Students who completed the final review in Book 2 with 85 percent or better accuracy should be ready to go on to Book 3, In addition, Book 3 is an appropriate starting place for students who test at levels 3 or 4 on the online *Challenger Placement Tool* and for students who test at levels 3.0–4.5 on standardized reading inventories.

Students working in Book 3 should be able to sound out or sight-read words on the word chart. They should also be able to read the stories and answer comprehension questions by themselves. They should, however, read all or most of the stories aloud when going over the homework.

Scheduling Considerations

One-hour sessions are appropriate for students in Book 3. This time frame allows students to do some oral reading, discuss the reading selection, go over the homework exercises, work on writing and/or reinforcement activities, and preview the next lesson.

Book 3 works well with students in a classroom setting or in a one-to-one or group tutorial setting, as described in the Introduction to *Challenger 2* on pages 70–72 of this manual. It is unlikely that students in Book 3 will need extensive individual tutoring. You should, however, allow some time to work with individual students on a regular basis.

Suggestions for Teaching the Lessons

It is important for you to read the material in the first five chapters of this manual if you have not already done so. These chapters discuss the concepts and procedures upon which *Challenger* is based and give general suggestions for using the series. The following are specific suggestions for Book 3.

THE WORD CHART

Book 3, like Book 1, uses common phonics principles to organize the introduction of new words. This helps students to recognize better the many regular patterns in English, which contributes to reading development. Have students read at least some of the chart words during either the lesson preview or the homework review. When appropriate, review the phonics principles involved. (See pages 8–10 for a listing of common phonics elements and principles.) How much emphasis you place on the phonics principles depends upon the needs of your students.

- Students who started in Books 1 and 2 but who still need practice on word attack skills should continue sounding out unfamiliar chart words according to methods they used in the earlier books.

- Students who start in Book 3 usually have a good sight vocabulary but often have difficulties arising from careless habits. It is often enough for you to pronounce an unfamiliar word and point out a specific phonics element, such as a double vowel that represents a long vowel sound. These students can often correct a misread word themselves if you say, "Look at it again."

- Plan to incorporate troublesome words into reinforcement activities.

WORDS FOR STUDY

This section, which precedes the story in each lesson, lists words that appear in the story and exercises for the first time in the series. The words appear in the same form in which they initially appear in the lesson, often giving students practice in reading word endings.

THE STORY

Make sure students understand that the readings in Book 3 are stories rather than articles such as those in Book 2. The terms *fiction* and *nonfiction* can be introduced. The following ideas may be helpful in your planning.

- The initial reading should be done for homework following one or more pre-reading activities during the homework preview. Suggestions for these activities are given in the individual lesson notes.

- As students move through the book, review with them what they already know about the characters from stories in earlier lessons.
- As often as possible, have students read the stories aloud before discussing them during the homework review.
- The lesson notes give suggestions for inferential- and applied-level questions to stimulate discussion and allow you to assess comprehension.

THE EXERCISES

Students should preview the exercises to be done for homework following procedures established in Books 1 and 2. Encourage students to develop the habit of reading directions carefully.

The wide variety of exercises helps students to develop recall and reasoning abilities. Keep the following points in mind when working on the exercises.

- Encourage students to refer to the reading selection when answering the comprehension questions in Exercise 1. Remind them that a long line under a question indicates that the answer should be a complete sentence.
- Remind students to answer all questions. If they aren't sure of an answer, they should use such strategies as intelligent guessing, the process of elimination, and context clues. Remind them also that they can learn from their mistakes. A fundamental premise of this series is that mistakes can be valuable sources of learning. If students have a problem with an exercise, help them to recognize what went wrong. Point out also what they did well.
- Students should correct all exercises during the homework review. Any grading that is required should be done on corrected work. Consider an average of 80 percent or better an excellent score.

Writing Activities

Student writing is discussed in Chapter 3 of this manual. Use those suggestions to help plan appropriate writing activities. Students in Book 3 should have weekly opportunities for extended writing, including projects that involve formal writing. For these projects, students can work together in pairs or small groups, helping each other to generate and organize ideas, reacting to each other's drafts, and helping each other to polish and edit pieces of writing.

Students should pick their own topics for writing activities. Topics related to the lessons are suggested in the lesson notes. Personal hobbies and interests and current issues can also provide appropriate topics for writing assignments. Writing Book 3 also provides writing activities to extend the lesson content and to help students develop and practice their writing skills.

The Lesson Segments

After the session in which Lesson 1 is completed and Lesson 2 is previewed for homework, the procedure for each session should be as consistent as possible. You may want to vary the order of the following segments to suit your particular situation.

1. **Homework Review.** Have students read aloud at least some of the story in the lesson studied for homework. Have them summarize the story, go over their answers to the comprehension questions in Exercise 1, and discuss the story. Then go over the rest of the exercises and have students make any necessary corrections.
2. **Writing Activity.** Students may work alone or in groups on the current writing activity, depending on what it is.
3. **Reinforcement Activity.** When time permits, focus on an area of difficulty in a way that is fun for the students. See Chapter 4 of this manual for suggestions.
4. **Homework Preview.** Preview the next lesson, which students will complete for homework. Have students read some of the words in the word chart either now or during the homework review. Have them read the Words for Study and the title of the story and predict what they think it will be about. Do one or more pre-reading activities. Have students read the directions for the exercises and do one item in any exercise that might be confusing.

Individual Lesson Notes

The individual lesson notes that begin on page 95 contain specific suggestions and procedures for Book 3 lessons.

LESSON 1
Review of Long and Short Vowels

Primary emphasis
- Comprehension and literary understanding
- Long and short vowels
- Phonics, word analysis, and context clues
- New vocabulary
- Writing and study skills

Secondary emphasis
- Oral reading skills
- Spelling (adding -*ing*)
- The -*er* ending
- Compound words

Word Chart
1. Long vowel patterns reviewed:
   - the silent *e* (VCe): *ape, eve, vine, owe, Luke*
   - the open syllable (V): *ivy*
2. Short vowel patterns reviewed:
   - closed syllables (VC, CVC, CVCC): *ad, van, raft*
3. Point out the apostrophes in *she's* and *she'd* and make sure students recognize these contractions.

Words for Study
Tell students that these are words that appear in this lesson for the first time in the *Challenger* series. Point out the contractions *they're, we'll,* and *how's.*

Pre-reading Activities
1. Introduce the terms *fiction* and *nonfiction,* giving examples of each. Tell students that the reading selections in *Challenger 3* are short fiction pieces about a group of young adults.
2. After reading the title, ask what it means to "take advice." Tell students to think about how Steven is persuaded to take his sister's advice. Have students read the story aloud. Assign a second reading for homework.

Post-reading Activities
1. Discuss the questions in Exercise 1.
   Ask or say:
2. Did Steven see a need to exercise at the beginning of the story? At the end of the story, why did he change his mind?

3. Do you think Ruth often gives Steven advice? What clues in the story support your answer?
4. Find the place in the story where Ruth manages to turn an argument into a challenge.
5. In your opinion, did Ruth give Steven good advice? Explain your answer.
6. Do you think Steven and Ruth care about each other? Explain.
7. If this story continued, what do you think would happen next?

Writing Activities
1. Do you have a favorite form of exercise? If so, write about it.
2. Explain why exercise is important.

Additional Activities
1. Do you ever feel your life is in a rut? What are some things you can do to get out of a rut?
2. Is exercise a good way to relieve tension? What are some other benefits of exercise?

Exercises

1 ABOUT THE STORY
During the homework preview, tell students to answer the questions in complete sentences. Explain that the answers to "What do you think?" questions should reflect students' own opinions.

2 THE ENDING -*ing*
During the homework preview, study the examples and ask, "Were any letters added, dropped, or changed when -*ing* was added?" Review the three rules for adding endings that start with a vowel:
- For column 1 words, add -*ing* to the base word.
- For column 2 words, drop the silent e before adding -*ing.*
- For column 3 words, double the final consonant before adding -*ing.*

3 HOW DO THESE PEOPLE EARN A LIVING?
During the homework preview, review the process of elimination. Tell students they don't have to do items in order. They should do the ones they know first. Then they can go back and do any skipped ones when fewer choices remain.

L E S S O N   2
Review of Consonant Blends and Digraphs: Part 1

Primary emphasis
- Comprehension and literary understanding
- Consonant blends and digraphs *ch, sh, st*
- Phonics, word analysis, and context clues
- New vocabulary
- Writing and study skills

Secondary emphasis
- Oral reading skills
- Spelling (adding *-est*)
- Identifying terms
- Compound words

Word Chart
1. Have students pronounce the digraphs and blend before reading the words.
2. Special notes:
   - The *l* in *chalk* is silent.
   - *Shove* and *breast* have short vowel sounds although they have long vowel spelling patterns (VCe and VV).

Words for Study
If students ask for definitions of any of these words, encourage them to try to figure out the meanings from the story.

Pre-reading Activities
1. Briefly review the story in Lesson 1 in which Steven was introduced. What did students learn about Steven? What did Steven decide to do at the end of the story?
2. The title of this story is "Meet Jerome." A character named Jerome is introduced in this story. Ask students to list things that make a good impression on them when they meet a person for the first time. Say:
3. In this story, Steven has begun his class at the YMCA. He is practicing his exercises when his friend Jerome arrives. Read to find out what kind of exercise class Steven is taking and why.

Note: From this lesson on, the first reading can be done for homework. Oral reading practice is important, however. Have some or all of the story read aloud during the homework review whenever time allows.

Post-reading Activities
1. Ask students to summarize the story.
2. Discuss the questions in Exercise 1. Ask or say:
3. The title of the story is "Meet Jerome." What things did you learn about Jerome from this first meeting?
4. Why was Jerome shouting his questions about yoga to Steven?
5. Did Steven consider the cost of the class?
6. What was Steven concerned about when he noticed Jerome shaking his head? What did he think Jerome was going to say?
7. Is this class helping Steven relax? What information supports your answer?
8. Do you think Steven was sorry he ended up in the yoga class, or do you think it worked out in his best interest? Explain.

Writing Activities
1. Write about your favorite way to relax.
2. Have you ever wandered into the wrong place? Write about your experience.

Additional Activities
1. Ask students to underline or highlight in color the conversation between Steven and Jerome. Discuss quotation marks, if necessary. Ask for volunteers to read the parts of Steven and Jerome and for a narrator to read the non-dialogue parts.
2. In this story, students meet Jerome. Discuss the skills involved in meeting new people. Make a list of suggestions for starting conversations and keeping them going. Ask for volunteers to role-play helping a new person feel welcome in class.
3. Ask if anyone is interested in reading about yoga and telling the class more about it. Have a book or article available if possible.

Exercise

2 ADDING -est TO WORDS
During the homework preview, have students state the spelling rule for each example.

LESSON 3
Review of Consonant Blends: Part 2

Primary emphasis
- Comprehension and literary understanding
- Consonant blends *bl, br, cl, cr, fl, fr*
- Phonics, word analysis, and context clues
- New vocabulary
- Writing and study skills

Secondary emphasis
- Oral reading skills
- Spelling (adding *-y*)
- Identifying terms
- Compound words

Word Chart
Have students pronounce the consonant blends before reading the chart words.

Pre-reading Activities
Ask or say:
1. Ask students what they know about yoga. Do any of them do yoga? What kind of yoga is it? When did they first start doing yoga? Is it fun?
2. Ask if anyone has ever wanted to try yoga but has kept putting it off. Ask them to talk about why. Are they concerned that they might look foolish, might not be good at it, or might get hurt?
3. Review what students learned about Jerome in the story in Lesson 2. The story in this lesson starts shortly after that one ended. Read this story to find out what Jerome learns about yoga.

Post-reading Activities
1. Ask students to summarize the story.
   Ask or say:
2. Why do you think that Jerome wanted to find out more about yoga rather than teasing Steven about something he didn't know much about?
3. How does the writer describe the person in the picture that Jerome finds on the Internet?
4. Why does Jerome think that yoga must be easier than it looks?
5. By the end of the story, Jerome has decided that yoga isn't easier than it looks. What has happened to make him change his mind?

6. What reason does Jerome give to explain why there are so many books on the yoga website?
7. Why does Jerome think he could use some help with his balance?
8. What does the word *crick* in paragraph 6 mean? How do you know?

Writing Activities
1. Write about the first time that you tried something new. It could be a new sport, a new food, or a new way to do something. Describe what you did and how you felt.
2. If you do yoga, describe how to stand on your head.
3. If you haven't already done so, introduce journal writing, and encourage students to write in their journals every day. Journal writing is described in Chapter 3 of this manual.

Additional Activities
Jerome finds his information on a website. Discuss with students how to be sure that what they find on the Internet is accurate and up-to-date. They need to find reputable websites. For example, if they are looking for medical information, they should look for sites maintained by organizations such as the American Medical Association and the American Cancer Society. For government information, they should look for sites that end in .gov.

Exercises

2 ADDING -*y* TO WORDS
Review the spelling rule for each example during the homework preview. Note that wool is an exception to the pattern. Generally, the final consonant is not doubled for words with double vowels.

3 WHO USES WHAT?
During the homework preview, tell students to read through each sentence before filling in the blank. Read the first sentence as follows: "A cook uses an *blank* to bake a cake." Tell students to reread the sentences after the words are filled in to be sure that they make sense. You might tell students that the *a* and *an* are hints about the missing word. The *a* signals that the missing word begins with a consonant and *an* signals that it begins with a vowel.

Review of Consonant Blends: Part 3

Primary emphasis
- Comprehension and literary understanding
- Consonant blends *gl, gr, pl, pr, sl, str*
- Phonics, word analysis, and context clues
- New vocabulary
- Writing and study skills

Secondary emphasis
- Oral reading skills
- Spelling (changing *y* to *i*)
- Identifying terms
- Compound words

Word Chart
Have students pronounce the blends before reading the words. The three-letter blend *str* is difficult for some people to pronounce.

Pre-reading Activities
Ask or say:
1. How do you react if you are interrupted by a phone call when you are busy or concentrating? Do you find it hard to be polite?
2. Review how the story in Lesson 3 ended and what you have learned about Jerome.
3. This story takes place shortly after the story in Lesson 3 ended. What do you think Jerome is doing at the beginning of this story?

Post-reading Activities
1. Discuss the questions in Exercise 1.
2. Ask volunteers to read this story aloud as a dialogue between Jerome and Ginger. Suggest that they underline or highlight the lines they will be reading. Point out that a new paragraph begins whenever a different person speaks. Encourage them to express the emotions felt by the two characters.
   Ask or say:
3. Describe Ginger's mood when the phone rang. What was Jerome's mood when he called Ginger?
4. Compare their moods at the beginning and end of the story.
5. Ginger says that she loves Jerome, but how well do you think that Ginger and Jerome know each other? What information from the story supports your answer?

6. In your opinion, who is more responsible for the argument, Ginger or Jerome? Why?
7. In your opinion, at what point in the story did trouble begin between Ginger and Jerome?
8. One of the benefits of yoga is that it helps people relax. How relaxed do you think Jerome was? Compare his reaction to being interrupted with Steven's reaction in Lesson 2.
9. What do you think will happen next?

Writing Activities
1. Think about what might have happened next if Ginger hadn't hung up. Write three or four more lines of dialogue.
2. Remind students to continue to write in their journals.

Additional Activities
1. Discuss why good phone skills are important.
2. Discuss ideas for dealing with difficult people or people in bad moods.
3. Practice phone skills. Ask students what kinds of phone calls they make. Then write a variety of telephone calling situations on slips of paper. Ask pairs of students to draw a slip and then to plan and role-play the various telephone conversations.
4. Suggested topics for a discussion on phone etiquette: phone calls at meal times, taking messages, answering machines, wrong numbers, and children and phones.

Exercises

2 CHANGING THE -y TO -i
During the homework preview, have students state the spelling rule for the -*y* to -*i* conversion. Point out that the -*y* is changed to -*i* before adding endings that begin with consonants, as well as endings that begin with vowels.

3 MORE WORK WITH THE ENDING -y
During the preview, tell students to write out the words in the top box before using them in the sentences.

5 COMPOUND WORDS
As a reinforcement activity, you might dictate 20 words that are parts of 10 compound words and then have students match them.

LESSON 5
Review of Consonant Blends: Part 4

Primary emphasis
- Comprehension and literary understanding
- Consonant blends *dr, tr, thr, sc, sk, sw*
- Phonics, word analysis, and context clues
- New vocabulary
- Writing and study skills

Secondary emphasis
- Oral reading skills
- The ending *-ly*
- Synonyms
- Compound words

Word Chart
1. The blend *thr* is difficult for some people to pronounce.
2. In these words, *sc* and *sk* sound alike.

Words for Study
Make sure students know that *etc.* stands for *et cetera,* a Latin term meaning *and so forth.* If necessary, review the term *abbreviation.*

Pre-reading Activities
1. Review what was learned about Ginger from the story in Lesson 4.
   Say:
2. In this story, we find out more about Ginger, including what she does for a living and how she met Jerome.
3. As you read, find out who influenced Ginger as a small girl and what information she keeps private from her mother and from Jerome.

Post-reading Activities
1. Discuss the questions in Exercise 1.
   Ask or say:
2. The title of this story is "Who Is Ginger?" What things did you learn about Ginger from reading the story?
3. Had Ginger made up her mind about how she felt about Jerome?
4. What does the sentence "As for Jerome—well, who knew what went on in his mind?" tell you about Jerome?

5. What does the saying "A penny saved is a penny earned" mean?
6. Do you think Ginger's grandmother would approve of how Ginger manages her money? Why or why not?
7. What information in the story indicates that Ginger is a talented and creative person?
8. Why do you think Ginger was not truthful with her mother?
9. If you were Ginger, would you spend some of your money to furnish your apartment? Why or why not?

Writing Activities
1. What lesson did Ginger's grandmother teach her? Write about how an older relative or friend influenced your life.
2. If you had money to invest, write about how you would invest it.

Additional Activities
1. Discuss in pairs or small groups the role of grandparents in raising children. Consider special circumstances such as divorce or families separated by distance. How may either of these situations change the grandparent's role? In what ways can the role of a grandparent be different from that of a parent?
2. Help students to understand financial transactions such as reading bills, writing checks, opening and using checking accounts, applying for safe deposit boxes, completing credit/loan applications, and using other banking services.

Exercises

2 THE ENDING *-ly*
During the preview, point out that no letters are added, dropped, or changed when *-ly* is added to these words. Note that *shyly* is an exception to the *-y* to *-i* conversion rule introduced in Lesson 4. Remind students to write the words in the left column before using them in the sentences.

3 WORDS THAT MEAN THE SAME
Remind students to use the process of elimination in this matching exercise.

LESSON 6

Review of Consonant Blends and Digraphs: Part 5

Primary emphasis
- Comprehension and literary understanding
- Consonant blends and digraphs *stn, sn, sp, scr, th, wh*
- Phonics, word analysis, and context clues
- New vocabulary

Secondary emphasis
- Oral reading skills
- The ending *-ly*
- Antonyms
- Compound words

Word Chart
1. The *th* is unvoiced, or soft, in these *th* words.
2. Some people pronounce the *wh* sound as /*hw*/; others pronounce it /*w*/. Either pronunciation is acceptable.

Pre-reading Activities
1. After reading the title, discuss the word *fate*. Ask what it means and what "a strange twist of fate" means.
2. Review what students know about Jerome and Ginger, including what they know about Jerome's job.
3. Tell students to read the story to find out how Jerome got himself into trouble at work.

Post-reading Activities
1. Discuss the questions in Exercise 1.
   Ask or say:
2. Describe how Jerome got into trouble at work. What is the "twist of fate" in this story?
3. Did Jerome care for Ginger? What information from the story supports your answer?
4. Compare how Jerome and Ginger think apartments should be furnished and kept.
5. Is entertaining friends more important to Jerome or to Ginger? Explain.
6. If Jerome gave Ginger a can of paint, do you think he would be giving her something she really wants? Why or why not?
7. What kind of a friend is Tony?
8. Why was Jerome concerned about telling his boss what happened? Do you think Jerome planned on telling his boss the whole truth?

9. Do you think Jerome should pay for the spilled paint? Why or why not?

Writing Activities
1. In Lesson 4, Ginger thinks of Jerome as "a jerk." After reading this story, do you agree or disagree? Write about why you think Jerome is or isn't a jerk.
2. Did you ever have to clean up a mess like Jerome's paint spill? Write about a situation you remember.
3. Write about a "twist of fate" in your life or someone else's life.

Additional Activities
1. The first sentence in the story states that Jerome was not a thief, but he did enjoy having sneaky ideas now and then. What is the difference?
2. Ask: If you were in Jerome's situation, what would you tell your boss?
3. Tony spent seven hours helping his friend Jerome clean up. Ask students to think about a time they helped a friend with a problem or a friend helped them. Invite volunteers to share their stories with the class.
4. Discuss the problem of employees who steal. Ask such questions as: How serious do you think this problem is? Do you think it is common? What can be done about it?
5. List some of the words for colors such as *emerald, vermilion, burgundy, ruby,* and *amber.* Ask students to match the colors to the common names *green, red, yellow,* etc.

Exercises

2 MORE WORK WITH THE ENDING *-ly*
Remind students to write all the words with *-ly* added first and to use the process of elimination when putting the words in the sentences.

3 WORD OPPOSITES
During the homework preview, make sure students understand the concept of opposite meanings.

LESSON 7
Review of Silent Letters

Primary emphasis
- Comprehension and literary understanding
- Silent letters *kn, wr, gn, tch, dge, gh, ght*
- Phonics, word analysis, and context clues
- New vocabulary
- Writing and study skills

Secondary emphasis
- Oral reading skills
- The endings *-ful* and *-less*
- Synonyms and antonyms
- Compound words

Word Chart
Have students identify the silent letters before reading the words. Students may want to cross out the silent letters in troublesome words.

Pre-reading Activities
1. Review what was learned about Steven in Lessons 1 and 2.
   Ask or say:
2. Think about the things that cause stress in your life. What can you do to help relieve or avoid stressful situations?
3. In this story, Steven learns that there is a lot more to yoga than he thought. Read to find out what is important besides the exercising.

Post-reading Activities
1. Discuss the questions in Exercise 1.
2. Ask for volunteers to read the parts of Holly and Steven, beginning with paragraph 4.
   Ask or say:
3. Did Steven seem to enjoy the yoga classes? What information in the story supports your answer?
4. How successful was Steven at learning the yoga exercises? What information in the story supports your answer?
5. After class, Steven's cold seemed to come back. Why did Steven notice his cold more before and after class than during it?
6. What things did you learn about Holly from this story?
7. What is important in yoga besides exercising?

8. Why does Holly suggest Steven should not eat chocolate cake?
9. Do you agree with what Holly's book says about sugar? Why or why not?

Writing Activities
1. Write two things you learned about yoga from reading this story.
2. Have you ever changed your diet to improve your health? Explain.
3. Write about a time when you got involved with something and found out there was more to it than you thought.

Additional Activities
1. Have students work in pairs or small groups to read a magazine or newspaper article on a health topic. Have them summarize what they read for the entire group.
2. Working in pairs or small groups, students can write down and report to the class on one or both of the following questions:
   - What are some things people can do to try to prevent illness?
   - What are some things people can do to help themselves get better when they are sick?

Exercises

2 THE ENDINGS *-ful* AND *-less*
During the homework preview, point out that no letters are added, changed, or dropped when *-ful* and *-less* are added to these words. Tell students to form the words indicated in Part A and then match those words to the definitions in Part B. During the homework review, ask students to explain what *-ful* and *-less* mean.

3 SAME OR OPPOSITE?
Occasionally students have trouble grasping the difference between *same* and *opposite* when they are combined in an exercise. For those students, use one or two pairs in sentences. For instance:
- He put the newspaper *on* the table.
  He took the newspaper *off* the table.
- You had a good *idea*.
  You had a good *thought*.

LESSON 8
Review of Vowel Combinations: Part 1

Primary emphasis
- Comprehension and literary understanding
- Vowel combinations *ai, ee, ēa, ĕa, ui*
- Phonics, word analysis, and context clues
- New vocabulary
- Writing and study skills

Secondary emphasis
- Oral reading skills
- Long and short vowel sounds
- The endings *-ful* and *-less*
- Synonyms and antonyms
- Compound words

Word Chart
Four of these combinations spell long vowel sounds. Note that *ea* also spells a short vowel sound. Point out the long and short vowel markings in the chart. If students have difficulty remembering the pronunciation of a troublesome word, suggest that they mark the vowel with the appropriate mark until they have learned the word.

Words for Study
Point out that *who's* is the contraction for both *who is* and *who has*. It is not the possessive form of *who*. Contrast *whose* and *who's*.

Pre-reading Activities
Ask or say:
1. In most families, parents and children sometimes disagree. What are some things that may cause conflicts between parents and children?
2. In the following story, Ginger helps her friend Gail begin to resolve her family problems. As you read, decide if Ginger is a good listener. Think about the kinds of questions Ginger asked Gail.

Post-reading Activities
1. Discuss the questions in Exercise 1.
2. Ask for volunteers to read the lines for Ginger and Gail as a dialogue.
   Ask or say:
3. Describe how Gail looked when Ginger opened the door.
4. Did Gail assume Ginger would let her stay? What information supports your answer?
5. Find a place in the story that shows Gail's father cares for her.

6. Ginger asked Gail questions to find out what had happened. Which questions helped Gail to see things in a different light?
7. Was Ginger a good listener? Explain.
8. What did Gail want from her parents? What did Gail's parents want from her? Did Gail understand? Did Ginger understand?
9. Compare how Gail feels about her father at the beginning and at the end of the story.

Writing Activities
1. Write one sentence about Ginger and one sentence about Gail.
2. Suggest a different title for this story, and explain why you think it would be a good one.
3. Gail shared her difficulties with her friend Ginger. In your opinion, is it a good idea for people to talk to friends and share their problems? Explain.

Additional Activities
1. Discuss what students think Ginger would advise Gail to do if the story continued.
2. Ask pairs or groups of students to discuss the following questions: When someone has a problem and asks for help, is it better to give advice or listen and ask questions? Why? Ask each pair or group to report to the class.
3. Say: Think about times you had arguments. Did you try to see the other viewpoint? Do you think it is a good idea to do this? Why?

Exercises

2 MORE WORK WITH THE ENDINGS *-ful* AND *-less*
Remind students to form the words indicated in **Part A** and then to match those words with the descriptions in **Part B.**

4 COMPOUND WORDS
During the preview, tell students to read the description on the right first and then to form a compound word that matches the description by using a word from **List A** and adding a word from **List B.** You may want students to complete Question 2 in class to make sure they understand how to do this exercise.

LESSON 9
Review of Vowel Combinations: Part 2

Primary emphasis
- Comprehension and literary understanding
- Vowel combinations *oa, oo, ou, oi, oy*
- Phonics, word analysis, and context clues
- New vocabulary
- Writing and study skills

Secondary emphasis
- Oral reading skills
- The ending *-en*
- Choosing the unrelated word

Word Chart
1. Point out the two pronunciations for *oo*.
2. Note that *oy* is usually at the end of a word or syllable, while *oi* is usually in the middle. *Joyce* is an exception.

Pre-reading Activities
1. Review with students what they have learned about Jerome, Ginger, Steven, and Holly.
   Say:
2. As you read, think about Jerome and how his pride is hurting all his friendships, not just his friendship with Ginger.
3. As you read, think about Jerome and why he is having trouble getting along with his friends.

Post-reading Activities
1. Discuss the questions in Exercise 1.
   Ask or say:
2. Why is Jerome's mood getting worse and worse?
3. What does Jerome do to fill time and try to feel better? Why do you think it isn't working?
4. Why do you think that Jerome thinks that Ginger will get in touch with him sooner or later? Could Ginger be thinking he will get in touch with her first?

5. If the e-card had been from Ginger, do you think that Jerome would have called or e-mailed her back? What do you think he would have said?
6. Does Steven know about Jerome's problem? What in the e-mail supports your answer?
7. Why does Jerome call Steven "a kind, loyal friend"?
8. How is pride involved in this story? Have you heard the expression "swallow your pride"? What do you think it means? What do you think that Jerome would do if he could swallow his pride?

Writing Activities
1. Complete the following sentences:
   - I think Jerome should . . .
   - I think Jerome should not . . .
2. Suggest another title for this story, and explain why you think it would be a good one.
3. Jerome offended Ginger and Steven. Think about what Jerome is doing or saying that is causing the trouble. What advice would you give Jerome?

Additional Activities
1. Jerome is trying to feel better by filling his time reading and cooking. Ask students what they do to cheer themselves up. Share ideas as a group.
2. Jerome calls Steven a loyal friend. What did Steven do that showed his loyalty and friendship to Jerome? What do you think is important in a friend?
3. Write about a time when a friend helped you when you were feeling sad about something.

Exercise

3 WHICH WORD DOES NOT FIT?
Have students do the first item during the preview so that they understand what to do. Ask students to explain the difference between *friend* and the other words (all relatives).

LESSON 10
The Sound for *au*

Primary emphasis
- Comprehension and literary understanding
- The sound for *au*
- Phonics, word analysis, and context clues
- New vocabulary
- Writing and study skills

Secondary emphasis
- Oral reading skills
- The ending *-en*
- Choosing the unrelated word
- Spelling scrambled words

Word Chart
The *au* sound may be difficult for students, and many of these chart words are difficult as well. If students have trouble with this chart, plan reinforcement activities for these words.

Words for Study
Review the /s/ sound in *machine*. Tell interested students that the /sh/ sound for *ch* occurs mostly in words of French origin.

Pre-reading Activities
1. Review what students already know about Jerome and Holly.
2. Ask students if they ever go to a laundromat. Ask how they feel about going to the laundromat. Tell them this is a story that takes place in a laundromat. Ask students to compare how they feel about laundromats with how Jerome feels.
   Say:
3. As you read the following story, decide if you agree more with Holly or with Jerome.

Post-reading Activities
1. Ask students to summarize the story.
2. Discuss the questions in Exercise 1.
   Ask or say:
3. What was Jerome's attitude toward doing the laundry?
4. Do you think Holly was being honest with Jerome? Why or why not?

5. Do you think Holly was interested in helping Jerome solve his problem? Explain.
6. What kind of person is Holly? What words would you use to describe her?
7. What did Jerome mean when he told Holly, "You women. You stick together like glue"?
8. Do you agree more with Holly or Jerome? Explain your answer.
9. What do you think will happen next? Do you think Jerome will call Ginger? Why or why not?

Writing Activities
1. Write one sentence about Jerome and one sentence about Holly.
2. Write about what you like to do on rainy days.
3. What household task do you dislike the most? Explain.

Additional Activities
1. Holly thought for a moment before she answered Jerome. Why is thinking for a minute before speaking often a good idea?
2. Laundromats frustrated Jerome. What kinds of things frustrate you? Why? What are some ways to deal with frustration?
3. In the laundromat, Holly writes two "Out of Order" signs. Ask students how they use their reading and writing skills in everyday places outside the classroom.

Exercises

3 WHICH WORD DOES NOT FIT?
If students had trouble with this type of exercise in Lesson 9, have them do the first item during the homework preview and explain the difference between *newspaper* (a thing) and the other words (people).

4 SPELLING CHECK
During the preview, have students do the first item so that they understand what to do. Suggest that students cross out letters as they use them to be sure the words are spelled correctly. Treat this exercise like a puzzle or game.

LESSON 11
Review of the *r*-Controlled Vowel

Primary emphasis
- Comprehension and literary understanding
- The r-controlled vowels *ar, er, ir, or, ur*
- Phonics, word analysis, and context clues
- New vocabulary
- Writing and study skills

Secondary emphasis
- Oral reading skills
- The prefix *re-*
- Synonyms
- Classifying words

Word Chart
Remind students that when *r* follows a vowel, the sound of the vowel is somewhat affected. Point out that *er, ir,* and *ur* sound alike.

Pre-reading Activities
1. After reading the title, ask students if they have ever been camping. Ask if they enjoy outdoor activities. Have them share their experiences.
   Say:
2. In this story Ginger goes camping alone. Read to find out what causes Ginger's camping trip to end suddenly.

Post-reading Activities
1. Discuss the questions in Exercise 1.
   Ask or say:
2. Why did Ginger have her phone taken out? Do you think Ginger was going to extremes since she had plenty of money? Why or why not?
3. Do you think Ginger was as concerned as Jerome about getting together again? Why or why not?
4. Is Ginger an experienced camper? What details in the story support your answer?
5. What made this story interesting or uninteresting for you?
6. If you thought you heard growling while eating lunch alone in the woods, would you react the same way that Ginger did? If not, what would you do differently?
7. Do you think the fishermen helped Ginger? What might they have done to help?

8. Do you think Ginger did the things she said she would do when she got back to the city? Why or why not?

Writing Activities
1. Write another title for this story, and explain why you think it would be a good one.
2. Write about a camping trip or some other outdoor activity that you or someone you know took part in.
3. Ask class members to imagine their favorite outdoor place. Next, ask each student to write a story or poem about that place. Help students get started by asking them questions. Share the poems and stories in class, or compile them in a book.

Additional Activities
1. Beginning after paragraph 3, where Ginger is eating her lunch, ask each student to contribute one or two sentences and create a different ending to the story.
2. Use catalogs from camping supply stores to practice filling out forms.
3. Read a short story or article about an outdoor adventure to the class. Ask students to summarize and react to what you read.
4. Help interested students find appropriate supplementary reading material on such subjects as outdoor adventure, nature, or high adventure nonfiction.

Exercises

2 WORDS THAT BEGIN WITH *re-*
During the homework review, have students read the words in the box. Most of these are new words. Encourage students to try to complete the exercise using the process of elimination. Discuss any words the students have questions about during the homework review.

4 AND 5 WHAT IS WHERE?
During the preview, explain that students should list each word in the box under the heading that tells where the item would most likely be found. Point out that there will be three words under each heading, so students can use the process of elimination if they are unsure about some of the words.

LESSON 12

Review of Vowels Followed by the Letter *l*

Primary emphasis
- Comprehension and literary understanding
- Vowels followed by *l: al, el, il, ol, ul*
- Phonics, word analysis, and context clues
- New vocabulary
- Writing and study skills

Secondary emphasis
- Oral reading skills
- The prefix *re-*
- Antonyms
- Compound words

Word Chart
1. Point out that the sound of *a* in *palm* is different from the *a* sound in the other words because the *l* in *palm* is usually silent.
2. Point out the double *l* spelling pattern for one-syllable short vowel words: *gall, mall, dill, sill, pill,* and *gull.*

Pre-reading Activities
1. Ask students if they enjoy baseball. Ask those who do to explain the game briefly. What are their favorite teams?
   Say:
2. In this story, Steven asks Holly to play a new video game with him. She becomes bored playing it and wants to do something else. Has this ever happened to you? You invited someone to do something like go to the movies and the other person doesn't like the movie you picked. What did you do?

Post-reading Activities
1. Ask students to summarize the story.
2. Discuss the questions in Exercise 1.
3. Ask for volunteers to read the story aloud as a dialogue between Holly and Steven, beginning with Holly's line: "So what's so special about this video game?"
   Ask or say:
4. Why did Holly want to change the game they were playing?
5. Why didn't Steven keep playing baseball and not play the dancing game?

6. What do you think that Holly's and Steven's choices say about them?
7. Do you think Steven will invite Holly to play his video game again? Why or why not?
8. Imagine the rest of Steven's afternoon. What do you think will happen next? Continue the story.

Writing Activities
1. Write about a sport you enjoy, and tell why you like it.
2. Suppose your family had given you a video game system. Write a thank-you note to them thanking them for the system.
3. If you could play any sport and be good at it, which sport would you choose? Why?

Additional Activities
1. Help students who are interested in sports to find stories at an appropriate reading level.
2. Read to the class a sports story, article, or excerpt from a biography or autobiography of a famous sports personality.
3. Read to the class a story, article, or excerpt from a biography or autobiography of a famous male or female dancer.
4. Bring the sports section of a newspaper to class. Help students find examples of statistics, human interest stories, sports writers' columns, and straight news articles. Talk about the differences in the types of articles.

Exercises

2 MORE WORK WITH WORDS THAT BEGIN WITH *re-*
During the homework preview, have students read the words in the box. Many of these words are new. Encourage students to use the process of elimination and make intelligent guesses when filling in the blanks in the sentences.

3 COMPOUND WORDS
Remind students that they did a similar exercise in Lesson 8.

LESSON 13
Review of the Hard and Soft *c* and *g*

Primary emphasis
- Comprehension and literary understanding
- The hard and soft *c* and *g*
- Phonics, word analysis, and context clues
- New vocabulary
- Writing and study skills

Secondary emphasis
- Oral reading skills
- The prefix *in-*
- Analogies
- Dividing words into syllables

Word Chart
1. Sounds for *c* reviewed:
   - *c* followed by *a, o,* or *u* sounds like /k/
   - *c* followed by *e, i,* or *y* sounds like /s/
2. Sounds for *g* reviewed:
   - *g* followed by *a, o,* or *u* and sometimes *e* or *i* sounds like /g/
   - *g* at the end of a word sounds like /g/
   - *g* followed by *e* or *i* often sounds like /j/

Words for Study
Point out the /sk/ sound in *scheme.* Tell students that this spelling for /sk/ is usually found in words from Greek.

Pre-reading Activities
1. After reading the story title and Words for Study, discuss the meaning of the word *scheme.* Ask students what they think Jerome's scheme might be in this story. Say:
2. Jerome really wants to see Ginger, but he is too proud to call her. In this story, he figures out a scheme to get back together again. Have students read the story to find out if his scheme is successful.

Post-reading Activities
1. Ask students to summarize this story in two or three sentences.
2. Discuss the questions in Exercise 1. Ask or say:
3. Why didn't Jerome invite Ginger to the party himself?
4. What do you think Ginger would say if she found out about the scheme?

5. Why do you think most people do not like to be the first guests to arrive at a party?
6. Did Jerome's guests seem to be enjoying themselves? What information from the story supports your answer?
7. Did Jerome blame Tony for his own unhappiness at the party? How do you know?
8. Compare how Jerome felt before and after the party. Did Jerome's scheme turn out the way he thought it would? Did it turn out the way you thought it would?

Writing Activities
1. Write about why you do or don't like parties.
2. Write a different ending to this story.
3. Describe the best or worst party you remember.
4. Write what you would need to do to prepare for giving a party.

Additional Activity
Celebrate the progress your students are making toward their goals by having a class party. Begin by discussing what kind of party to have and when and where to have it. Decide if there will be games or entertainment, what kind of food to have, and if anyone else will be invited. Help students to plan and organize the party.

Exercises

3 WHICH WORD FITS BEST?
During the homework preview, have students:
- read the first sentence saying "blank" where the blank occurs.
- explain the relationship between *salsa* and *dance.*
- read the four answer choices and decide which choice goes with *music* in the same way that *salsa* goes with *dance.*
- write *hip-hop* on the blank and read the complete sentence.

4 CONSONANTS
In this exercise, students discover that when words have a double consonant in the middle, the syllable break usually comes between the consonants, creating a closed first syllable. During the homework review, make sure students do not pronounce the double consonants twice. They should say /gŭt er/ not /gŭt ter/.

LESSON 14
The *gh* and *ght* Words

Primary emphasis
- Comprehension and literary understanding
- Words with *gh* and *ght*
- Phonics, word analysis, and context clues
- New vocabulary
- Writing and study skills

Secondary emphasis
- Oral reading skills
- Synonyms and antonyms
- Dividing words into syllables

Word Chart
1. Point out that *igh* is a common spelling for long *i* and that *eigh* is a less common spelling for long *a*.
2. Note that *gh* is pronounced /f/ in *laugh, laughter, tough, rough, enough,* and *cough*.
3. Note different pronunciations used for *ough*. (Examples: *bought, tough, cough, dough*)

Pre-reading Activities
1. Ask students to tell in their own words what happened in the story in Lesson 13.
2. After reading the title of this story, ask students to think about what might have happened to Tony and Ginger. Ask them to write down their ideas and then share them.

Post-reading Activities
1. Discuss the questions in Exercise 1.
   Ask or say:
2. When Tony first moved into the neighborhood, he got along with Mrs. Darkpill. What clue was there that trouble might lie ahead? What other clues suggest that Mrs. Darkpill was difficult to get along with?
3. What do you think it would be like to grow up in the Darkpill home? How do the Darkpill children behave? What clues in the story support your answer?

4. Find the place in the story where Tony recognizes he is going to have trouble with Mrs. Darkpill.
5. Tony's deed to the property proved he owned the tree. If you were Tony, what would you do to stop Mrs. Darkpill from sawing branches off your tree?
6. What do you think happened that led Tony and Ginger to end up at police headquarters?
7. How does the title create interest in reading the story?
8. What unanswered question is raised at the end of this story? What additional questions do you want answered?

Writing Activities
1. Write one sentence about Tony and one sentence about Mrs. Darkpill.
2. Write some advice for Tony about dealing with Mrs. Darkpill.
3. Write about a person you consider difficult to get along with.

Additional Activities
1. Ask: When Mrs. Darkpill started to saw branches off Tony's tree, what did he do to persuade her to stop? Did it work? Do you think talking to someone who offends you is a good first step in getting a problem solved? What suggestions do you have for a second step?
2. Discuss what Mrs. Darkpill did to Tony. Ask someone to explain the position of the police. Do police have to uphold the law even if they disagree with what the law says at times? Why or why not?

Exercise

4 MORE WORK WITH DOUBLE CONSONANTS
This exercise reviews the decoding strategy introduced in Lesson 13 for words with double consonants.

Review of *r*-Controlled Vowel Combinations

Primary emphasis
- Comprehension and literary understanding
- Combinations *air, ear, eer, oar, oor, our*
- Phonics, word analysis, and context clues
- New vocabulary
- Writing and study skills

Secondary emphasis
- Oral reading skills
- Syllables
- Identifying terms

Word Chart
As with single vowels, when *r* follows a vowel combination, the vowel sound is somewhat affected. Have students pronounce the vowel combinations before reading the words.

Pre-reading Activities
1. Before reading this story, ask students what they already know about Tony and Ginger. Ask what plans they had for the evening.
2. Tony and Ginger did not leave for the party immediately after Ginger stopped to pick up Tony. If they had left right away, the evening might have turned out very differently. Ask students to read the story to find out what the delay cost Tony and Ginger.

Post-reading Activities
1. Discuss the questions in Exercise 1.
   Ask or say:
2. Why do you think Tony had not told Ginger where they were going? Do you think Ginger would have agreed to go to Jerome's party if she knew that's where Tony planned to take her?
3. Do you agree with Tony that Mrs. Darkpill was looking for a fight? Why or why not?
4. What do you think would have happened if Ginger had not gotten involved in the argument?
5. What was Tony's attitude toward Mrs. Darkpill? What was Ginger's attitude toward Mrs. Darkpill? What was Mrs. Darkpill's attitude toward them?
6. Did Mrs. Darkpill have a right to be angry about where Ginger had parked? How could she have

persuaded Ginger to move her car without offending Ginger and Tony?
7. Did Tony's neighbors do the right thing in calling the police? Why or why not?
8. Is trying to get along well with neighbors a good policy? Explain.
9. What do you think will happen next? What do you think Jerome will say when he hears what happened to Tony and Ginger?

Writing Activities
1. Write one sentence each about Ginger, Tony, and Mrs. Darkpill.
2. List some of the ways Mrs. Darkpill offended other people.
3. Write about a good or bad experience you had with a neighbor.

Additional Activities
1. What were some of the mistakes made by people in the story? List them, and then rank them by importance.
2. Ask students to think about experiences in their lives where people have lost their tempers and were out of control. What are some ways of dealing with such people? What are some things not to do or say? What helps? Discuss in pairs, and have each pair report to the group.

Exercises

2 THE *ea* AND *ee* WORDS
Have students read all the words in the left column during the homework preview. Make sure they are reading them correctly.

3 SYLLABLES
During the preview, explain that a syllable is a unit of sound and that each syllable has one vowel sound. Go over the first example and point out that *board* is spelled with two vowels but that there is only one vowel sound. Some students have difficulty hearing syllables in words. Have students read the words orally, pausing briefly between syllables.

LESSON 16
Common Word Beginnings: Part 1

Primary emphasis
- Comprehension and literary understanding
- Common prefixes *de-, ex-, mis-, com-, con-*
- Phonics, word analysis, and context clues
- New vocabulary
- Writing and study skills

Secondary emphasis
- Oral reading skills
- Defining words containing *ow*
- Combining syllables to form words
- Reviewing factual information

Word Chart
Interested students might like to look up the meanings of these prefixes in a dictionary. The concept that a word part can have a meaning of its own may be new to students.

Pre-reading Activities
1. Ask students if they like to try new foods. Do they like to try out new recipes? Ask them to share experiences with trying new foods.
2. Tell students that in this story, Steven and Holly discuss Jerome. Read the story to find out what each one thinks about Jerome.

Post-reading Activities
1. Discuss the questions in Exercise 1.
2. This story is a dialogue between two people. Have volunteers read the two parts aloud.
   Ask or say:
3. This story has two different parts in which two different subjects are discussed. What are they? Find the place where the subject changes.
4. Does Holly agree with Steven's opinion of the prune whip? How do you know?
5. What kind of cookbook is Holly writing? (See Lesson 9.)
6. In the story, Holly asks if Jerome still thinks the world's giving him a raw deal. What does she mean by a "raw deal"?
7. Does Steven think Ginger had a good excuse for not coming to the party? Does Steven think Jerome should call Ginger? Why do you think so?
8. What do you think Steven meant when he said that Jerome was a very complex person? Do you agree?
9. Discuss the relationship between Steven and Holly. What words would you use to describe their relationship?

Writing Activities
1. Write about a good or bad experience you had when trying a new food. Your story could begin, "The first time I tried . . ."
2. Write a story about trying to cook or otherwise make something that did not turn out right.
3. Think of something you know how to cook or make. List the ingredients or materials needed, and write the steps in the process.

Additional Activities
1. Make a list of common cooking abbreviations and terms. Some cookbooks provide such a list. Help students with any terms or abbreviations they need to have explained. Read several recipes together, and clarify the terms used.
2. Ask students to bring to class copies of their favorite recipes. The recipes could be exchanged or compiled into a class cookbook. Volunteers might gather the ingredients and prepare one of the recipes.

Exercises

3 MORE WORK WITH SYLLABLES
After students have read the directions and studied the example during the preview, have them do one item in class. Tell students to read the sentences and pick one they know the answer to. Explain that the process of elimination is important in this exercise. Remind them to cross out the syllables in the box as they use them.

4 BRAIN BENDERS
During the preview, emphasize that students should make a good guess even if they don't know the answer. Tell students that newspapers and magazines often have self-quizzes similar to this.

LESSON 17
Common Word Beginnings: Part 2

Primary emphasis
- Comprehension and literary understanding
- Common prefixes *de-*, *ex-*, *com-*, *con-*, *un-*
- Phonics, word analysis, and context clues
- New vocabulary
- Writing and study skills

Secondary emphasis
- Oral reading skills
- Compound words with *ow*
- Choosing the unrelated word
- Syllables

Word Chart
Students probably know the meaning of *un-*. If they don't, have them figure it out by reading the base words without *un-*.

Pre-reading Activities
Ask or say:
1. What do you like to do in your free time or on your days off?
2. Do you know someone who got a day off by calling in sick when he or she wasn't sick?
3. As you read this story, find out why Tony gets more than he bargained for at a clothing sale.

Post-reading Activities
1. Discuss the questions in Exercise 1.
   Ask or say:
2. Had Tony planned to call in sick the morning of the story? How do you know?
3. Based on his manner on the telephone, what kind of boss do you think Mr. Dennis was?
4. Where did Tony expect Mr. Dennis to be? Where did Mr. Dennis expect Tony to be?
5. What did Mr. Dennis mean when he told Tony he had "all the time in the world"?
6. Do you think Tony regretted telling his boss he was sick so that he could have the day off? How did he feel when he hung up the phone? When do you think he regretted it?

7. In your opinion, did Tony deserve to get fired? Why or why not?
8. Did this story turn out the way you thought it would? Did it turn out the way Tony thought it would? Explain.
9. If you were Tony, what would you do next?

Writing Activities
1. Write one sentence about Tony and one about Mr. Dennis.
2. Imagine the perfect day off. If you could do anything you wanted, what would it be? Write about it.

Additional Activities
1. Discuss what Tony might have done differently. What might Mr. Dennis have done differently?
2. Tony found the clothing sale by reading an advertisement in the newspaper. Bring some newspaper ads to class, and discuss them. What store is advertising? Where is it located? When is the store open? What is being advertised?
3. Discuss good phone manners. Tony's boss answered the phone in an extremely unfriendly manner. Do you think this was his usual way to answer the phone? Why or why not? Name businesses that depend on having a good relationship with telephone customers. List some suggestions for good telephone manners.
4. Copy key action sentences from this story, and cut them apart. Rearrange the sequence. Have students put the sentences in the correct sequence.

Exercises

3 WHICH WORD DOES NOT FIT?
During the homework review, discuss the relationships among the words in any group that caused students trouble.

4 MORE WORK WITH SYLLABLES
During the preview, point out that the number of blanks for each word indicates the number of syllables in the word. If necessary, have students do Question 4 in class.

Common Word Beginnings: Part 3

Primary emphasis
- Comprehension and literary understanding
- Common prefixes *ex-, dis-, un-, im-, in-*
- Phonics, word analysis, and context clues
- New vocabulary
- Writing and study skills

Secondary emphasis
- Oral reading skills
- Classifying words
- Spelling scrambled words

Word Chart
Interested students might look in a dictionary to see how many words start with these prefixes.

Words for Study
Point out that *you'd* is the contraction for both *you had* and *you would*.

Pre-reading Activities
1. Review what students have learned about why Ginger didn't come to Jerome's party. Then tell students that when this story takes place, Jerome and Ginger still haven't spoken.
   Ask or say:
2. Who do you think has a talk with Jerome? What do you think the talk will be about?
3. As you read the story, decide if you think Jerome gets some good advice.

Post-reading Activities
1. Discuss the questions in Exercise 1.
2. Ask for volunteers to read the story as a dialogue. You might also make an audiotape of the reading after students have had an opportunity to rehearse their lines.
   Ask or say:
3. What was Steven trying to persuade Jerome to do?
4. Did Ginger ever find out where Tony intended to take her the evening they spent at the police station?
5. Why do you think Steven felt like he was talking to a child?
6. Find the place in the story where Steven feels like giving up on Jerome. Why do you think he continues to try to help Jerome?

7. Did Steven's talk with Jerome do any good? Why do you think Jerome finally decided to call Ginger?
8. What do you think will happen when Jerome calls Ginger?

Writing Activities
1. What might Jerome say to Ginger when he calls her? How might she respond? Write the first few lines of their conversation.
2. Do you agree with Steven that you have to do something to get what you want out of life? Write about something you want in life and what it will take to get it.

Additional Activities
1. In this story, Steven gives Jerome his opinion. Sometimes it is hard to know when to get involved and when not to get involved in someone else's business. Discuss what is helpful to people when they have a problem and what is not helpful.
2. Steven told Jerome that he should forget about what other people should do. He told Jerome to think about what he should be doing for himself. Do you consider this good advice? How does this relate to what Holly said about Jerome in Lesson 16?
3. Does someone you know have trouble admitting mistakes? Why do you think it is so difficult? What do you think about people who do admit their mistakes? Do you admire them? Why or why not?

Exercises

2 SHORT STORIES
Review the words in the left column during the homework preview. Point out that there are three paragraphs on separate topics, each with five missing words. Students should read a whole paragraph before filling in the blanks. Remind them to reread the paragraphs with the words filled in to be sure they make sense.

3 SPELLING CHECK
Remind students to cross out the letters in each group as they are used.

LESSON 19
Up-, Down-, Out-, Over-, and Under-

Primary emphasis
- Comprehension and literary understanding
- Words with *up-, down-, out-, over-, under-*
- Phonics, word analysis, and context clues
- New vocabulary
- Writing and study skills

Secondary emphasis
- Oral reading skills
- Reviewing calendar information
- Classifying terms
- Identifying terms

Word Chart
Be sure students recognize the individual words that make up these compound words. Remind students that when compound words are formed, the pronunciation and the spelling of the individual words stay the same.

Pre-reading Activities
1. After they have read the story title and Words for Study, ask students to predict what this story will be about.
Ask:
2. Do you think Jerome and Ginger will finally make up, or do you think they'll have another fight?

Post-reading Activities
1. Discuss the questions in Exercise 1.
2. Ask a student to summarize the first four paragraphs, and then ask for volunteers to read the rest of the story as a dialogue. You might record the dialogue after students have had a chance to rehearse their lines.
Ask or say:
3. How did you feel after reading the first sentence in the story? Were you disappointed that Jerome had decided not to call Ginger? Jerome decided to go to see her in person. Do you think this was a good idea? Why or why not?
4. When Jerome saw Ginger at the nightclub, do you think he was sorry he waited so long to see her? Why or why not?
5. When Ginger walked over to Jerome's table, what do you think she wanted Jerome to say?

6. Why do you think Jerome lied to Ginger about why he had come to see her? What does "beat around the bush" mean? Why did Ginger accuse Jerome of beating around the bush? Why did Ginger insist that Jerome be honest with her?
7. Did Ginger forgive Jerome? Find information in the story to support your answer.
8. Do you think Ginger and Jerome will get along with each other in the future? Why or why not?
9. Did the story turn out the way you thought it would? Were there any surprises in the story? What were they?

Writing Activities
1. Write two sentences about Ginger and two sentences about Jerome.
2. Find a picture of a music-related activity in a magazine or newspaper. Ask students to write one or two statements about the picture.
3. If any students are interested in music, ask them to write about their interest.

Additional Activities
1. Ginger was a singer in a band that played in clubs around the city. Ask students to describe the kind of band they imagine Ginger sang with. What instruments would probably be in the band? What type of music would they play? Why do you think so?
2. When Jerome decided to act, he no longer felt downhearted. Think about a time in your life when you had a difficult decision to make. How did you feel before you made the decision? How did you feel afterward?

Exercise

3 THE FOUR SEASONS
Students will have to use the process of elimination to do this exercise. Tell them to fill in the items they are sure of first and then to make intelligent guesses for the rest of the items. Students who live in a warm climate may well question which season *flowers blooming* and *beach* belong to. Treat this exercise as a game to avoid confusion or frustration.

More Work with Compound Words

Primary emphasis
- Comprehension and literary understanding
- Compound words
- Phonics, word analysis, and context clues
- New vocabulary
- Writing and study skills

Secondary emphasis
- Oral reading skills
- Identifying terms
- Synonyms and antonyms

Word Chart
Most of these compound words are fairly long. Remind students that each word is made up of two shorter words. If they have trouble decoding any of the compound words, they should identify the two shorter words and read them first.

Pre-reading Activities
Say:
1. This is the last story in the book. Before reading it, write down a few of your own ideas about how you would like the book to end.
2. After reading the title of the story, ask students what they think this story will be about. Does knowing that it is the last story in the book influence their thinking? Do they expect a happy ending? What unanswered questions do they have about the group of friends in this book?

Post-reading Activities
1. Discuss the questions in Exercise 1.
   Ask or say:
2. Compare your ideas about how you wanted the book to end with the story the author wrote. Were you surprised? Pleased? Disappointed? Satisfied?
3. How did Holly thank Steven for testing her recipes?
4. What was Jerome concerned about when he called Holly? In what ways was Jerome helpful when he called?
5. Does Jerome expect some trouble in his future? What else does he expect? Support your answer with information from the story.

6. Why did Holly make prune whip? What did Steven mean when he said, "Now I know why they call a joke a gag"?
7. Did Ginger show a strong interest in yoga? What information from the story supports your answer?
8. Recall Jerome's attitude at the beginning of the book. In what ways did he change?
9. Think about Steven's life at the beginning of the book. Is he better off now for having taken his sister's advice? Explain.

Writing Activities
1. Write a one- or two-sentence description of each of the following characters: Steven, Jerome, Ginger, and Holly.
2. In the last paragraph of the story, Jerome says, "One minute you're down, and the next minute you're up. You just never know what's going to happen next!" Do you agree? Explain.
3. Have you experienced situations or feelings similar to those of the characters in this book? Write about them.
4. Write down some of the ways you are using reading in your life. Review and update your reading goals.

Additional Activities
1. Plan a class party to celebrate the progress students have made in *Challenger 3*. Help students to organize, plan, and divide up the tasks.
2. For each student, compare a writing sample done at the beginning of the book with one done near the end of the book to show the progress made.

Exercises
2 MORE WORK WITH COMPOUND WORDS
Some of the word choices are new compound words. Remind students to identify the two shorter words in any compound they have trouble decoding.

5 FEELINGS
After students have read the directions, have them do the first item in class so they understand what to do. Make sure they understand that their answers should be appropriate responses to the situations described and that their sentences should explain their choices.

Review: Lessons 1–20

The purpose of this review is to give students one more opportunity to work with many of the words and concepts emphasized in *Challenger 3*. Preview each exercise, and if necessary, have students complete an item during the review.

The following exercises include new material for students and may require a bit of extra time during the preview.

1 WORD STUDY

No new words are introduced in this exercise, but the format is new. Tell students to select the answer choice that best defines the italicized word and to write the letter for their choice on the line provided.

6 SPELLING CHECK

During the preview, make sure students understand that they are to use the first letter of each answer word to spell the name of the dessert at the bottom of the page.

After going over the review, discuss what students have learned and accomplished while working in *Challenger 3*.

Book 4 Introduction

The format of *Challenger 4* corresponds to that of *Challenger 2*. The 20 lessons in Book 4 reinforce vocabulary, reasoning skills, and phonics principles introduced in earlier books and continue to develop reading comprehension skills.

Book 4 contains brief nonfiction selections on a wide variety of subjects. Written comprehension questions follow each reading selection. After every five lessons there is a review that provides additional opportunities to review words and reinforce concepts. Each review is followed by a word index listing the words introduced in lessons up to that point.

Book 4 is generally used by students who have completed *Challenger 3*. Book 4 is also an appropriate starting place for students who test at level 4 on the online *Challenger Placement Tool* and those who read at levels 4.0–5.0 as determined by standardized reading tests.

Scheduling Considerations

One-hour sessions are appropriate for students in Book 4. This allows time for students to do some oral reading, discuss the reading selection, go over the homework exercises, work on writing and/or reinforcement activities, and preview the next lesson.

Book 4 works well with students either working together in a classroom setting or working independently in a tutorial setting. Students working in Book 4 usually do not need intensive skill development and are often able to assist each other, requiring less supervision from you. A more detailed description of these instructional settings can be found in the Introduction to *Challenger 2* on pages 70–72 of this manual.

Suggestions for Teaching the Lessons

It is important for you to read the material in the first five chapters of this manual if you have not already done so. These chapters discuss the concepts and procedures upon which *Challenger* is based and give general suggestions for using the series. The following are specific suggestions for Book 4.

WORDS FOR STUDY

This section, which precedes the story in each lesson, lists words that appear in the reading. The words appear in the same form in which they initially appear in the lesson, often providing practice in reading word endings.

THE READING SELECTIONS

Tell students that the readings in Book 4 are articles containing information about a variety of subjects. Review the terms *fiction* and *nonfiction*. Students whose long-range goal is to pass the high school equivalency exam are particularly motivated when they learn that brief readings in science and social studies are included in those tests. The following ideas may be helpful in your planning.

*   With the exception of the first lesson, the initial readings should be done for homework, following pre-reading activities during the homework preview. Pre-reading suggestions are given in the individual lesson notes.
*   Oral reading of the selections should be done as often as possible during the homework review, before discussing the selection. Inferential- and applied-level comprehension questions, suggested in the lesson notes, stimulate discussion and help students to develop their reasoning skills.

THE EXERCISES

Preview the exercises during the class session, and have students complete them for homework. Make sure students know how to do each exercise. The wide variety of exercises helps students to develop recall and reasoning abilities. Keep the following points in mind.

*   Encourage students to refer to the reading selection when answering comprehension questions in Exercise 1. Remind them that a long line under a question signals that the answer should be a complete sentence.
*   Remind students to answer all questions. If they aren't sure of an answer, they should use such strategies as intelligent guessing, the process of elimination, and context clues. Remind them also that they can learn

from their mistakes. If students have a problem with an exercise, help them to recognize what went wrong. Point out also what they did well.

- Students should correct all exercises during the homework review. Any grading that is required should be done on corrected work. Consider an average of 80 percent or better an excellent score.

Writing Activities

Student writing is discussed in Chapter 3 of this manual. Use those suggestions to help plan appropriate writing activities. Book 4 students should have extended writing opportunities at least weekly. For formal writing projects, students can work together in pairs or small groups to generate ideas, plan the organization and development of the theme, give feedback to each other's drafts, and help each other to polish and edit pieces of writing.

Allow students to pick their own topics for writing activities. Topics related to the lessons are suggested in the lesson notes. Personal interests, hobbies, and current issues and events can also provide appropriate topics for writing assignments. Writing Book 4 also provides writing activities to extend the lesson content and to help students develop and practice their writing skills.

The Lesson Segments

After the first session, the procedure for each session should be as consistent as possible. You may want to vary the order of the following segments to suit your particular situation.

1. **Homework Review.** Have students read aloud at least some of the reading selection studied for homework. Have them summarize the selection, and go over their answers to the questions in Exercise 1. Discuss the selection, using some of the inferential- and applied-level questions suggested in the lesson notes. Then go over the rest of the exercises, and have students make any necessary corrections.

2. **Writing Activity.** Students may work in groups or singly on the current writing activity, depending on what it is.

3. **Reinforcement Activity.** When time permits, focus on an area of difficulty in a way that is fun for the students. See Chapter 4 of this manual for suggestions.

4. **Homework Preview.** Preview the next lesson, which students will complete for homework. Have students read the Words for Study and the title of the selection and predict what they think the selection will be about. Do one or more pre-reading activities. Have students read the directions for the exercises to be sure they know what is required for each of them.

Individual Lesson Notes

The individual lesson notes that begin on page 118 contain specific suggestions and procedures for Book 4 lessons.

LESSON 1
The Heart

Primary emphasis
- Literal/inferential/applied comprehension
- Phonics, word analysis, and context clues
- New vocabulary
- Writing and study skills
- Common expressions

Secondary emphasis
- Oral reading and listening skills
- Spelling (adding *-er*)
- Syllabication
- Identifying vowel sounds

Words for Study
These words appear in this lesson for the first time in the *Challenger* series. Have students read the words that they recognize. Pronounce any word that students don't recognize, and have them repeat the word several times while looking at it.

Pre-reading Activities
1. The reading passages in Book 4 are nonfiction. Discuss *fiction* and *nonfiction*.
   Say:
2. Where is your heart located? What is the size of a heart? What does the heart do? This article will help answer these questions.
3. For this first lesson, have students read the article aloud in class. Assign a second reading for homework.

Post-reading Activities
1. Discuss the questions in Exercise 1.
   Ask or say:
2. Does a heart weigh more than a pound?
3. How and where does blood get oxygen? Is oxygen necessary for our bodies?
4. What do veins and arteries do? How are they similar? How are they different?
5. Is the heart in a protected location in the body? How do you know?

Writing Activities
1. Write something you learned about hearts from this lesson.
2. Write about one thing you do that is good for your heart and one thing you do that is not good for your heart.

Additional Activities
1. Bring to class additional diagrams and pictures showing the circulatory system. Help students trace the route blood takes through the heart, to the lungs, back to the heart, and out to the rest of the body. Explain why the blood flows to the lungs.
2. Ask students to share information they have heard about how to keep hearts healthy. What types of food and exercise are good for the heart? What types are not good?
3. Ask if anyone has ever donated blood. Discuss how and why it is done.

Exercises

1 ABOUT THE READING
Tell students to write *true* or *false* on each line based on facts from the reading.

2 THE HUMAN BODY
During the homework preview, review the process of elimination. Tell students to do the items they know first, skipping the ones they aren't sure of. Then they can go back and do the skipped ones when fewer choices remain.

3 THE ENDING *-er*
During the preview, study the examples and ask, "Have any letters been added, dropped, or changed in the examples when *-er* was added?" Then review the three rules for adding endings that start with a vowel.
- For column 1 words, add *-er* to the base word.
- For column 2 words, drop the silent *e* before adding *-er.*
- For column 3 words, double the final consonant before adding *-er.*

4 SYLLABLES
During the preview, remind students that each syllable will have one vowel sound, although there may be more than one vowel letter in the syllable.

LESSON 2
Danica Patrick

Primary emphasis

- Literal/inferential/applied comprehension
- Phonics, word analysis, and context clues
- Writing and study skills
- Choosing the unrelated word
- Synonyms and antonyms

Secondary emphasis

- Oral reading and listening skills
- New vocabulary
- Spelling (adding -*er*)
- Syllabication
- Identifying vowel sounds

Words for Study

Encourage students to figure out the meanings of unfamiliar words from the context of the lesson. Plan reinforcement activities for any words that cause difficulty.

Pre-reading Activities

Ask or say:

1. Do you have a hero? If so, who is it, and why is this person special to you?
2. Do you like learning about the lives of famous people? Do you like sports? Do you know anything about auto racing? List the things that students mention.

Post-reading Activities

1. Discuss the questions in Exercise 1.
2. Ask students to summarize the article.
   Ask or say:
3. What does "caught the eye of " in paragraph 3 mean?
4. Explain in your own words why 2005 was a big racing season for Patrick.
5. Why was 2008 an important year for Patrick?
6. Do you think that the governor of Illinois should have named a day in her honor? Why or why not?
7. Do you think that people pay too much attention to athletes? Why or why not?

Writing Activities

1. Write about why you think that people need heroes.
2. For practice in requesting information, write an e-mail to NASCAR, the National Association for Stock Car Auto Racing, asking for information, for example, its history (who founded it, when, where, and why), famous races, and record holders. Include your name and address in case the information needs to be mailed.
3. Write a list of questions that you would like to ask Danica Patrick. They could be about her career or about stock car racing.

Additional Activities

1. Locate on a map or atlas places Danica Patrick lived.
2. Read to the class an article or an excerpt from a book about another well-known sports figure, or have students read one together.
3. Help interested students to find other stories about heroes to read for pleasure. In *American Lives,* New Readers Press offers stories of sports heroes and other famous and not-so-famous Americans who helped shape U.S. history.

Exercises

2 GAMES AND SPORTS

During the preview, encourage students to ask friends or fellow class members for help if they don't know about some of these games or sports.

4 WORDS THAT MEAN THE SAME AND 5 WORD OPPOSITES

During the homework preview, suggest that students use a dictionary to check on any words here they don't know. Make sure that students know how to use a dictionary efficiently.

6 SYLLABLES

Point out the following general principles on where syllable breaks occur:

- between double letters in the middle of words (item 5)
- between consonants (items 8 and 9)
- between the smaller words in compound words (item 10)
- between prefixes and roots and between roots and suffixes (items 3, 7)

LESSON 3
Energy Crisis

Primary emphasis
- Literal/inferential/applied comprehension
- Phonics, word analysis, and context clues
- New vocabulary
- Writing and study skills
- Reviewing factual information

Secondary emphasis
- Oral reading and listening skills
- Spelling (adding -*y*)
- Syllabication
- Identifying vowel sounds

Words for Study
Continue encouraging students to figure out the meanings of unfamiliar words from the context of the lesson.

Pre-reading Activities
1. As a way to tap students' background knowledge, ask if they remember the rise in gas prices in 2008. What do they remember about it? Did they notice the rise in the prices of food and other goods because of the rise in gas prices? Ask why the prices of other things rise when the price of gas rises.
2. Say that many people think that the United States is headed for an energy crisis. Tell students to read the article to find out what an energy crisis is and what we can do to stop it from happening.

Post-reading Activities
1. Discuss the questions in Exercise 1.
   Ask or say:
2. A cause is something that makes something else—an effect—happen. If the cause is a greater demand for energy than there is energy, what will the effect be?
3. What was the cause of the rise in gas prices in the summer of 2008?
4. How will turning down the heat at night help keep an energy crisis from happening?

5. The word *hybrid* means something made of unlike parts. Why is this a good name for the energy-saving cars described in the article?
6. Do you think that everyone has a duty to help keep the nation from having an energy crisis?
7. If we had an energy crisis, what do you think life would be like?

Writing Activities
1. Write a slogan, or saying, to help you remember to save energy, such as "Walk more. Drive less."
2. If you were going to buy a car, what questions would you ask about it? List your questions.

Additional Activities
1. Have students work out a dialogue that they could have at home to convince their family members or roommates to turn down the heat, turn off unused lights, recycle, or take part in a similar energy-saving strategy. Students should first decide on the energy-saving strategies they want to present at home.
2. One way to save energy is to drive less and take public transportation. Give a copy of a bus or train schedule to each student. Help them to read the schedule. Ask question such as, "What bus would you need to take to get downtown by 1 P.M.? What bus goes to (blank) and (blank)?"

Exercise

3 THE ENDING -*y*
Review the rules for adding endings that start with a vowel, and have students state the rule that applies to each column of words.
- For column 1, add -*y* to the base word.
- For column 2, drop the silent -*e* before adding -*y*.
- For column 3, double the final consonant before adding -*y*.

If students don't know or remember the rules, ask, "Have any letters been added, dropped, or changed in the examples when -*y* was added?"

LESSON 4
Insects

Primary emphasis

- Literal/inferential/applied comprehension
- Phonics, word analysis, and context clues
- Writing and study skills
- Reviewing factual information
- Analogies

Secondary emphasis

- Oral reading and listening skills
- New vocabulary
- Spelling (adding -*y*)
- Syllabication

Pre-reading Activities

1. Tell students there is information in the reading that explains how to define an insect. Ask them to locate it as they read.
2. Have the class list ways we benefit from insect life. Then list problems caused by insects. Add new information to both lists after reading the article. Say:
3. Read the following article to find out what important jobs insects perform on Earth. Think about what problems would result if insects disappeared from Earth.

Post-reading Activities

1. Discuss the questions in Exercise 1.
   Ask or say:
2. Name some creatures that depend on insects as a source of food.
3. Do you think that in the future people will learn new information about insects, or is the study of insects finished? Explain.
4. What are some things that all insects have in common? Why isn't a spider an insect?
5. Name some places on earth that are likely to have large insect populations.
6. What are some sheltered places where insects might live during the winter?
7. Why would it be useful for people who study forest management to study insects?
8. Do you think the author was trying to persuade readers to like insects? Explain.
9. If there were no insects, what would some of the resulting problems be?

Writing Activities

1. Write about an experience you have had that involved an insect or insects.
2. Write what you like and what you don't like about insects.
3. After reading the article in this lesson, did your opinion about insects change in any way? Explain.

Additional Activities

1. With students, contrast cold- and warm-blooded animals, and give examples of each.
2. Ask students if they have seen caterpillars. Then ask, "Do insects look the same in all stages of their lives?" Show pictures of the stages in an insect's life: egg, nymph or larva, pupa, adult.
3. Read information to students about the journey of the monarch butterfly. Using a book with color photos, share with students the beauty of butterflies and moths. Ask students if they recognize any of the butterflies or moths.
4. What are insecticides? What are some of the problems caused by overuse or improper use of insecticides? Are there other ways to control insect populations?

Exercises

2 NAME THAT BUG

Before beginning the exercise, have students read the list of words in the box to become more familiar with them.

3 WHICH WORD FITS BEST?

During the homework preview, have students:

- read the first sentence saying "blank" where the blank occurs.
- explain the relationship between *termite* and *wood*. (Termites feed on wood.)
- read the four answer choices and decide which choice goes with *blood* in the same way that *termite* goes with *wood*.
- write *tick* in the blank and read the complete sentence.

Have students complete item 2 if they seem confused.

L E S S O N   5
Cell Phones

Primary emphasis
- Literal/inferential/applied comprehension
- Phonics, word analysis, and context clues
- Writing and study skills
- Sequencing events
- Categorizing

Secondary emphasis
- Oral reading and listening skills
- New vocabulary
- Syllabication

Words for Study
Point out the prefix *trans-* in the word *transmitters,* and say that it means "over, through, across, on the other side of, to the other side." Ask for other words that students know that begin with *trans-*. Look them up in a dictionary as a class activity to see if students can figure out how the prefix fits with each definition. (Examples: *transparent:* see through; *transport:* to carry across, over, or through)

Pre-reading Activities
Ask or say:
1. Have you ever thought about how cell phones work? This article gives some information about how cell phones send and receive phone calls.
2. Have you ever thought about how different cell phones are from the old tabletop or wall phones that some people grew up with? All you could do with those phones was make or receive phone calls. Do you have a wired phone in your home? Or do you only have a cell phone? As you read this article, think about all the things that you can do with your cell phone besides talk to someone.

Post-reading Activities
1. Discuss the questions in Exercise 1.
2. Ask students to summarize the article.
   Ask or say:
3. Think of another title for this article. Why do you think it is a good title?
4. Choose one of the ways that people use cell phones. Explain how to do it step by step.
5. When you use a cell phone, people can reach you wherever you are, day or night. Do you think this is a good thing? Why or why not?

Writing Activities
1. Write a list of at least five things to do or not to do when you are talking on a phone—cell phone or landline. (Example: don't eat while on the phone.)
2. What is the farthest place that you have called using a cell phone? Tell to whom you talked.

Additional Activity
Bring in several brochures advertising cell phone plans from different cell phone carriers. Go over the different plans with students. Ask them to compare the plans in terms of length of contract, number of minutes per month or unlimited calling, if unused minutes can be saved from month to month, if the phone works in other countries, the cost for text messaging, and similar plan features. Have students construct tables to help them organize their data.

Exercise

4 WORKING WITH HEADINGS
During the preview, have students explain why "Spending Time with Friends" is the correct heading for the example. Point out to students that this skill (categorizing) can help them to construct tables to organize data, as they did in "Additional Activity."

Review: Lessons 1–5

Explain that reviews appear after every five lessons. Tell students that they may refer to previous lessons or a dictionary to review factual information.

In addition to the review, you might also have students do a research-and-report activity in which they select one topic from lessons 1–5 and find out more about it. Students can work alone, in pairs, or in groups and give oral and/or written reports.

Explain that the word index after this review lists words introduced in Lessons 1–5.

LESSON 6
The Sun

Primary emphasis
- Literal/inferential/applied comprehension
- Phonics, word analysis, and context clues
- Writing and study skills
- Classifying
- Definitions

Secondary emphasis
- Oral reading and listening skills
- New vocabulary
- Spelling (adding -ing)
- Distinguishing between similar words

Pre-reading Activities
1. Bring in books with illustrations and pictures of the sun, stars, and moon to build interest and help students understand the lesson.
   Ask:
2. What do you know about the sun? Is the sun a star? What is the difference between a star and a planet? Why does life on Earth depend on the sun? How long do you think life would last without the sun?

Post-reading Activities
1. Discuss the questions in Exercise 1.
   Ask or say:
2. Explain in your own words the connection between the sun and the Earth's food chain.
3. Have people understood the importance of the sun for a long time?
4. Why do you think ancient people worshipped the sun? What does it mean to call someone a "sun worshipper" today?
5. Is there more than one sun? Explain.
6. Find a place in the article where the author uses an example to help readers understand information. As a class, draw it. (Examples: the skyscraper, the man, the dog)
7. Does the Earth receive most of the sun's light and heat? Explain.
8. How have scientists learned about the possibilities for the future of the sun?

Writing Activities
1. What are some ways the sun is a friend of the Earth? What are some problems related to the sun?
2. Do you think there is life on planets in other solar systems? Why or why not?
3. What does "powered by solar energy" mean? Write about something you have heard about or seen that is powered by solar energy.

Additional Activities
1. From what direction does the sun rise in the morning? In what direction does it set in the evening? Can north and south be determined from seeing a sunrise? Give other examples of how this information can be useful.
2. Use a globe and a light to demonstrate night, day, moonlight, and eclipses. Follow up with questions: Where does moonlight come from? When it is day where you live, where is it night? What is an eclipse?
3. Students may want to learn more about the solar system and the universe. Help them to find materials at an appropriate reading level.

Exercises

2 WORKING WITH HEADINGS
During the homework preview, make sure students understand that solids, liquids, and gases are the three states of matter. Ask students to give examples of each. Remind students to use the process of elimination to do this exercise.

3 COMPOUND WORDS
During the homework preview, remind students that compound words are made up of two or more smaller words. During the review, have students say the two words that make up each compound word.

4 THE ENDING -ing
Have students state the spelling rules for adding endings that start with a vowel.

5 SOME CONFUSING -ing WORDS
During the preview, have students read the pairs of -ing words. Remind them that doubling the final consonant keeps the preceding vowel short.

LESSON 7
Thomas Edison

Primary emphasis

- Literal/inferential/applied comprehension
- Phonics, word analysis, and context clues
- New vocabulary
- Writing and study skills
- Analogies

Secondary emphasis

- Oral reading and listening skills
- Forming and defining compound words
- Syllabication

Words for Study

Point out the *-or* endings of the words *inspector, conductor,* and *inventor,* and ask students what they think *-or* means in these words. (It means *someone who does something*)

Pre-reading Activities

Ask or say:

1. What do you know about Thomas Edison? When do you think he lived? Why do you think he is famous?
2. As you read the following article, find some things about Edison's early life that show he was an intelligent child. Find one person who understood that he had great promise.

Post-reading Activities

1. Discuss the questions in Exercise 1.
   Ask or say:
2. Do you think Edison was an unusual child? Why or why not?
3. What do you think was more important to Edison, being careful or satisfying his curiosity?
4. Why do you think the teacher thought Edison was crazy? Are people who are different, for whatever reason, often considered crazy? Why or why not?
5. Mrs. Edison thought learning could be fun. This was unusual for her time. Do you agree or disagree with her belief? Explain.
6. How would your life be different if Edison hadn't invented the lightbulb?

7. How have items invented by Edison changed over the years (in particular, lightbulbs, movies, and records)? What do you think might happen to them in the future?
8. Which of Edison's inventions listed at the beginning of the article do you consider the most important? Why?

Writing Activities

1. If you could invent something, what would you invent? Why?
2. Edison is quoted as saying, "Genius is 99 percent perspiration and 1 percent inspiration." Explain what this means in your own words.

Additional Activities

1. Sometimes adults are so busy they do not take time to answer children's questions. Why is it important for adults to listen to children and answer their questions?
2. Edison conducted 10,000 failed experiments on a storage battery. Failure did not seem to discourage him. Why is the ability to overcome failure important in an inventor? Why is the ability to overcome failure important to people in their everyday lives?
3. Students who enjoyed this article may be interested in learning about other inventors such as Robert Fulton, Alexander Graham Bell, Samuel Morse, and the Wright brothers.

Exercises

3 MORE WORK WITH COMPOUND WORDS

After students have read the directions and studied the example, suggest that they do one item together in class. If they have trouble with item 2, have them read the descriptions until they come to one they know. Remind students to check off the words in both columns as they use them.

4 WHICH WORD FITS BEST?

If students had trouble with this type of exercise in Lesson 4, review the process for determining the relationships between the word pairs.

LESSON 8
Knives, Forks, and Spoons

Primary emphasis
- Literal/inferential/applied comprehension
- Phonics, word analysis, and context clues
- Writing and study skills
- Reviewing factual information
- Singular and plural words

Secondary emphasis
- Oral reading and listening skills
- New vocabulary
- Spelling (changing *f* to *v*)

Pre-reading Activities
1. As students read the article, ask them to compare how the early humans ate with how we eat today. Ask them to think about how culture changes as life becomes less difficult.
2. Bring into class a pair of chopsticks, and ask students what they are, what they are used for, and in what countries they are used.
   Say:
3. This article gives some advice about what to do in situations in which you are uncertain about what behavior is correct. Look for this advice as you read.

Post-reading Activities
1. Discuss the questions in Exercise 1. Make sure students understand the meaning of *key* as it is used in question 5. Ask or say:
2. Compare how the early humans ate with how people eat today.
3. What do you think the early humans' spoons were made from? Explain.
4. Why do you think the early humans ate only enough food to stay alive? Do you think it was difficult for them to get food?
5. People use forks in many places around the world today. How and why do you think the popularity of forks spread?
6. Why do you think spoons and knives were invented before forks?

7. What happens to cultures of people when life becomes less difficult? What are some changes that take place?
8. What advice does the author give to people who are uncertain about what to do in a given situation? Think of another situation in which this advice can be useful.

Writing Activities
1. What foods do you find difficult to eat even with a knife, fork, or spoon? Write about what it's like to eat them.
2. Eating habits have changed since the time of early humans. Write about something else that has changed.
3. Write about a situation in which you did not know what was the correct thing to do.

Additional Activities
1. Bring kitchen gadgets to class. Ask students about the intended uses, and brainstorm additional uses for them.
2. Each historical time and culture is different, and rules constantly change. Discuss the fairness of judging other people by their behavior when they may have been raised under different circumstances.
3. How do you think people today know how early humans ate? Some people make their living by studying ancient humans and cultures. Would you like this type of job? Why or why not?

Exercises

4 SINGULAR AND PLURAL WORDS
During the preview, make sure students understand the concepts *singular* and *plural*. Point out that the most common way to form plurals in English is to add *-s* to a word but that some plurals, such as *men,* take a different form.

5 ONE KNIFE/TWO KNIVES
During the preview, state this spelling rule: Change *f* to *v* and add *-es.* Then have students write the five plural words. Point out that they will use both the singular and the plural words in the sentences.

LESSON 9
Internet Dating

Primary emphasis

- Literal/inferential/applied comprehension
- Phonics, word analysis, and context clues
- Writing and study skills
- Choosing the unrelated word
- Sequencing

Secondary emphasis

- Oral reading and listening skills
- New vocabulary
- General information (manners)
- Singular and plural words

Pre-reading Activities

Say:

1. Online dating used to be thought of as something only for people who couldn't get a date any other way. Many people no longer think of it that way. As you read, decide what you think about online dating.

Post-reading Activities

1. Discuss the questions in Exercise 1.
   Ask or say:
2. What do you think a matchmaker is?
3. What does the phrase "Mr. or Ms. Right" mean?
4. Suppose you had used an Internet dating site. Would you answer "yes" if asked if you had? Why or why not?
5. Suppose you wanted to meet someone through an Internet dating service. What would you want to know about the person?
6. How soon do you think that you should meet someone in person whom you met through an online dating service?
7. Do you think that Internet dating services are a good idea? Why or why not?

Writing Activities

1. Which do you think is most important in dating someone: having the same background, religion, or interests?

2. Tell a funny story about the meeting of two people who are matched by an online dating site but haven't told the truth about what they look like or what their interests are.
3. Work out the description of the "perfect" person you would want to meet through an online dating service. Have male students as a group make up their ideal version and female students as a group create their ideal version. Then ask how realistic they think it would be to find such a person online—or anywhere. What would be a more realistic description of a Mr. or Ms. Right?

Additional Activity

Work out a list of safe dating practices with your students. You might wait until students have finished Exercise 5, The Ending -*ly*, and use that as a jumping-off point for this activity. While some of your students may be married, this activity could help them understand how online dating works.

Exercises

2 WHICH WORD DOES NOT FIT?

The format of this exercise may seem new to students, but the process used is the same as in Lesson 3, Exercise 4. If students seem unsure of what to do after studying the example, have them do item 2 during the homework preview.

3 SINGULAR AND PLURAL WORDS

During the homework preview, review the meanings of *singular* and *plural* and the fact that many plurals are formed by adding -*s* or -*es*.

5 THE ENDING -*ly*

During the preview, point out that no letters are added, dropped, or changed when -*ly* is added to these words. Remind students to write the words in the box before they begin filling in the blanks in the sentences.

LESSON 10
Solar System

Primary emphasis
- Literal/inferential/applied comprehension
- Phonics, word analysis, and context clues
- Writing and study skills
- Inferring meanings from context clues
- Choosing the related word

Secondary emphasis
- Oral reading and listening skills
- New vocabulary
- Multiple meanings and pronunciations

Words for Study
Use the names of the planets to review the capitalization of proper nouns. Point out that the word *Earth* is capitalized when referring to the planet, but when we are talking about earth as land, it is not capitalized. (Example: He dug up the earth in his garden to plant seeds.)

Pre-reading Activities
Ask or say:
1. What is the *solar system*? What do you think is in our solar system?
2. Have you ever seen a picture of Earth taken from outer space? What did it look like to you? Read this article to see what the writer thinks Earth looks like from outer space.

Have students look at the picture. Then ask if they have ever seen a model of our solar system. Find a picture of the solar system in a book or on the Internet. Show students the picture and have them identify the sun, moon, and planets.

Post-reading Activities
1. Discuss the questions in Exercise 1.
   Ask or say:
2. Why is the sun so important to the solar system?

3. Why is the sun so important to Earth?
4. Do you think any other planets have life on them? Discuss.
5. Explain why experts decided that Pluto wasn't a planet anymore.

Writing Activities
1. Space travel used to be thought of as science fiction. If you like science fiction, explain the plot of your favorite science fiction story or movie.
2. Suggest another title for this article, and write why you think it would be a good one.
3. Would you like to be an astronaut? Why or why not?

Additional Activity
Bring in articles about the latest space flight, and read them to the class or help students read them. Discuss the space flight's mission and how it added to our knowledge of space.

Exercises

2 ABOUT METEORS
During the preview, have students read the list of words to be filled in. Suggest that they read the whole passage first, saying "blank" for each missing word. Next, students should fill in the words they are sure of and check them off. Then they can fill in the rest of the words when they have fewer choices.

3 CHOOSING THE RIGHT WORD
During the homework review, have students tell whether each correct answer describes, means the same thing, or is an example of the first word. Some students confuse examples with synonyms, and this exercise provides an opportunity to help them clear up the confusion.

Review: Lessons 1–10

During the review, remind students to refer to previous lessons or a dictionary to review factual information.

5 SYLLABLES

Stress that the process of elimination is very important in this exercise. Suggest that students read the sentences and do the ones they know the answers to first. Remind them to cross out the syllables in the box as they use them.

Encourage students to select one topic from Lessons 6–10 to research and report on. Students can work alone, in pairs, or in groups and give oral and/or written reports.

LESSON 11
Accepting Who You Are

Primary emphasis
- Literal/inferential/applied comprehension
- Phonics, word analysis, and context clues
- New vocabulary
- Writing and study skills

Secondary emphasis
- Oral reading and listening skills
- Spelling (changing *y* to *i* and puzzle)
- Word endings
- Silent letters

Pre-reading Activities
Ask or say:
1. What does it mean to accept who you are? What information would you expect an article with this title to have?
2. As you read this article, watch for the author's main points, and notice how examples are used to support them.

Post-reading Activities
1. Discuss the questions in Exercise 1.
Ask or say:
2. Discuss fact and opinion. Find examples of facts and opinions in this article.
3. Discuss the major thesis of this article. Then ask students to find one of the main ideas and supporting examples of that main idea.
4. Reread the first paragraph. How can what we choose not to do send messages to other people? Think of something you chose not to do. What does that say about you?
5. Which comes first, being an open and friendly person or being a person who accepts herself or himself?
6. What can we do to help other people, especially children, to accept who they are?

Writing Activities
1. What information in this article was useful to you? Write about something you would like to remember.
2. Is there something about yourself that you have tried to change? Write about it.

Additional Vocabulary Practice
self-esteem – having confidence in yourself; accepting and respecting yourself

Additional Activities
1. Discuss self-esteem. What are some signs that a person has high self-esteem? What are some signs of low self-esteem?
2. Discuss how students' accomplishments and progress in improving reading skills relate to self-esteem.

Exercises

2 CHANGING THE -*y* TO -*i*
During the preview, tell students to add the endings -*er,* -*est,* and -*ness* to each word after changing the -*y* to -*i.* Point out that -*y* is changed to -*i* before endings that start with consonants as well as endings that start with vowels. Note that -*y* is not changed if the ending starts with -*i.*

3 WORD ENDINGS
During the homework preview, have students read the words in the box. Tell them to read each sentence through before selecting the word to write in the blank.

4 SILENT LETTERS
During the preview, have students read the words to be sure they are pronouncing them correctly.

5 HAPPINESS
If students have never done this type of puzzle, have them do two or three items during the preview. Tell them to fill in the letters in the quotation as they answer each item. Tell them to work back and forth between the clues and the quotation, using context clues in the quotation to complete partially filled-in words.

LESSON 12
Anne Frank: Part I

Primary emphasis
- Literal/inferential/applied comprehension
- Phonics, word analysis, and context clues
- New vocabulary
- Writing and study skills
- Synonyms and antonyms

Secondary emphasis
- Oral reading and listening skills
- Word beginnings
- Hard and soft *g*

Words for Study
Use these words to introduce background information on World War II.

Pre-reading Activities
1. Find out how much students already know about Adolf Hitler, World War II, and Anne Frank. What were some countries that fought on the same side as Germany? What were some countries that fought against Germany? Who was Adolf Hitler? What did he want to do? Discuss Hitler's attempt to destroy Europe's Jewish population during the war.
2. Bring in pictures, maps, and books about World War II to enhance understanding and create interest in the lesson. Find Germany and Holland on a world map or atlas.
   Say:
3. As you read the article about Anne Frank, think about how hard it would be to live hiding in an attic for two years.

Post-reading Activities
1. Discuss the questions in Exercise 1.
   Ask or say:
2. Anne Frank lived from 1929–1945. How old was she when she died?
3. What do you think would happen to a Jewish person who carried a suitcase in a country occupied by Nazis?
4. Did Anne think Germany had changed since Hitler became powerful? What did Anne mean when she wrote, "Hitler took away our country long ago"?

5. How do you think the people hiding in the attic were able to get the supplies and food they needed? (Many people in Holland risked their own lives to hide and help Jewish people.)
6. What do you think would be the most difficult part of hiding in an attic for two years?
7. Do you think discrimination and racism still exist today? Give examples. Have you experienced discrimination? Discuss.
8. Is reading a diary an interesting way to learn about history? Would you prefer to read a diary or a history book to learn about events in the past? Why?

Writing Activities
1. Write what you are feeling and thinking after reading parts of Anne Frank's diary.
2. Write a few sentences or a poem about Anne Frank.
3. What are some things you would try to take with you if you were forced into hiding?
4. Point out that journals are like diaries. Remind students to write in their journals.

Additional Activities
1. During the year 1933, Anne Frank's family moved to the Netherlands (Holland) from Germany to avoid trouble following Hitler's rise to power. Find these places on a world map or atlas.
2. How do you think it was possible for a person such as Hitler to become so powerful? Do such people continue to reach positions of power in the world today? Discuss.
3. Anne wrote, "I want to go on living after my death." Things a person writes are often read years after the writer has died. Think of examples of other people who have died but whose writings are still read. Do you consider their work a means for them to be "living after . . . death"?

Exercise

2 WORD BEGINNINGS
Information in the reading and background information about World War II should help students to answer these questions.

LESSON 13
Anne Frank: Part II

Primary emphasis
- Literal/inferential/applied comprehension
- Phonics, word analysis, and context clues
- Writing and study skills
- Inferring meanings from context clues
- Classifying

Secondary emphasis
- Oral reading and listening skills
- New vocabulary
- Word endings

Words for Study
Find the places listed on a world map or atlas.

Pre-reading Activities
1. Review the selection in Lesson 12.
   Ask or say:
2. What would you miss the most if you had to live in an attic for two years? List the things you would miss. After completing the reading, compare your ideas with the list of things in Anne's diary.
3. As you continue to read about Anne Frank, find something that Anne was hopeful about.

Post-reading Activities
1. Discuss the questions in Exercise 1.
   Ask or say:
2. Describe how you picture the hiding place.
3. Why do you think Anne feels she cannot show her rage?
4. Did the people living in hiding wish for expensive things or simple things? Explain.
5. Did you find Anne's diary interesting? If so, what did you find interesting about it? Do you think Anne's diary helped her survive the two years in hiding? Explain.
6. Did Anne think she would survive? Find a sentence that supports your answer.
7. Think about a time when you were very afraid. Imagine what it must have been like to live year after year in fear of losing your life. Imagine having to be quiet at all times and often go hungry. Discuss the problems of living with a group of eight people who are under great stress and in fear.

Writing Activities
1. Write about what you would miss the most if you had to live under the circumstances that Anne's family did.
2. If you had been hiding in an attic for two years and were suddenly freed, what would you want to do first?
3. What can each of us do in our lives to work toward a better world?

Additional Activities
1. Students may have questions about how Anne Frank's story ended. Germany was defeated in 1945. Anne died in a concentration camp less than two months before the end of the war. Anne's father, Otto, was the only survivor among the eight people in the attic. After the war, he visited the people who had hidden his family. They had found Anne's diary, and they gave it to him.
2. Read other excerpts from *Anne Frank: The Diary of a Young Girl* if the class is interested. Many books written about Anne Frank have pictures of Anne and the secret hiding place. Some students may want to read the entire diary.
3. Watch a movie or film about Anne Frank, and have students discuss it or write a review.
4. Think about the article "Accepting Who You Are" in Lesson 11. Do you think Anne Frank accepted who she was? Find details from her diary that support your answer.

Exercises

2 WORLD WAR II
Suggest that students read the entire passage before filling in the missing words.

3 CITIES, STATES, AND COUNTRIES
Tell students that they can find this information in most dictionaries. During the homework review, have maps of the United States and the world available to help students locate all these places.

LESSON 14
The Ship of the Desert

Primary emphasis
- Literal/inferential/applied comprehension
- Phonics, word analysis, and context clues
- New vocabulary
- Writing and study skills
- Forming and defining compound words

Secondary emphasis
- Oral reading and listening skills
- Word endings
- Syllabication
- Identifying vowel sounds

Pre-reading Activities
1. After looking at the pictures, ask students if they have ever seen camels at a zoo. Ask them to describe what they saw. Find out why they think camels are called "ships of the desert."
2. Ask if students have seen a desert. If so, have them describe it. If no one has been to a desert, ask students to imagine what one is like.
3. Find the deserts of Asia and Africa on a world map or atlas.

Post-reading Activities
1. Discuss the questions in Exercise 1.
   Ask or say:
2. What are Asia and Africa? Can you name the other continents? Find them on a world map or atlas.
3. Is it always hot in a desert? (No. Nights are often cold.) Are all deserts hot? (No.) Are all deserts dry? (Yes.)
4. How is a camel's body well suited to life in the desert? Why is fat stored in the hump? (Fat provides energy when food is scarce.)
5. Do people have to be careful around camels? Explain.
6. Find a place in the article where the author expresses a personal opinion about camels. Does this article contain more facts or more opinions?
7. Compare horses and camels. What are the similarities? What are the differences? Consider such things as how

their bodies are built, how they are used by people, and the parts of the world where they are found.
8. Would you like to ride a camel? Why or why not?

Writing Activities
1. According to an old joke, a camel is a horse that was designed by a committee. Write what you think the joke means.
2. Just for fun, design an animal that would be useful to you. Write a description or draw a picture of your animal.
3. Write a humorous short poem about a camel.

Additional Activities
1. How do you think camels came by the name "ships of the desert"? One explanation for the name is found in the article. Another explanation is that when a camel paces, both legs on the same side of its body move up and down together. This causes it to sway and pitch like a ship on waves. The swaying motion sometimes makes riders "seasick."
2. Some camels grow thick, long hair under certain conditions. What do you think those conditions are? (Examples: in winter or in cold regions)
3. Some camels can tolerate water loss of up to 25 percent of their body weight. Humans die at water losses of only 12 percent. Figure out how much you would weigh if you lost 25 percent of your body weight.
4. Help interested students find information on the two types of camels, those with one hump (Arabian) and those with two (Bactrian). Look for pictures of the two types.
5. Find pictures of other animals that illustrate how their bodies are especially suited to their habitat. (Examples: anteaters, armadillos, giraffes, mountain goats, sharks)

Exercise

2 COMPOUND WORDS
Students may want to use a dictionary to do this exercise.

LESSON 15
Cloning

Primary emphasis
- Literal/inferential/applied comprehension
- Phonics, word analysis, and context clues
- New vocabulary
- Writing and study skills
- Common expressions

Secondary emphasis
- Oral reading and listening skills
- Singular and plural words

Words for Study
Remind students to try to figure out the meanings of unfamiliar words from the context of the reading.

Pre-reading Activities
1. Point out that this article is set up like a set of "Frequently Asked Questions." Ask students what this phrase means. Point out that on websites, the acronym "FAQ" is often listed. What do students think these letters stand for? Where have students found lists of FAQs?
2. Explain that cloning is making a copy of something living or dead such as a plant or animal. As they read, students should think about whether they think cloning is a good idea or a bad idea.

Post-reading Activities
1. Discuss the questions in Exercise 1.
   Ask or say:
2. How did cloning Dolly the sheep change what experts thought about cloning?
3. Why is cloning animals helpful in medical research?
4. Why do some people think that using human cells for cloning is wrong?

5. Where does the debate about using human embryos for cloning research stand?
6. Do you think that using the FAQ format to explain cloning helped you better understand what it is and the issues about it? Why or why not?

Writing Activities
1. Write one fact from the article that surprised you. Explain why it surprised you.
2. How would you feel if there was another one of you walking around—but 20 years younger? Write a funny story about what it would be like to have a younger clone of you.
3. Do you think that cloning animals is a good idea or a bad idea? Why?
4. Do you think that cloning human cells for medical research is a good idea or a bad idea? Why?

Additional Activities
1. Help students to do research about Dolly the sheep and what happened to her.
2. Help students turn the reading into a series of FAQs. Point out that asking *who, what, when, where, how,* and *why* questions when they read can help students pull apart something they are reading to understand it better.

Exercise

4 SINGULAR AND PLURAL WORDS
During the homework review, have students identify the various ways these plurals are formed:
- adding -*s* or -*es*
- changing -*y* to -*i* and adding -*es*
- changing *f* to *v* and adding -*es*
- making no change (Example: deer)
- making an irregular change (Examples: oxen, cattle)

Review: Lessons 1–15

During the review, remind students to refer to previous lessons or a dictionary to review factual information.

Encourage students to select one topic from Lessons 11–15 to research and report on. Students can work alone, in pairs, or in groups and give oral and/or written reports.

LESSON 16
Some Thoughts about Dying

Primary emphasis
- Literal/inferential/applied comprehension
- Phonics, word analysis, and context clues
- New vocabulary
- Writing and study skills
- Sequencing events

Secondary emphasis
- Oral reading and listening skills
- The ending -ly
- Compound words

Words for Study
If students ask for definitions for unfamiliar words, encourage them to try to figure out the meanings from the context of the reading.

Pre-reading Activities
Ask or say:
1. This article talks about dying. Briefly discuss how, when, and why living things die. Injury and the effects of old age are two common causes of death. Can you think of a third? (Example: disease)
2. As you read, think about what the author's message is about dying.

Post-reading Activities
1. Discuss the questions in Exercise 1.
2. Summarize the author's message about dying. Ask or say: What is the main idea of the article? Would you describe the article as positive or negative? Why?
3. Why do you think so many people have written books about death?
4. Describe the death of the elm tree. Why do we treat a tree's death as "normal"?
5. Why does the author say that a dying person feels no pain?
6. Do you think this would be a good article for a dying person to read? Why or why not?

Writing Activities
1. Write some of your thoughts about dying.
2. Write some of your thoughts about pain.

Additional Activities
1. People may disagree about the definition of death. Is a person dead when his or her heart stops? When the brain ceases to have activity? Discuss drugs, medical advances, and other means used to continue body functions. When do students think they should be used? Should they always be used? What about cost? Who should have access first to limited resources? Who should make these important decisions?
2. What are "right to die" groups concerned about?
3. In years past, so many people died at home that death was viewed as a natural part of life. Many people today have not had the experience of being around a dying person. Do you think this makes it more difficult to view death as a natural part of life? Explain.

Additional Vocabulary Practice
hospice – a program that provides home-like care for dying people

DNR – Do Not Resuscitate—an order stating that a person does not want to be kept alive with life-support systems in the event of a terminal illness

brain dead – the absence of brain activity

Exercises

2 WHAT DO YOU THINK?
If students feel comfortable discussing their feelings, have them compare and discuss their answers.

3 THE ENDING -ly
Tell students to write the words with -ly added before using them to fill in the blanks in the sentences.

5 MORE WORK WITH COMPOUND WORDS
During the homework review, briefly discuss the meanings of any of the answer choices that students don't know.

LESSON 17
The Number One Eater in America

Primary emphasis

- Literal/inferential/applied comprehension
- Phonics, word analysis, and context clues
- New vocabulary
- Writing and study skills
- Common expressions

Secondary emphasis

- Oral reading and listening skills
- The ending -ful
- Forming words with syllables

Pre-reading Activities

Ask or say:

1. Did you ever eat too much? How did you feel? This is an article about a man who ate too much every day for years.
2. List some questions that you might have about James Brady. Was James Brady rich? How old do you think he was when he died?
3. List what you ate today. Then read the article to find out what Diamond Jim Brady would have eaten in the same period of time. Compare your list to what he would have eaten.

Post-reading Activities

1. Discuss the questions in Exercise 1.
   Ask or say:
2. Would you like to have been a friend of Diamond Jim Brady? Why or why not?
3. Do you think Diamond Jim was a hard worker? Why or why not?
4. What kind of qualities do you think an "extremely successful salesman" has?
5. Did Jim Brady live near the ocean? What clues in the article did you use to decide?
6. What did the restaurant owner mean when he said Diamond Jim was "the best twenty-five customers we had"?
7. Was $100,000 worth more in Diamond Jim's time than it is today?
8. Discuss tone. Did the author admire Jim Brady? Was the author impressed? Would the tone change if Brady

had been referred to as "the Number One Glutton"? How would the tone be different if the article were written by or for people who could not get enough to eat?

Writing Activities

1. If you could afford to eat any foods you wanted, write about what you would eat.
2. If you were as rich as Diamond Jim Brady, write about what you would do with your wealth.

Additional Vocabulary Practice

glutton – a person who consumes excessive amounts of food and drink

gluttony – excessive eating or drinking

Additional Activities

1. Find Atlantic City and New York on a map or atlas.
2. Diamond Jim drank a gallon of orange juice for breakfast. Bring in empty containers that hold different volumes. Make labels for each container. Ask students to match the labels to the containers. Ask about equivalent measures. For example: How many quarts are in a gallon? How many cups are in a pint? In a quart? In a gallon?
3. What health problems are associated with overeating?
4. People like Diamond Jim Brady eat too much while many people in the world do not get enough to eat. Do you think this is fair? Can anything be done about it?

Exercises

2 FOOD FOR THOUGHT

During the homework preview, discuss any expressions here that are unfamiliar to students.

3 THE ENDING -ful

Tell students to add -ful to each word listed at the top of the page before filling in the blanks in the sentences.

4 WORKING WITH SYLLABLES

Remind students to use the process of elimination and to cross out the syllables in the box as they use them.

LESSON 18
The Great Hunger

Primary emphasis
- Literal/inferential/applied comprehension
- Phonics, word analysis, and context clues
- Inferring meanings from context clues
- Writing and study skills
- Word associations

Secondary emphasis
- Oral reading and listening skills
- New vocabulary
- The ending -less

Pre-reading Activity
Ask students what they know about Ireland. Does anyone have relatives or ancestors who came from Ireland? Can anyone name some Irish symbols or traditions? (Examples: St. Patrick's Day, shamrocks, leprechauns) Find Ireland on a world map or atlas.

Post-reading Activities
1. Discuss the questions in Exercise 1.
   Ask or say:
2. List some facts given that illustrate the poverty in Ireland during the 1800s.
3. Do you think it is wise to depend on only one crop for food? Why do you think the people in Ireland did so?
4. What are two reasons why the population of Ireland decreased during the years of potato blight?
5. Why do you think people waited so long before they left the country? Why do you think some people never left?
6. Besides starvation, what are some other reasons that people immigrate to another country?
7. Contrast the famine described in this article with the feasting described in Lesson 17.

Writing Activities
1. Explain what the phrase "at the end of their rope" means.

2. Write about what you would have done if you had lived in Ireland at the time of the potato blight.

Additional Activities
1. Students may want to learn more about Ireland's history. Help them to find appropriate materials.
2. Did the people from Ireland speak the same language as the people in the United States? Do you think that knowing the language is an advantage to people who immigrate? What difficulties result when people move to countries where a different language is spoken?
3. Read to the class about an immigrant or immigrant family. What was it like for people to have to be separated from their relatives and friends and move to another country?
4. Some students may have ancestors or relatives who migrated to or from other countries. If any students know their family stories, ask them to share these stories with the class or to write about them.
5. Does famine exist in the world today? Find places on a world map or atlas where people have suffered from food shortages or famine in recent years. Are there people in your community who do not have enough food? Why? What can be done to help them?

Exercises

2 MORE ABOUT POTATOES
Remind students to take their time and to use context clues and the process of elimination while completing this exercise. During the review, trace on a world map or atlas the path potatoes took to get from South America to North America.

3 WHERE WOULD YOU FIND IT?
General background knowledge is needed to do this exercise. During the preview, discuss any items that are unfamiliar to students.

LESSON 19
Digestion

Primary emphasis
- Literal/inferential/applied comprehension
- Phonics, word analysis, and context clues
- New vocabulary
- Writing and study skills
- Cause-and-effect relationships

Secondary emphasis
- Oral reading and listening skills
- Factual information
- Word endings

Pre-reading Activities
Ask or say:
1. What does *digestion* mean, and what do you know about it? What kind of information do you expect to find in this article on digestion?
2. This article traces the path of food people eat as it goes through the body. Read to find out where food goes after you swallow it.

Post-reading Activities
1. Discuss the questions in Exercise 1.
   Ask or say:
2. After swallowing, where does the food go? Trace the path through the digestive system.
3. Using information from the article, explain why after eating a really big meal, you feel really full.
4. Do you think it takes longer to digest scrambled eggs or steak? Eggs or orange juice?
5. Why is food broken down into smaller and smaller parts? (It must enter the bloodstream through the intestinal walls to be carried to all parts of the body.)
6. Do you think this article has more facts or opinions? Was it written to inform or to persuade?

Writing Activities
1. Write two new things you learned about the digestive system.

2. Write about any information in this article that can be useful in your daily life.

Additional Activities
1. Ask students what other systems are in the body. Can students name any body parts that belong to the skeletal system, the respiratory system, the nervous system, and/or the circulatory system? Pictures illustrating these other systems would enhance the lesson.
2. What does the phrase "empty calories" mean? Why is it important to eat food that is useful to our bodies?
3. Either go online ahead of time and download information about the U.S. Department of Agriculture's food guidelines or help students go online to find the information at the website of the Food Nutrition Information Center (fnic.nal.usda.gov). Look for "Dietary Guidelines for Americans." The food pyramid focuses on grains, vegetables, fruits, milk, meat and beans, and oils. Notice that sweets are not included but can be eaten as part of a person's discretionary calories. The website has life cycle food advice as well as a pyramid for kids, dietary information for pregnant women, and an "Ethnic/Cultural Food Guide," which includes dietary guidelines for Latino/Spanish, Native American, and Asian groups.

Exercises

2 MORE ABOUT DIGESTION
During the preview, be sure students understand the two parts to this exercise. First, they are to write the six body parts in order. Then they are to describe briefly how each aids digestion.

3 CAUSE AND EFFECT
During the preview, explain that an *effect* is a *result*. Advise students to number each effect with the number of the corresponding cause before writing the effects on the lines provided.

LESSON 20
Nail Soup

Primary emphasis

- Literal/inferential/applied comprehension
- Phonics, word analysis, and context clues
- New vocabulary
- Writing and study skills
- Reading a menu

Secondary emphasis

- Oral reading and listening skills
- Synonyms and antonyms
- Using context clues
- Word endings

Pre-reading Activities

1. Unlike the nonfiction articles in the rest of this book, this is a well-known folktale. After reading the title, ask if anyone is familiar with the story. (There is also a version called "Stone Soup.") Discuss some of the differences between fiction and nonfiction.

2. Ask students to think of stories they have heard about a clever person living by his or her wits. There are many examples in fairy tales, fables, and folk stories. There are also examples in history and in the news today.

Post-reading Activities

1. Discuss the questions in Exercise 1.

2. Have students underline in different colors the text of this story according to speaking parts. The speaking parts are the little old lady (Granny), the stranger, and the neighbor, Martha. Any lines not in quotation marks can be read by a narrator. Have students practice reading the parts in groups of four students. Then have volunteers read it for the class.
   Ask or say:

3. Did the story turn out the way you thought it would? What was the point of the story?

4. Was the little old lady on her guard against anyone taking advantage of her? Was she a hard worker? Why do you think so?

5. Do you think the stranger had a plan in mind before he met the old lady? Do you think it was the first or only time he made nail soup?

6. Do you think the woman would have helped the young stranger if he had told her he was hungry? Why or why not?

7. Find the place in the story where Granny begins to change her attitude.

8. Do you think the old woman understood what the stranger was doing?

9. The young man said he always earns his dinner. Do you think he earned the nail soup? Why or why not?

Writing Activities

1. Write about something someone did or said that you consider clever.

2. Write about something you do now that you didn't do when you started *Challenger 4*.

Additional Activities

1. Read another story about someone clever who lived by his or her wits. Some sources are fairy tales, fables, folk stories, and human interest news stories. New Readers Press publishes a series of such stories titled *Timeless Tales*.

2. This is the last lesson in *Challenger 4*. Review students' goals, and discuss their progress. Look back at some of the writing students have done since beginning the book.

Exercises

2 MAY I TAKE YOUR ORDER?

There is no one right answer for questions 3, 4, and 5. Accept any answers that make sense.

3 SAME OR OPPOSITE?

Encourage students to use a dictionary for any items that give them difficulty.

Review: Lessons 1–20

The purpose of this review is to give students one more opportunity to work with many of the concepts emphasized in Book 4. Preview each exercise as usual. Advise students to refer to the lessons for answers they don't remember. After going over the review, discuss what students have learned and accomplished while working in *Challenger 4*. Help students to plan and prepare for some sort of celebration.

ANSWER KEY FOR WRITING BOOKS
Challenger Writing 1

Lesson 1

1 FILL IN THE MISSING WORD
1. o'clock
2. fired
3. late
4. quit

2 ANSWER THE QUESTIONS
1. Bob was late for work.
2. Eddie and Mike rode to the park with Bob.
3. Bob woke up at nine o'clock.
4. Bob hates his job.
5. Eddie did not have a job at the time.
6. Mr. Jones fired Bob.

3 PUT THESE SENTENCES IN ORDER
1. Bob was late for his job.
2. Bob hoped Mr. Jones would not fire him.
3. Mr. Jones did fire Bob.
4. Bob rode to the park with Eddie and Mike.

4 WHAT DO YOU THINK?
Answers may vary.

5 UNSCRAMBLE THE SENTENCES
1. Bob got a ride to his job.
2. Bob rode with Eddie.

Lesson 2

1 FILL IN THE MISSING WORD
1. job
2. bikes
3. bad
4. Eddie
5. hire

2 ANSWER THE QUESTIONS
1. Dan Rose was a friend of Bob's dad.
2. Bob had a date to see Dan Rose.
3. The job was fixing bikes.
4. Bob said he did not have to see Dan until five o'clock.
5. Eddie did not want to let his friend down.

3 PUT THESE SENTENCES IN ORDER
1. Bob said, "I hope I feel relaxed when I meet Dan."
2. Eddie said, "Let's ride around until it is time to see him."
3. Bob was relaxed by the time he got to Dan's home.
4. Dan said he would hire Bob to fix bikes.

4 WHAT DO YOU THINK?
Answers may vary.

5 UNSCRAMBLE THE SENTENCES
1. Bob had a date to see Dan Rose.
2. The job was fixing bikes.

Lesson 3

1 FILL IN THE MISSING WORD
1. loved
2. bank
3. met
4. jeep
5. week

2 ANSWER THE QUESTIONS
1. Kate was Eddie's girlfriend.
2. Dave had a jeep.
3. Eddie was with Mike and Dave in the jeep.
4. Dave beeped the horn so Kate would see Eddie.
5. Kate seemed mad at the beeping.
6. Eddie and Kate had fun at the lake.

3 PUT THESE SENTENCES IN ORDER
1. Eddie rode to the lake with Mike and Dave.
2. Eddie made Dave beep the horn.
3. Kate loved Eddie at first sight!
4. Kate rode off with Eddie in Dave's jeep.

4 WHAT DO YOU THINK?
Answers may vary.

5 UNSCRAMBLE THE SENTENCES
1. Eddie hoped that Kate loved him.
2. She rode off with him in Dave's jeep.

Lesson 4

1 ANSWER THE QUESTIONS
1. Kate lived with her aunt.
2. Louise was Kate's aunt.
3. Kate wanted to bake the cake without help.
4. Kate dug a hole behind her home and put the cake in it.

2 PUT THESE SENTENCES IN ORDER
1. Kate wanted to bake a cake for Eddie.
2. Aunt Louise said she would help Kate.
3. Kate refused her Aunt Louise's help.
4. The cake looked like a joke and was bad.
5. Kate put the cake in a hole she dug.

3 UNSCRAMBLE THE SENTENCES
1. Kate didn't know how to bake.
2. Kate ate a bite of the cake.
3. She fed the cake to the cat.
4. The cat hated the cake.
5. Kate was mad at herself.

4 WHAT DO YOU THINK?
Answers may vary.

Lesson 5

1 ADD ANOTHER WORD
1. mitt   3. home
2. Ben   4. hug

2 ANSWER THE QUESTIONS
1. Kate's friends liked to talk to her Aunt Louise.
2. Bob went to see Aunt Louise after work.
3. Aunt Louise was fixing beef for dinner.
4. Bob talked to women who needed to have bikes fixed.

3 WHAT DO YOU THINK?
Answers may vary. Some possible answers are:
1. she talked to him about his problems.
2. she listened to them.

4 UNSCRAMBLE THE SENTENCES
1. I have a problem at work.
2. Would you like to have dinner with us?
3. It was fun to talk and joke with Aunt Louise.

5 PERSONAL QUESTIONS
Answers may vary.

Lesson 6

1 FILL IN THE MISSING WORD
1. sick   3. phone   5. ducks
2. laptop   4. refund   6. won

2 ANSWER THE QUESTIONS
Answers may vary. Some possible answers are:
1. Eddie wanted to get Kate something nice.
2. Eddie had the idea to win lots of money.
3. Eddie won by picking good cards from the pack.
4. Eddie was down in the dumps because he ran out of money.

3 WHAT DO YOU THINK?
Answers may vary. Some possible answers are:
1. he won six hands at the online casino.
2. he was too greedy and his luck ran out.

4 PUT THESE SENTENCES IN ORDER
1. Eddie got his laptop and went to the online casino.
2. He bet the money he had and won.
3. He won the next five hands.
4. Eddie lost a game, but he played again and again.

5 PERSONAL QUESTIONS
Answers may vary.

Lesson 7

1 ADD ANOTHER WORD
1. dozed   3. looked
2. honk   4. sang

2 ANSWER THE QUESTIONS
Answers may vary. Some possible answers are:
1. Dave wanted to sink back into the bed when the clock rang.
2. Dave needed to take money out of the bank so he could go downtown and look for a new car.
3. Dave needed a new car because he had junked his jeep.
4. The cat banged into a box of fuses.

3 WHAT DO YOU THINK?
Answers may vary. Some possible answers are:
1. he didn't want to look for a new car.
2. Dave put the jam away.

4 UNSCRAMBLE THE SENTENCES
1. Dave had to get to the bank by nine o'clock.
2. The jam pot hit the sink with a bang.
3. Dave wiped up the jam and went back to bed.

5 PERSONAL QUESTIONS
Answers may vary.

Lesson 8

1 FILL IN THE MISSING WORD
1. fuss   3. huge   5. ago
2. amusement   4. keeled   6. stayed

2 ADD ANOTHER WORD
1. Jack   3. male   5. games
2. beef   4. hum   6. home

3 ANSWER THE QUESTIONS
Answers may vary. Some possible answers are:
1. Aunt Louise and Jack rode to the amusement park in a cab.
2. Aunt Louise was happy again once they were at the amusement park.
3. The rides were fifty cents years ago.

4 PUT THESE SENTENCES IN ORDER
1. Jack and Aunt Louise rode in a cab.
2. Aunt Louise was getting mad.
3. Jack said that they should go home.

5 WHAT DO YOU THINK?
Answers may vary.

Lesson 9

1 FILL IN THE MISSING WORD
1. guy   3. joy
2. birthday   4. myself

2 CHOOSE THE RIGHT WORD
1. safely   2. quickly   3. jack

3 UNSCRAMBLE THE SENTENCES
1. Bob is going to be twenty-four on Wednesday.
2. They only had six bucks to get something nice.

4 ANSWER THE QUESTIONS

Answers may vary. Some possible answers are:

1. Bob's friends didn't have any money because payday wasn't until Friday.
2. Kate didn't bake the cake because Eddie wanted her aunt to bake it.
3. Dave said Bob's friends should buy him some toys.
4. They all got into Mike's car and went downtown.
5. Yes, Min-hee went downtown with them.

5 WHAT DO YOU THINK?

Answers may vary.

Lesson 10

1 FILL IN THE MISSING WORD

1. ditch
2. write
3. wrong
4. fight

2 CHOOSE THE RIGHT WORD

1. knife
2. waited
3. right

3 UNSCRAMBLE THE SENTENCES

1. Kate wanted to know where Eddie was.
2. All Eddie wanted to do was see a movie.

4 ANSWER THE QUESTIONS

Answers may vary. Some possible answers are:

1. Eddie was going to meet Kate and go to a movie.
2. Eddie didn't want to get into a fight with Kate.
3. Eddie hit the gas, and the car hit a patch of ice.
4. Eddie was numb, and his stomach was in a knot.
5. Eddie hurt his knee and his wrist.
6. Kate said not to worry.
7. Eddie sat down and waited for Kate.

5 PERSONAL QUESTIONS

Answers may vary.

Lesson 11

1 FILL IN THE MISSING WORD

1. nerve
2. work
3. purse

2 CHOOSE THE RIGHT WORD

1. care
2. jerk
3. breath

3 ANSWER THE QUESTIONS

Answers may vary. Some possible answers are:

1. Kate took a card out of her purse.
2. Aunt Louise said that fortune-telling was silly.
3. Eddie would jeer at Kate.

4 PUT THESE SENTENCES IN ORDER

1. Aunt Louise and Kate were out walking.
2. Kate wanted Aunt Louise to go to the fortune-teller with her.
3. They went into the store where the fortune-teller worked.

4. Mary said she tells fortunes by looking at cards, charts, and palms.
5. Mary peered at Kate's palm.
6. Mary said Kate would live a long and happy life.

5 COMPLETE THE SENTENCES

Answers may vary. Some possible answers are:

1. she would not feel scared.
2. that Kate wanted her fortune told.
3. peered at the lines on her palm.
4. said that Eddie would act like a jerk.

Lesson 12

1 FILL IN THE MISSING WORD

1. paid
2. lie
3. join

2 CHOOSE THE RIGHT WORD

1. loudly
2. foot
3. join

3 ANSWER THE QUESTIONS

Answers may vary. Some possible answers are:

1. Kate didn't have the money to buy a new coat.
2. Eddie wanted to celebrate his new job.
3. Kate was sorry she shouted at Eddie.

4 PUT THESE SENTENCES IN ORDER

1. Kate was in a bad mood today.
2. Eddie came into the room.
3. Kate was in no mood to put up with Eddie's bad temper.
4. Eddie said maybe Bob would celebrate with him.
5. Kate said she was sorry.

5 WHAT DO YOU THINK?

Answers may vary.

Lesson 13

1 FILL IN THE MISSING WORDS

1. fair/hair
2. part/dark
3. smart/aid
4. dear/year

2 ANSWER THE QUESTIONS

Answers may vary. Some possible answers are:

1. Dave had made up his mind to take a class at night school.
2. Dave could pick up some hints on how to paint better.
3. Dave was painting a picture of a pear.
4. Joan's pear looked like a box.
5. Dave felt that night school was going to be a lot more fun than he thought it would be.

3 UNSCRAMBLE THE SENTENCES

1. Dave had failed art in high school.
2. A lovely woman was painting near Dave.
3. Dave said he had been painting for years.
4. I would like to buy you a Coke.

4 COMPLETE THE SENTENCES

Answers may vary. Some possible answers are:

1. he was getting tired of just going to work, looking at television, hanging out with his friends, or seeing Min-hee in the evenings.
2. tear it up and forget all about night school.
3. Joan said it really looked like a pear.
4. he had been painting for years.

Lesson 14

1 CHOOSE THE RIGHT WORD

1. belt	3. wild	5. yell
2. pull	4. fill	6. cold

2 PUT THESE SENTENCES IN ORDER

1. Eddie stopped at Jack's house on his way home.
2. Eddie could hear Jack laughing loudly in the den.
3. Eddie could see Jack wasn't reading a book.
4. Eddie asked Jack what was so funny.
5. Jack handed Eddie his phone bill.

3 ANSWER THE QUESTIONS

Answers may vary. Some possible answers are:

1. Jack was paying his bills and laughing.
2. Jack's phone bill was for only ten cents.
3. Eddie was so happy to have a job that he didn't mind paying bills.

4 FILL IN THE MISSING WORDS

1. useful/useless	3. helpful/helpless
2. harmful/harmless	4. careless/careful

5 WHAT DO YOU THINK?

Answers may vary.

Lesson 15

1 FILL IN THE MISSING WORDS

1. loud/loudest	3. lovely/loveliest
2. big/biggest	4. lucky/luckiest

2 ANSWER THE QUESTIONS

Answers may vary. Some possible answers are:

1. Kate wanted to buy a cheap chair.
2. Kate asked Eddie if it is too much of a risk to shop online.
3. Eddie said that shopping at online auctions is easy and safe.
4. Kate hit "Buy Now."
5. Eddie shook his head and couldn't stop laughing.

3 UNSCRAMBLE THE SENTENCES

1. The online auction had a lot of stuff for sale.
2. Kate was mad people were wasting money.
3. Kate was in shock at the bidding for the toast.
4. Kate did not think shopping online was safe.

4 COMPLETE THE SENTENCES

Answers may vary. Some possible answers are:

1. a chair at an online auction.
2. chairs, desks, chests, and all sorts of stuff.
3. so she could choose all the things that she wanted.
4. can see what sorts of odd things people are selling."
5. hit the "Buy Now" key and got the piece of toast shaped like Elvis.

Lesson 16

1 PUT THESE SENTENCES IN ORDER

1. Bob slammed his hand in the car door.
2. He saw that his thumb was cut.
3. Bob asked June to go out Saturday night.
4. Bob said they could talk about the good old days.

2 ANSWER THE QUESTIONS

Answers may vary. Some possible answers are:

1. Bob wrapped his hand in an old cloth.
2. Dr. Chase's place was in the middle of the next block.
3. June Baker was the nurse at Dr. Chase's.
4. June thought Bob's hand looked bad, but the rest of him looked just fine.
5. Bob and June planned to go out Saturday night.

3 FILL IN THE MISSING WORDS

1. payday/paycheck	3. birthday/birthday cake
2. rain/raincoat	4. weekends/week

4 WHAT DO YOU THINK?

Answers may vary.

Lesson 17

1 CHOOSE THE RIGHT WORD

1. shirt	3. prize	5. cleaner
2. brave	4. free	

2 ANSWER THE QUESTIONS

Answers may vary. Some possible answers are:

1. Running into June at Dr. Chase's was like a dream come true.
2. Dan Rose yelled because Bob wasn't strong enough to go back to work yet.
3. Dan was upset because his prize worker was out sick.
4. Bob planned to take June to the Steak House for dinner.
5. Bob froze because he didn't have any money.

3 UNSCRAMBLE THE SENTENCES

1. Bob was proud of his clothes.
2. Bob had to decide where to take June.
3. Bob put on his jacket to go downtown.
4. Bob didn't have a dime to his name.

4 COMPLETE THE SENTENCES

Answers may vary. Some possible answers are:
1. he was going out with June that night.
2. his hand was all wrapped up.
3. what June would want to do.
4. he had missed work yesterday.

Lesson 18

1 CHOOSE THE RIGHT WORD
1. sneeze   3. three   5. thin
2. wheel   4. snake

2 ANSWER THE QUESTIONS
Answers may vary. Some possible answers are:
1. Billy smashed Jack in the chest with a toy.
2. Jack thought Billy might need a good spanking.
3. Jack said that he was over six feet tall and that Billy was maybe three feet tall.
4. Billy was sitting calmly on the floor and playing with his toy trucks.
5. She said, "You sure do have a way with kids."

3 PUT THESE SENTENCES IN ORDER
1. Mary's mother and father wanted to take Mary to a play.
2. Mary's mother told Jack to be firm with Billy.
3. Billy wheeled his bike into the room and rolled it right into Jack's legs.
4. Jack asked Billy if he had learned about numbers in math.
5. Billy was sitting calmly on the floor.

4 WHAT DO YOU THINK?
Answers may vary.

Lesson 19

1 CHOOSE THE RIGHT WORD
1. shrink   3. squeeze   5. Christmas
2. scar   4. splint

2 ANSWER THE QUESTIONS
Answers may vary. Some possible answers are:
1. Kate had saved her money to buy a bike.
2. The scooter cost more than Kate had to spend.
3. Kate did not want to hit a squirrel.
4. The chrome was scratched, and the tires were shredded.
5. She had to pay for the scooter.

3 UNSCRAMBLE THE SENTENCES
1. Kate would make a splash riding the red scooter.
2. Kate did not want to squash the squirrel.
3. The scooter swerved, and the brakes squealed.
4. The squirrel was saved, but Kate got a ticket.

4 COMPLETE THE SENTENCES
Answers may vary. Some possible answers are:
1. headed toward the park.

2. she was going to squash a squirrel in the street.
3. if it would leave a scar.
4. stepped out of his car and put a splint on her knee.

5 WHAT DO YOU THINK?
Answers may vary.

Lesson 20

1 FILL IN THE MISSING WORDS
1. Pork chops/beef roast
2. pancakes/eggs
3. candy bar/ice cream cone

2 PUT THESE SENTENCES IN ORDER
1. Bob asked Aunt Louise to lend him some money.
2. Bob called June and explained what happened.
3. Bob said, "Maybe we can go out next week."
4. June said she would fix a nice meal.
5. June said, "I'm really glad to see you."

3 ANSWER THE QUESTIONS
Answers may vary. Some possible answers are:
1. He had no money and wanted Aunt Louise to lend him some.
2. He had a date and hadn't had a chance to pick up his paycheck.
3. She was mending a top to wear that night.
4. June asked Bob to come over and eat dinner at her home.

4 WHAT DO YOU THINK?
Answers may vary.

Review

1 FILL IN THE MISSING WORD
1. safely   4. next   6. remind
2. celebrate   5. almost   7. useful
3. surprise

2 UNSCRAMBLE THE SENTENCES
1. I pay cash for my food.
2. Mary takes the train to work.
3. A loud knock on the door woke me up.

3 PUT THESE SENTENCES IN ORDER
1. Joan was driving her car downtown.
2. She was driving very fast in the rain.
3. Her car began to slip.
4. Joan crashed into another car.
5. Joan was lucky that nobody was hurt.

4 WHAT DO YOU THINK?
Answers may vary.

5 PERSONAL QUESTIONS
Answers may vary.

Challenger Writing 2

Lesson 1

1 CHOOSE THE RIGHT WORD
1. children
2. draw
3. touch
4. over
5. mouth
6. sense

2 PERSONAL QUESTIONS
Answers may vary.

3 UNSCRAMBLE THE SENTENCES
1. Donna Griffiths had the worst sneezing fit.
2. Most people cover their noses when they sneeze.

4 COMBINE THE SENTENCES
Answers may vary. Some possible answers are:
1. Somebody may hear you sneezing and say, "God bless you."
2. Donna Griffiths was twelve years old when she had the worst sneezing fit ever recorded, *or* Donna Griffiths had the worst sneezing fit ever recorded when she was twelve years old.

5 WHAT DO YOU THINK?
Answers may vary.

Lesson 2

1 CHOOSE THE RIGHT WORD
1. catbird
2. barking
3. paws
4. cats

2 UNSCRAMBLE THE SENTENCES
1. Cats like to have their own way.
2. Cats have sharp senses of smell and hearing.

3 WHAT DO YOU THINK?
Answers may vary.

4 COMBINE THE SENTENCES
Answers may vary. Some possible answers are:
1. Dogs and cats make good pets.
2. A doctor who lived on the West Coast died in 1963.
3. The doctor left his money to his two cats in his will, *or* In his will, the doctor left his money to his two cats.

5 PERSONAL QUESTIONS
Answers may vary.

Lesson 3

1 CHOOSE THE RIGHT WORD
1. ten
2. hundred
3. eighty
4. Five

2 UNSCRAMBLE THE SENTENCES
1. Seven is a lucky number for many people.
2. I always forget the names of the Seven Wonders of the World.

3 WHAT DO YOU THINK?
Answers may vary.

4 COMBINE THE SENTENCES
Answers may vary. Some possible answers are:
1. Seven-Up is a soft drink, and it is even the name of a children's card game.
2. There are twenty-four hours in a day, and there are seven days in a week.
3. There are thirty days in the month of June and thirty-one days in the month of January.

5 PERSONAL QUESTIONS
Answers may vary.

Lesson 4

1 CHOOSE THE RIGHT WORD
1. drink
2. grown
3. Japan
4. eaten
5. bunch
6. sneeze

2 COMBINE THE SENTENCES
Answers may vary. Some possible answers are:
1. You can tell time in hours and seconds.
2. The word *ugly* is the opposite of the word *cute*.
3. June always walks home from work the same way.
4. The United States is big, but the world is bigger.

3 WHAT DO YOU THINK?
Answers may vary.

4 UNSCRAMBLE THE SENTENCES
1. Ketchup is made from tomatoes.
2. I sometimes eat cold pizza for breakfast.

5 PERSONAL QUESTIONS
Answers may vary.

Lesson 5

1 CHOOSE THE RIGHT WORD
1. pepper
2. chain
3. wrote
4. person
5. letters

2 UNSCRAMBLE THE SENTENCES
1. The lover did not write the letter himself.
2. The lover hired a scribe to write the letter.
3. The words were written over and over.
4. This must have been a boring job.

3 WHAT DO YOU THINK?
Answers may vary.

4 COMBINE THE SENTENCES
Answers may vary.
1. A scribe is a person who writes for a living.

2. The lover stayed there and said "I love you" 1,875,000 times.

5 PERSONAL QUESTIONS

Answers may vary.

Lesson 6

1 USE THESE WORDS IN SENTENCES

Answers may vary.

2 PERSONAL QUESTIONS

Answers may vary.

3 COMBINE THE SENTENCES

Answers may vary. Some possible answers are:

1. Anne had a checkbook that was easy to use.
2. John had a girlfriend, and her name (whose name) was Min-hee.
3. It is hard to be a good shortstop.
4. Dan said, "Please give me some gingerbread and milk."

4 WHAT DO YOU THINK?

Answers may vary.

Lesson 7

1 UNSCRAMBLE THE SENTENCES

1. There are hidden pouches under a skunk's tail.
2. Each pouch has enough liquid for six rounds.
3. It takes a week to form more liquid.

2 COMBINE THE SENTENCES

Answers may vary. Some possible answers are:

1. The problem that looked hard was really easy to do.
2. Sometimes I forget important things, but I remember them later.
3. Mary saved money buying a used car, but she still spent a lot.

3 USE THESE WORDS IN SENTENCES

Answers may vary.

4 PERSONAL QUESTIONS

Answers may vary.

Lesson 8

1 CHOOSE THE RIGHT WORD

1. breathe	3. smart	5. twelve
2. sank	4. chicken	

2 WHAT DO YOU THINK?

Answers may vary.

3 COMBINE THE SENTENCES

Answers may vary. Some possible answers are:

1. Jack took the dozen eggs and put them in the refrigerator.

2. Joan has a pet chicken named "Sandy."
3. I eat ham and eggs for breakfast every day because I like them.

4 UNSCRAMBLE THE SENTENCES

1. The plane landed on the beach.
2. I do not think a chicken lived to be twenty years old.
3. You have to put holes in potatoes to cook them in a microwave.

5 PERSONAL QUESTIONS

Answers may vary.

Lesson 9

1 COMBINE THE SENTENCES

Answers may vary. Some possible answers are:

1. Gold was found on land owned by John A. Sutter.
2. The real gold rush began in 1849 when 100,000 men rushed to California.

2 UNSCRAMBLE THE SENTENCES

1. His word was as good as gold.
2. People told a story about a land rich in gold called El Dorado.

3 WHAT DO YOU THINK?

Answers may vary.

4 USE THESE WORDS IN SENTENCES

Answers may vary.

5 PERSONAL QUESTIONS

Answers may vary.

Lesson 10

1 CHOOSE THE RIGHT WORD

1. through	3. stuck
2. sport	4. rhyme

2 UNSCRAMBLE THE SENTENCES

1. Mother Goose rhymes have been around for hundreds of years.
2. One queen of England loved to tease her lords.

3 WHAT DO YOU THINK?

Answers may vary.

4 PUT THESE SENTENCES IN ORDER

1. The people who served the queen had nicknames.
2. A lady-in-waiting was called *Spoon*.
3. The *Dish* and the *Spoon* ran off to get married.
4. Somebody made up a rhyme about the *Dish* and the *Spoon*.

5 PERSONAL QUESTIONS

Answers may vary.

Lesson 11

1 USE THESE WORDS IN SENTENCES
Answers may vary.

2 COMBINE THE SENTENCES
Answers may vary. Some possible answers are:
1. Most dreaming takes place during the fourth stage of sleep, which is called *REM*.
2. During REM, the fourth stage of sleep, the body can't move at all.
3. We need to move during the time we sleep so we will not get sick.

3 WHAT DO YOU THINK?
Answers may vary.

4 COMPLETE THESE PARAGRAPHS
Answers may vary.

Lesson 12

1 CHOOSE THE RIGHT WORD
1. beekeeper
2. simply
3. sunny
4. noisy
5. quickly
6. cheaply
7. dwarves

2 COMBINE THE SENTENCES
Answers may vary. Some possible answers are:
1. Bees are important because they help fruit to grow.
2. Bees live in colonies that may have 50,000 bees.

3 USE THESE WORDS IN SENTENCES
Answers may vary.

4 COMPLETE THESE PARAGRAPHS
Answers may vary.

Lesson 13

1 USE THESE WORDS IN SENTENCES
Answers may vary.

2 WHAT DO YOU THINK?
Answers may vary.

3 UNSCRAMBLE THE SENTENCES
1. Handwriting experts look at many factors.
2. The slant of the letters tells about the writer.

4 COMBINE THE SENTENCES
Answers may vary. Some possible answers are:
1. Yesterday, I paid the bill that is due tomorrow.
2. The young woman won the race, but the older woman also did very well.

5 COMPLETE THESE PARAGRAPHS
Answers may vary.

Lesson 14

1 CHOOSE THE RIGHT WORD
1. heater
2. diver
3. brought
4. batter
5. beat

2 WHAT DO YOU THINK?
Answers may vary.

3 PUT THESE SENTENCES IN ORDER
1. As early as 1858, some doctors worried about smoking and health.
2. For the first time, smoking was tied to lung cancer.
3. Ads for smoking could not be shown on television.
4. Planes had to have nonsmoking seats.
5. The United States Army banned smoking.

4 COMPLETE THESE PARAGRAPHS
Answers may vary.

Lesson 15

1 USE THESE WORDS IN SENTENCES
Answers may vary.

2 WHAT DO YOU THINK?
Answers vary.

3 UNSCRAMBLE THE SENTENCES
1. Hold Fast is the name of a kind of barbed wire.
2. Barbed wire swizzle sticks were sold to a store.
3. Some kinds of barbed wire are no longer around.

4 COMBINE THE SENTENCES
Answers may vary. Some possible answers are:
1. The doctor uses wire cutters to cut off a strand of wire.
2. Some rare barbed wire may sell for forty dollars a strand.

5 COMPLETE THESE PARAGRAPHS
Answers may vary.

Lesson 16

1 CHOOSE THE RIGHT WORD
1. bank
2. which
3. happier
4. sweater
5. lost

2 WHAT DO YOU THINK?
Answers may vary.

3 PUT THESE SENTENCES IN ORDER
1. There were almost no gray whales left by 1946.
2. The United States passed a law banning the hunting of ocean mammals in United States waters.
3. The Endangered Species Act was passed to protect plants and animals.
4. The California gray whale was taken off the list of endangered species.

5. Beluga whales were added to the list of protected animals.

4 COMPLETE THESE PARAGRAPHS
Answers may vary.

Lesson 17

1 USE THESE WORDS IN SENTENCES
Answers may vary.

2 WHAT DO YOU THINK?
Answers may vary.

3 UNSCRAMBLE THE SENTENCES
1. Black Bart's real first name was Charles.
2. He broke a stick from a bush to use as a gun.

4 COMBINE THE SENTENCES
Answers may vary.
1. He always laid careful plans, which he kept to himself.
2. He knew the driver and thought he'd give him a scare.

5 COMPLETE THESE PARAGRAPHS
Answers may vary.

Lesson 18

1 CHOOSE THE RIGHT WORD
1. useless   3. near   5. stairs
2. swung   4. happily

2 USE THESE WORDS IN SENTENCES
Answers may vary.

3 UNSCRAMBLE THE SENTENCES
1. Laws were passed to help clean up pollution in our air and water.
2. People learned to recycle paper, cans, and boxes.
3. Earth Day helped to make people aware of threats to the environment.

4 COMBINE THE SENTENCES
Answers may vary. Some possible answers are:
1. Earth Day is important because it celebrates the Earth.
2. Every day can be Earth Day if we protect the environment every day.

5 COMPLETE THIS PARAGRAPH
Answers may vary.

Lesson 19

1 USE THESE WORDS IN SENTENCES
Answers may vary.

2 COMBINE THE SENTENCES
Answers may vary. Some possible answers are:
1. The convicts would push the oar, dip it into the water, and pull with all their might.

2. Until the end of his days, a convict lived with the men in his gang, *or* A convict lived with the men in his gang until the end of his days.

3 UNSCRAMBLE THE SENTENCES
1. A convict on the galleys was no longer a man.
2. Life on board a galley at sea was a living hell.

4 WHAT DO YOU THINK?
Answers may vary.

5 COMPLETE THIS PARAGRAPH
Answers may vary.

Lesson 20

1 USE THESE WORDS IN SENTENCES
Answers may vary.

2 WHAT DO YOU THINK?
Answers may vary.

3 PUT THESE SENTENCES IN ORDER
1. George Washington was born on February 11.
2. Men tried to kidnap Washington in order to kill him.
3. His friends had to lend him money to go to New York.
4. He served two terms as president.

4 COMPLETE THESE PARAGRAPHS
Answers may vary.

Review

1 UNSCRAMBLE THE SENTENCES
1. It hit him like a ton of bricks.
2. Don't wear your heart on your sleeve.
3. Don't put all your eggs in one basket.
4. A penny saved is a penny earned.

2 WHAT DO YOU THINK?
Answers may vary.

3 PUT THESE SENTENCES IN ORDER
1. Mike drove two of his friends to a party.
2. Mike drank a number of beers at the party.
3. Mike gave his car keys to a friend who wasn't drinking.
4. Mike's friend drove everyone home from the party.

4 COMBINE THE SENTENCES
Answers may vary. Some possible answers are:
1. Sixty people went to the dance, and they all had a good time.
2. Teachers help people learn, but people must learn things for themselves.
3. Eating good food, getting enough sleep, and working out are things you can do to take care of yourself.

5 COMPLETE THESE PARAGRAPHS
Answers may vary.

Challenger Writing 3

Lesson 1

1 USE THESE WORDS IN SENTENCES
Answers may vary.

2 WHAT DO YOU THINK?
Answers may vary.

3 COMBINE THE SENTENCES
Answers may vary. Some possible answers are:
1. I put the dirty dishes in a dishpan and then washed them.
2. Today's newspaper had a story about a plan that backfired.
3. The city will fix the broken sidewalk in front of my house.
4. Many workers carry in their toolboxes the tools they need to do their jobs.

4 COMPLETE THESE PARAGRAPHS
Answers may vary.

Lesson 2

1 USE THESE WORDS IN SENTENCES
Answers may vary.

2 WHAT DO YOU THINK?
Answers may vary.

3 PUT THESE SENTENCES IN ORDER
1. Steven was standing on his head.
2. Jerome was feasting on beef stew.
3. Jerome said he did not think Steven was crazy.
4. Steven treated Jerome to a steak dinner.

4 COMPLETE THESE PARAGRAPHS
Answers may vary.

Lesson 3

1 USE THESE WORDS IN SENTENCES
Answers may vary.

2 WHAT DO YOU THINK?
Answers may vary.

3 COMBINE THE SENTENCES
Answers may vary. Some possible answers are:
1. Divers use flashlights to see in deep water.
2. You can use these folders to file your reports.
3. Students use notebooks to write down important information.
4. Swimmers use towels to dry (themselves) off when they come out of a pool.
5. People use mats in yoga class to sit or lie on when they do moves.

4 COMPLETE THESE PARAGRAPHS
Answers may vary.

Lesson 4

1 USE THESE WORDS IN SENTENCES
Answers may vary.

2 WHAT DO YOU THINK?
Answers may vary.

3 PUT THESE SENTENCES IN ORDER
1. Ginger let the phone ring a few times before she picked it up.
2. Ginger asked Jerome if he was coming over.
3. "I always come over to your place," complained Jerome.
4. Jerome yelled at Ginger to stop screaming.

4 COMPLETE THESE PARAGRAPHS
Answers may vary.

Lesson 5

1 USE THESE WORDS IN SENTENCES
Answers may vary.

2 WHAT DO YOU THINK?
Answers may vary.

3 COMBINE THE SENTENCES
Answers may vary. Some possible answers are:
1. Anne was madly in love with Ben and wanted to marry him, *or* Anne, who was madly in love with Ben, wanted to marry him.
2. The boxer swung wildly, slipped, and fell against the ropes.
3. John had been away a lot lately, so we hadn't seen him for a while, *or* Because John had been away a lot lately, we hadn't seen him for a while.

4 COMPLETE THESE PARAGRAPHS
Answers may vary.

Lesson 6

1 USE THESE WORDS IN SENTENCES
Answers may vary.

2 WHAT DO YOU THINK?
Answers may vary.

3 PUT THESE SENTENCES IN ORDER
1. Jerome thought about snatching a can of blue paint.
2. Jerome reached for the can.
3. Five gallons of blue paint poured over him.
4. Tony laughed so hard that he nearly slipped on the paint.

4 COMPLETE THESE PARAGRAPHS
Answers may vary.

Lesson 7

1 USE THESE WORDS IN SENTENCES
Answers may vary.

2 WHAT DO YOU THINK?
Answers may vary.

3 COMBINE THE SENTENCES
Answers may vary.
1. Steven had a cold and didn't feel well, but he went to his yoga class anyway.
2. Holly told Steven he should not eat sugar because it makes people grouchy and restless.
3. Holly went to the yoga class for exercise and because it made her feel peaceful and more relaxed.

4 WRITE A PARAGRAPH
Answers may vary.

Lesson 8

1 USE THESE WORDS IN SENTENCES
Answers may vary.

2 WHAT DO YOU THINK?
Answers may vary.

3 PUT THESE SENTENCES IN ORDER
1. Gail slouched against Ginger's doorway.
2. "Is it okay if I stay here for a day or two?" asked Gail.
3. "My father lost his temper," Gail said.
4. "You know very well your father's proud of his job," said Ginger.
5. "Go wash your face, and I'll fix you some breakfast," Ginger said.

4 WRITE A PARAGRAPH
Answers may vary.

Lesson 9

1 USE THESE WORDS IN SENTENCES
Answers may vary.

2 WHAT DO YOU THINK?
Answers may vary.

3 COMBINE THE SENTENCES
Answers may vary. Some possible answers are:
1. I left the frozen beef out to thaw and then used it to make a stew.
2. Ginger has written a health food cookbook that is selling well.
3. Joyce stopped to loosen the straps on her backpack because they were too tight.

4 WRITE A PARAGRAPH
Answers may vary.

Lesson 10

1 USE THESE WORDS IN SENTENCES
Answers may vary.

2 WHAT DO YOU THINK?
Answers may vary.

3 PUT THESE SENTENCES IN ORDER
1. Jerome threw his laundry in the trunk of his car.
2. Jerome found Holly at the laundromat.
3. Jerome told Holly that Ginger should say she is sorry.
4. Holly said that Jerome is a jerk.
5. Jerome said women stick together like glue.

4 WRITE A PARAGRAPH
Answers may vary.

Lesson 11

1 USE THESE WORDS IN SENTENCES
Answers may vary.

2 WHAT DO YOU THINK?
Answers may vary.

3 COMBINE THE SENTENCES
Answers may vary. Some possible answers are:
1. I don't recall my first party, but I remember my first dance and my first date.
2. Sam often sounds edgy the first time he talks to a woman because women make him nervous.
3. Mike doesn't like to brag about things he does well, but Mary wants people to know how good Mike is, so she boasts for him.

4 WRITE A PARAGRAPH
Answers may vary.

Lesson 12

1 USE THESE WORDS IN SENTENCES
Answers may vary.

2 WHAT DO YOU THINK?
Answers may vary.

3 PUT THESE SENTENCES IN ORDER
1. Steven showed Holly how to swing her arms like she was playing golf.
2. Steven swung his arms like he was swinging a baseball bat.
3. Holly wanted to play a game that was more like yoga.
4. Steven tripped and missed steps in the dance game.
5. Holly said she could play this game all day.

4 WRITE A PARAGRAPH
Answers may vary.

Lesson 13

1 USE THESE WORDS IN SENTENCES
Answers may vary.

2 WHAT DO YOU THINK?
Answers may vary.

3 COMBINE THE SENTENCES
Answers may vary. Some possible answers are:
1. Jerome had a scheme that involved Tony and Ginger.
2. Jerome bought bug spray, swept the cobwebs from the ceiling, and scrubbed the carpet.
3. Jerome went online to get hip-hop music, burned a CD of the songs, and added some Cuban music, too.

4 WRITE A PARAGRAPH
Answers may vary.

Lesson 14

1 USE THESE WORDS IN SENTENCES
Answers may vary.

2 WHAT DO YOU THINK?
Answers may vary.

3 PUT THESE SENTENCES IN ORDER
1. Tony bought a small house.
2. Mrs. Darkpill complained about the chestnut tree.
3. Tony heard the sound of a buzz saw.
4. Tony yelled at Mrs. Darkpill's kids.
5. Mrs. Darkpill called the police.

4 WRITE A PARAGRAPH
Answers may vary.

Lesson 15

1 USE THESE WORDS IN SENTENCES
Answers may vary.

2 WHAT DO YOU THINK?
Answers may vary.

3 COMBINE THE SENTENCES
Answers may vary. Some possible answers are:
1. Last month Gail had a baby girl that (who) weighed seven pounds, eleven ounces.
2. I take weekly dancing lessons that last one hour.
3. I went to the store yesterday and bought one quart of milk and a can of Coke, too.

4 WRITE A PARAGRAPH
Answers may vary.

Lesson 16

1 USE THESE WORDS IN SENTENCES
Answers may vary.

2 WHAT DO YOU THINK?
Answers may vary.

3 COMBINE THE SENTENCES
Answers may vary. Some possible answers are:
1. The elbow, knee, and wrist are joints in the body.
2. We have a new bathroom with a towel rack and a shower.
3. Martin, who is a good bowler, is on a (bowling) team that bowls every Thursday.

4 WRITE A PARAGRAPH
Answers may vary.

Lesson 17

1 USE THESE WORDS IN SENTENCES
Answers may vary.

2 WHAT DO YOU THINK?
Answers may vary.

3 PUT THESE SENTENCES IN ORDER
1. Tony shut off the alarm.
2. Tony told Mr. Dennis he was sick.
3. Tony went to the clothing sale at the men's store.
4. Tony chose two pairs of slacks to try on.
5. Tony told the person in the fitting booth to hurry up.
6. Mr. Dennis fired Tony.

4 WRITE A PARAGRAPH
Answers may vary.

Lesson 18

1 USE THESE WORDS IN SENTENCES
Answers may vary.

2 WHAT DO YOU THINK?
Answers may vary.

3 COMBINE THE SENTENCES
Answers may vary. Some possible answers are:
1. The carpenter needed some nails and a saw, but she had a drill, *or* The carpenter had a drill, but she needed some nails and a saw.
2. A fisherman uses a rod, hooks, and bait for fishing.
3. A baker uses a rolling pin to roll out dough that is put in pie plates.

4 WRITE A PARAGRAPH
Answers may vary.

Lesson 19

1 USE THESE WORDS IN SENTENCES
Answers may vary.

2 WHAT DO YOU THINK?
Answers may vary.

3 PUT THESE SENTENCES IN ORDER
1. Jerome decided to see Ginger in person.
2. Jerome went to the club where Ginger was singing.
3. Ginger felt Jerome's stare and looked up.
4. Ginger was angry and turned to walk away.
5. Jerome said he missed Ginger very much.
6. Ginger said she would sing "September Song."

4 WRITE A PARAGRAPH
Answers may vary.

Lesson 20

1 USE THESE WORDS IN SENTENCES
Answers may vary.

2 WHAT DO YOU THINK?
Answers may vary.

3 COMBINE THE SENTENCES
Answers may vary. Some possible answers are:
1. Ben likes to cook spaghetti and cheesecake.
2. I like to play sports like baseball but tennis is my favorite.
3. I carry heavy gear for camping in a knapsack on my back, *or* I carry heavy camping gear in a knapsack on my back.

4 WRITE A PARAGRAPH
Answers may vary.

Review

1 COMBINE THE SENTENCES
Answers may vary. Some possible answers are:
1. Ginger finally painted her apartment blue and hung new curtains.
2. Steven practiced yoga every day and got so good that he became a yoga instructor.
3. Holly got food from the refrigerator, cooked it, and ate her dinner in thirty minutes, *or* In thirty minutes, Holly got food from the refrigerator, cooked it, and ate it.

2 WHAT DO YOU THINK?
Answers may vary.

3 PUT THESE SENTENCES IN ORDER
1. Tony drove his car to work.
2. Tony had a blowout as he drove.
3. Tony was fixing his flat tire when a police car stopped.
4. The policeman waited while Tony changed the tire.
5. Tony thanked the policeman for keeping other cars from hitting him.
6. Tony was only ten minutes late for his new job.

4 WRITE PARAGRAPHS
Answers may vary.

Challenger Writing 4

Lesson 1

1 USE THESE WORDS IN SENTENCES
Answers may vary.

2 WHAT DO YOU THINK?
Answers may vary.

3 PUT THESE SENTENCES IN ORDER
1. The heart is really two pumps in one.
2. The right side pumps blood into the lungs.
3. The left side collects blood from the lungs.
4. Then the left side of the heart pumps blood to the body.
5. Veins bring the blood back into the heart.

4 WRITE A PARAGRAPH
Answers may vary.

Lesson 2

1 USE THESE WORDS IN SENTENCES
Answers may vary.

2 WHAT DO YOU THINK?
Answers may vary.

3 COMBINE THE SENTENCES
Answers may vary. Some possible answers are:
1. Danica Patrick first raced go-karts but moved up to auto racing when she was 16.
2. Patrick's biggest dream was winning the Indianapolis 500, but when she drove in it for the first time in 2005, she came in fourth.
3. The governor of Illinois named April 26, 2008, "Danica Patrick Day" to honor her for her win at the 2008 Japan 300 *or* The governor of Illinois named April 26, 2008, "Danica Patrick Day" in honor of her win at the 2008 Japan 300.

4 WRITE A PARAGRAPH
Answers may vary.

Lesson 3

1 USE THESE WORDS IN SENTENCES
Answers may vary.

2 WHAT DO YOU THINK?
Answers may vary.

3 COMBINE THE SENTENCES
Answers may vary. Some possible answers are:
1. The price of gas rose quickly from $40 or $50 to $100 to fill a tank, causing many people to cut back on spending so they would have money to pay for gas.

2. Many people felt the pinch when energy prices caused the prices of many goods and services to rise, which made it hard for some people to afford them.
3. People can save energy in many ways, such as turning off lights when they are not being used, driving less, and buying hybrid cars.

4 WRITE A PARAGRAPH
Answers may vary.

Lesson 4

1 USE THESE WORDS IN SENTENCES
Answers may vary.

2 WHAT DO YOU THINK?
Answers may vary.

3 COMBINE THE SENTENCES
Answers may vary. Some possible answers are:
1. Some people think insects should be wiped out because they sting people and animals and (they) harm forests.
2. Some insects are food for other kinds of insects or for other animals, and many insects help plants to grow.
3. Insects are cold-blooded animals that move very quickly when it is hot but become slower when it is cold.

4 WRITE A PARAGRAPH
Answers may vary.

Lesson 5

1 USE THESE WORDS IN SENTENCES
Answers may vary.

2 WHAT DO YOU THINK?
Answers may vary.

3 PUT THESE SENTENCES IN ORDER
1. You decide to make a call and punch in the number.
2. Low-power transmitters in your cell phone send out radio signals.
3. The radio equipment in the nearest base station picks up the radio signals from your cell phone.
4. The base station sends out radio waves to the cell phone of the person you called.
5. As you move around and talk, your phone's signal is passed from cell to cell.

4 WRITE A PARAGRAPH
Answers may vary.

Lesson 6

1 USE THESE WORDS IN SENTENCES
Answers may vary.

2 WHAT DO YOU THINK?
Answers may vary.

3 COMBINE THE SENTENCES
Answers may vary.
1. There is life on Earth that depends on a bright star called the sun. *or* All life on Earth depends on the sun, which is a bright star.
2. All living things are part of a process called the food chain, which starts with green plants that make food with the help of sunlight.
3. People long ago worshipped the sun as a god and offered prayers and gifts to the sun god.

4 WRITE A PARAGRAPH
Answers may vary.

Lesson 7

1 USE THESE WORDS IN SENTENCES
Answers may vary.

2 WHAT DO YOU THINK?
Answers may vary.

3 PUT THESE SENTENCES IN ORDER
1. As a small child, Edison was known for asking questions.
2. When Al was seven, his family moved to Michigan.
3. Al upset his teacher with all his questions.
4. Al overheard the teacher say he was crazy.
5. Al told his mother what the teacher said.
6. Al's mother took him out of school and taught him herself.

4 WRITE A THREE-PARAGRAPH SUMMARY
Answers may vary.

Lesson 8

1 USE THESE WORDS IN SENTENCES
Answers may vary.

2 WHAT DO YOU THINK?
Answers may vary.

3 COMBINE THE SENTENCES
Answers may vary. Some possible answers are:
1. Guests brought their own knives, used them at mealtime, wiped them off, and stuck them back into their belts.
2. In 1100, forks were first used in Italy by a rich man's wife because she thought people looked like animals when they ate meat with their hands.
3. As people started to use knives and forks, they made up rules about how to set a table, such as where to put knives and spoons.

4 WRITE A THREE-PARAGRAPH SUMMARY
Answers may vary.

Lesson 9

1 USE THESE WORDS IN SENTENCES
Answers may vary.

2 WHAT DO YOU THINK?
Answers may vary.

3 COMBINE THE SENTENCES
Answers may vary. Some possible answers are:
1. Meeting people can be just a mouse click away when you use an online dating website.
2. Some dating sites are for all kinds of people, but some sites are for people with the same backgrounds, religions, and interests. *or* While some dating sites are for all kinds of people, other sites are for people with the same backgrounds, religions, and interests.
3. Meeting by chance, placing personal ads in magazines and newspapers, and going to a matchmaker are some ways to meet someone.

4 WRITE A THREE-PARAGRAPH SUMMARY
Answers may vary.

Lesson 10

1 USE THESE WORDS IN SENTENCES
Answers may vary.

2 WHAT DO YOU THINK?
Answers may vary.

3 COMBINE THE SENTENCES
Answers may vary. Some possible answers are:
1. Earth, the third planet from the sun, is the only planet with liquid water, which is needed for life.
2. Other planets have moons, and some are larger than our own, whereas others are just small broken pieces of rock. *or* The moons of other planets may be larger than our own or just small broken pieces of rock.
3. The sun is important to our solar system because it holds the solar system together and gives off heat, light, and energy.
4. The new solar system, which is smaller than ours, has a smaller central sun. *or* The new solar system is smaller than ours and has a smaller central sun.

4 WRITE A THREE-PARAGRAPH SUMMARY
Answers may vary.

Lesson 11

1 USE THESE WORDS IN SENTENCES
Answers may vary.

2 WHAT DO YOU THINK?
Answers may vary.

3 COMBINE THE SENTENCES

Answers may vary. Some possible answers are:

1. Patrick is an unhappy, angry person who is lonely because other people stay away from him.
2. Sue has many friends because she is a happy person who impresses other people as being friendly and open.
3. Tommy accepts himself and other people, so he doesn't often get upset or angry.

4 WRITE A THREE-PARAGRAPH SUMMARY

Answers may vary.

Lesson 12

1 USE THESE WORDS IN SENTENCES

Answers may vary.

2 WHAT DO YOU THINK?

Answers may vary.

3 COMBINE THE SENTENCES

Answers may vary. Some possible answers are:

1. Anne Frank was a young Jewish girl who lived in an attic with seven other people for more than two years.
2. Anne kept a diary she called "Kitty," which she started when she was thirteen and wrote in until she was fifteen. *or* When she was thirteen, Anne started a diary that she called "Kitty" and wrote in until she was fifteen.
3. On October 9, 1942, Anne had depressing news about her family's friends, who were loaded into cattle trucks and taken to a large Jewish camp.

4 WRITE A THREE-PARAGRAPH SUMMARY

Answers may vary.

Lesson 13

1 USE THESE WORDS IN SENTENCES

Answers may vary.

2 WHAT DO YOU THINK?

Answers may vary.

3 PUT THESE SENTENCES IN ORDER

1. Hitler's army invaded Poland.
2. Hitler's war machine took over five countries in three months.
3. Japan attacked Pearl Harbor, Hawaii.
4. The United States declared war on Japan and Germany.
5. Anne Frank died in one of Hitler's camps.
6. World War II ended.

4 WRITE PARAGRAPHS

Answers may vary.

Lesson 14

1 USE THESE WORDS IN SENTENCES

Answers may vary.

2 WHAT DO YOU THINK?

Answers may vary.

3 COMBINE THE SENTENCES

Answers may vary. Some possible answers are:

1. The camel is a desert animal that can carry people and cargo hundreds of miles with little food or water.
2. The United States tried using camels in the 1850s when the army brought camels from Africa and Asia to carry cargo from Texas to California.
3. The camel has a hump that can weigh eighty pounds or more and is used to store fat, not water.

4 WRITE PARAGRAPHS

Answers may vary.

Lesson 15

1 USE THESE WORDS IN SENTENCES

Answers may vary.

2 WHAT DO YOU THINK?

Answers may vary.

3 PUT THESE SENTENCES IN ORDER

1. Researchers wanted to show that no gene matter was lost as cells grew and split.
2. A frog was cloned by putting gene matter from the egg cell of one frog into another frog.
3. Researchers cloned human cells using human embryos.
4. Dolly was cloned from the cell of another adult sheep.
5. Live mice were cloned from the cells of frozen mice.

4 WRITE PARAGRAPHS

Answers may vary.

Lesson 16

1 USE THESE WORDS IN SENTENCES

Answers may vary.

2 WHAT DO YOU THINK?

Answers may vary.

3 COMBINE THE SENTENCES

Answers may vary. Some possible answers are:

1. In libraries and bookstores, there are many books about dying, and there are many websites about death and dying, too.
2. After the elm tree died of blight, a tree disease, it had to be chopped up and carted away.
3. Although a lot is written about death being pain-free, no one has proved it, so we don't really know if it is true.

4 WRITE PARAGRAPHS
Answers may vary.

Lesson 17

1 USE THESE WORDS IN SENTENCES
Answers may vary.

2 WHAT DO YOU THINK?
Answers may vary.

3 PUT THESE SENTENCES IN ORDER
1. James B. Brady was born in 1856.
2. Brady was first hired as a bellhop.
3. He became a successful salesman.
4. He was taken to the hospital.
5. Doctors learned that Brady's stomach was six times as large as normal.
6. Diamond Jim died in 1917.

4 WRITE PARAGRAPHS
Answers may vary.

Lesson 18

1 USE THESE WORDS IN SENTENCES
Answers may vary.

2 WHAT DO YOU THINK?
Answers may vary.

3 COMBINE THE SENTENCES
Answers may vary. Some possible answers are:
1. Life was hard in Ireland in the 1800s when people depended on potatoes for their main food.
2. People only needed a spade to grow potatoes, but potatoes were a dangerous crop because they did not keep and couldn't be stored until the next season.
3. More than a million people fled Ireland and went to America and England.

4 WRITE PARAGRAPHS
Answers may vary.

Lesson 19

1 USE THESE WORDS IN SENTENCES
Answers may vary.

2 WHAT DO YOU THINK?
Answers may vary.

3 PUT THESE SENTENCES IN ORDER
1. Glands in the mouth make saliva.
2. Our teeth break up food we eat into small bits.
3. The food moves down the esophagus.
4. The stomach receives the food.
5. The food is churned by muscles in the stomach.
6. The most important part of digestion happens in the small intestine.
7. The large intestine removes water from the liquid paste that was once food.

4 WRITE PARAGRAPHS
Answers may vary.

Lesson 20

1 USE THESE WORDS IN SENTENCES
Answers may vary.

2 WHAT DO YOU THINK?
Answers may vary.

3 COMBINE THE SENTENCES
Answers may vary. Some possible answers are:
1. A little old lady looked up and saw a stranger who had ragged clothes but wore them without shame.
2. The stranger put the washtub on the fire and then went to the well, got some water, and put it in the washtub.
3. The young man was busy making soup, adding beans and tomatoes, but Granny did not see him do that. *or* The young man was busy adding beans and tomatoes to the soup, but Granny didn't see him do that.

4 WRITE PARAGRAPHS
Answers may vary.

Review

1 WHAT DO YOU THINK?
Answers may vary.

2 WRITE PARAGRAPHS
Answers may vary.

3 WRITE A THREE-PARAGRAPH STORY
Answers may vary.

4 WRITE A THREE-PARAGRAPH STORY
Answers may vary.